Land Rover

Other titles in the Crowood AutoClassic series

AC Cobra	Brian Laban
Aston Martin: DB4, DB5 and DB6	Jonathan Wood
Aston Martin and Lagonda V-Engined Cars	David Styles
Austin-Healey 100 and 3000 Series	Graham Robson
BMW M-Series	Alan Henry
Ford Capri	Mike Taylor
The Big Jaguars: 3½-Litre to 420G	Graham Robson
Jaguar E-Type	Jonathan Wood
Jaguar XJ Series	Graham Robson
Jaguar XK Series	Jeremy Boyce
Jaguar Mk 1 and 2	James Taylor
Lamborghini Countach	Peter Dron
Lotus and Caterham Seven: Racers for the Road	John Tipler
Lotus Elan	Mike Taylor
Lotus Esprit	Jeremy Walton
Mercedes SL Series	Brian Laban
MGA	David Styles
MGB	Brian Laban
Morgan: The Cars and the Factory	John Tipler
Porsche 911	David Vivian
Porsche 924/928/944/968	David Vivian
Range Rover	James Taylor and Nick Dimbleby
Sprites and Midgets	Anders Ditlev Clausager
Sunbeam Alpine and Tiger	Graham Robson
Triumph TRs	Graham Robson
Triumph 2000 and 2.5PI	Graham Robson
TVR	John Tipler
VW Beetle	Robert Davies
VW Golf	James Ruppert

LAND ROVER

The Original 4x4

JOHN TIPLER

First published in 1996 by
The Crowood Press Ltd
Ramsbury, Marlborough
Wiltshire SN8 2HR

British Library Cataloguing-in-Publication Data
A catalogue record for this book is available from the British Library

ISBN 1 85223 946 8

Picture Credits
All illustrations supplied by John Cameron, Nick Dimbleby, Kriss and Sheila Evitts, Land Rover Press Office, Bob Morrison, the National Motor Museum, Beaulieu, Richard Pomeroy, Carl Rogerson, James Ruppert, Johnny Slavin and the author.

Printed and bound by BPC Books Ltd, Aylesbury

Contents

Acknowledgements

First and foremost, I have to thank Nick Dimbleby for his outstanding photographs which form the bulk of the illustrations in the book. I often meet Nick while working as an off-road journalist, and never cease to be impressed by his tenacity and eye for a good shot.

I also want to thank everyone at Land Rover for their help with research, particularly Corporate Affairs PRO Nick Argent, who laid on several factory visits; Josephina Zacarolli-Walker who made the Scottish off-roading press trip so enjoyable; while Roger Crathorne of the 'Land Rover Experience' was a fine instructor out in the wilderness.

I met many key figures in the Land Rover world while working with Carlton Rogerson as a journalist on *Land Rover Owner* magazine. They included Vince Cobley, Duncan Barbour, Ken, Julie and Johnny Slavin, Bob Morrison, Richard Thomas, Dave Barker, and many, many others. Thanks to all for help, direct and indirect, in putting together this book. For a thorough Land Rover history and chassis number breakdown, I commend readers to James Taylor's *Land Rover Collector's Guide.* Also important reference books are *Land Rover, the Unbeatable 4x4*, by K. & J. Slavin, G.N. Mackie and D. McDine, and *Modern Military Land Rovers* by James Taylor and Bob Morrison.

I am also grateful to Andy Robinson for information on Land Rovers 'down under', to Vicky Hanson for telling us about those in South Africa, Steve Wiles for travellers' tales, Geoff Browne of *Classic Car Weekly* for reference material, Kriss and Sheila Evitts for restoration guidance as well as fun in the Lakes, and John and Alison Cameron for the Land Rover gymkhana experience.

I should like to dedicate the book to my children Julius and Kerry, who could actually do with a Land Rover in the wilds of Cumbria. However, they like being able to miss school when it snows, and a Land Rover would change that.

Introduction

The badge of the true 'Best 4 × 4 by Far'.

To start with, I should present my credentials for doing a Land Rover book. The enthusiasm goes way back to early childhood. My introduction to the joys of Land Rovering was in the early 1950s, when my family used to visit an uncle – Derek Findley – who was a land agent on an estate in Shropshire, and who had a Series I. My cousins took it all a bit for granted as they only ever travelled by Land Rover, but nothing thrilled me more than the 'expeditions' we would go on over Wenlock Edge and the Long Mynd, top down off-roading.

These sunny memories have not been distilled by time, but there was a long gap before my next serious Land Rover experience. This was with a couple of friends, Kriss and Sheila, Landie fans who ran an 88in (2,235mm) Series IIA and a 109in (2,768mm) Series III, both hard-tops. They eventually restored the Series IIA, and I talk about that in the restoration section; the Series III was eventually sold off, but not before we had done some enjoyable off-roading in the Lake District, spending several weeks mucking about, easing our way along boulder-strewn pot-holed tracks, following drove roads and sometimes venturing into uncharted tracts of moorland. The four of us camped out beneath the awning pitched to the side of the Series III wherever we ended up – usually with the local farmer's permission – and despite the rain which you expect in the Lake District, we

The author's uncle introduced him to Land Rover 'expeditions' on Wenlock Edge as a small boy.

had excellent fun. The capacious Series III was like a mother-ship, providing a base where we slept, brewed up and cooked camp-fire dinners. Occasionally we'd make use of washing facilities in hotels and public conveniences, and it paid to be handy with a spade when nature called. Somehow you couldn't really do an expedition like this with a regular road car: only a Land Rover is appropriate.

The Land Rover has been such a success that anyone could be forgiven for assuming it was the result of a careful long-term design process. Of course it wasn't, and the prototype was hurriedly put together in 1947 from cannibalized Jeep parts and whatever else could be conveniently sourced from Rover's car parts bins. Market research didn't come into it, although it proved to be absolutely right for its market niche as an agricultural and industrial runabout. It became such a familiar sight in so many walks of life that there was a danger of it being taken for granted.

As I found out while features editor of *Land Rover Owner* magazine, there is something about older Land Rovers that makes owners want to keep on driving them, no matter what the season. Like sports cars in the Caterham Seven mould, the Land Rover is the sort of vehicle that keeps you in touch with the elements – camping on wheels, if you like – and it is this basic, no-nonsense quality that fires one's enthusiasm for the year-round air-conditioning. Even through the depths of winter, owners still regard their Land Rovers as virtually their best friend and would never want to drive anything else. There is a very addictive survival element about it which appeals to one's adventurous streak, and it also separates the real men and women from the rest of the motoring mediocrity.

In the course of doing my job on *Land Rover Owner* I encountered countless Land Rover devotees from all manner of backgrounds, from Camel Trophy types to *concours* buffs, and safari travellers to trials merchants. It entailed commissioning and harvesting Land Rovering tales, and provided access to the Lode Lane headquarters at Solihull where I met and interviewed members of the workforce.

Looking at the pros and cons of vehicles in the 4 × 4 market in general – evidence from owners who cover hundreds of thousands of miles off-road in forestry, field projects and expeditions, using a broad spec-

As an off-roading journalist on Land Rover Owner, *the author used a Series III Station Wagon. It was known as Old Smoky, and the kids loved it.*

trum of vehicles from Land Rover Series IIs and IIIs, 110s, Range Rovers, Toyota Land Cruisers, Isuzu Troopers and Nissans – it is clear that the toughest, most reliable and versatile vehicles are the leaf-sprung Land Rovers. A good set of muscles is the only necessary accessory, apart from winches and high-lift jacks. Punctures are rare, too.

It's not just the vehicles which are characterful. Many owners fit that category too, and they flock in their hundreds to club events, both social and competitive. Probably the biggest on the UK calendar is Billing, Northamptonshire, organized by John Cornwall and his team at the Land Rover Owner bookshop at Diss, in Norfolk.

Billing is always an impressive show, and 1995 produced record crowds of 200,000 – that's easily as many as attend the British Grand Prix. Many Land Rover enthusiasts bring caravans, and the campsites are full. Wander round the site and you'll see every different type of Land Rover product. You'll inevitably spend ages chatting to people on the trade stands and having a look around the various club stands. Without exception, everyone is friendly; in the Land Rover scene you simply don't get the snobbery and one-upmanship which lurk among the upper echelons of the classic car scene. If you want to make new contacts in the Land Rover scene or simply look up old ones, Billing is the place to do it.

The latest round of enthusiasm for off-roading has brought controversy in the shape of so-called bull-bars and green-laning. Some people wonder what bull-bars are for, and perhaps with good reason: I spent a couple of years living in the depths of Herefordshire cattle country, and never once met a bull at large. It seems they originated 'down under' as 'roo-bars', but since you're more likely to meet a bull in Britain than a kangaroo, that is why the name was changed. Safety considerations aside, I happen to think they do the purity of the vehicle's lines no favours whatsoever, and are best left to the Japanese brigade, who perhaps need to bolster their egos with macho accessories. Land Rovers really have no such need – apart, that is, from when indulging in competitive trialling when we get into the realms of roll-cages.

Green lanes are a vexed issue, and I think you have to stand on one side of the argument or the other: either you approve of driving an off-road vehicle – Land Rover or moto-cross bike, or whatever – along a limited section of hitherto unspoiled countryside, or you don't. I happen to enjoy walking and mountain biking on green lanes, and can appreciate the view of those who are incensed when confronted by 4 × 4s churning their way through virgin lane. Another side of the argument is that gamekeepers and farmers may already use green lanes in this way in the course of their work, and so the damage, if that's what you call it, has already been done. It comes down to a common sense attitude to off-roading: if it looks reasonable to drive it without spoiling it for the other sections of the community, then fair enough; if not, there are plenty of other places to enjoy driving Land Rovers to your heart's content.

Today, Land Rover itself defines its marque values as individualism, authenticity, freedom, adventure, guts and supremacy. That's a great deal to live up to, and many lesser makes simply could not measure up. But Land Rover can lay claim to all those concepts, with justification and in good measure.

One of the issues currently taxing off-roaders is use of green lanes. Some are less green than others.

1 The Series I

The saga of Britain's best loved off-roader is well known and has already been documented in several books and videos, notably those by historian James Taylor, with more specialized works by Ken and Julie Slavin and Lindsay Porter. However, no book would be complete without a synopsis of Land Rover's history.

Before the Land Rover came out, several four-wheel drive precedents existed, notably the Dutch Spijker, Citroën Kégresse, Japanesse Kurogame and the Second World War US Jeep. But the Land Rover was the first fully commercial 4 × 4.

The Solihull factory was built as an aero-engine plant and did not make any road-going vehicles until the end of 1945. When this factory became redundant after the war, the Rover car company took advantage of the spare capacity. There was strong government pressure to build cars for export, in spite of the fact that steel was rationed and in short supply.

Coincidentally, Rover's chief engineer and chief executive at the time were the brothers Maurice and Spencer Wilks, and the former also owned Blackdown Manor, a farm on the isle of Anglesey. Here he used an ex-US army jeep to drive around on the fields, and it was soon obvious to the brothers that while the four-wheel-drive concept was good, they could do something rather better.

There were other factors at play. Rover had planned to build a new small car code-named M1, but the marketing people put them off and there was still a gap in the company's plans. At the same time there was a growing trend towards mechanization on farms, demonstrated by the success of the Ferguson tractor. A complementary utility vehicle made sense, and they would sell it to farmers as well as the military.

LAND ROVER PROTOTYPES

The Land Rover body was to be made of aluminium alloy because sheet steel was in short supply in the late 1940s, although the more expensive aircraft-quality alloy was plentiful. The alloy was also much easier to work by hand, thus saving Rover the expense of buying machine tools to make the Land Rover's body. If they built it in aluminium it would neatly side-step the steel shortage, yet be eminently suitable as an export commodity. It was conceived as a short-term product, of simple construction, but robust and easy to operate. A prototype was ready in six months, by the summer of 1947, and to this end, it had a central steering wheel so there was no need for a left- or right-hand-drive bias. It might thus prove attractive to farmers used to the centre-steer layout of tractors and traction engines, and would not require conversion for export markets. As it turned out, of course, it proved impractical in practice, and a conventional steering position was adopted.

The centre-steer Land Rover prototype

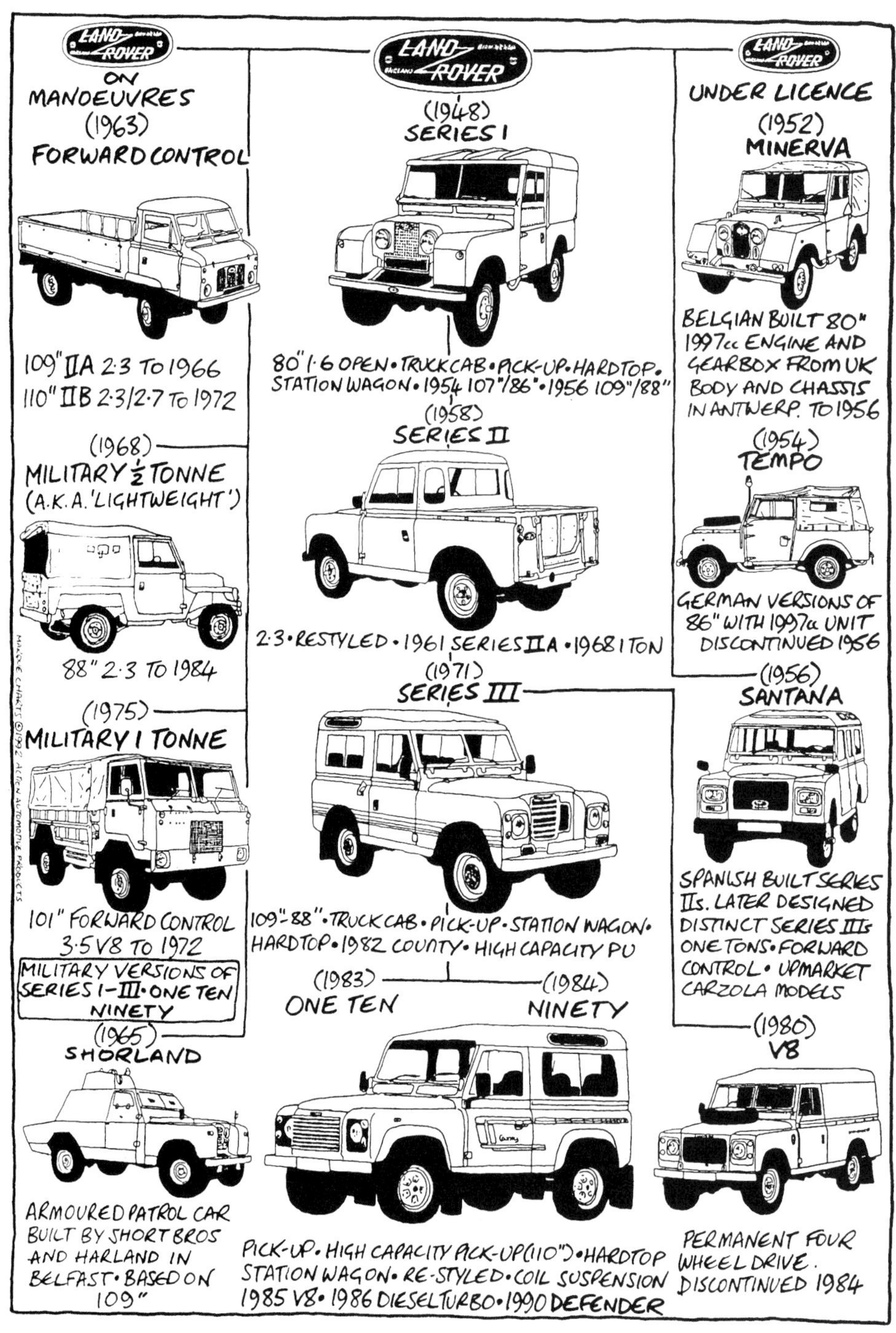

Land Rover family tree and derivatives, courtesy of James Ruppert.

Some of the very first Land Rovers near the end of the line at South Works; mesh radiator grilles have yet to be fitted.

was painted grey; this vehicle was restored in 1956 by Land Rover apprentices, although many of the parts used were later production items. The light green paint used on the first forty pre-production Land Rovers was actually aircraft cockpit green, of which there were plentiful supplies in the immediate post-war years.

Because the Rover chassis wasn't ready in time for the projected launch, the Jeep chassis was used, incorporating the 1,389cc engine, rear axle and suspension from the Rover 10 saloon car, with as many hand-formed alloy body parts as were necessary. However, although the prototype used the Jeep chassis, the proper Land Rover chassis was a far stronger box-section design, unlike the Jeep's channel-section version. Other prototypes were tried with power take-offs pulling ploughs, harrows and other farm implements. The Brockhouse 15cwt (762kg) trailer designed for the Land Rover used the same wheels and tyres and had the same track as the vehicle itself. With all these possibilities, it soon became apparent that a more powerful engine was needed, and that of the forthcoming Rover 60 P3 was drafted into service. A vehicle called the Road Rover was an early 1950s project which was half car, half Land Rover. Its name was resurrected in 1968 for the styling mock-up of the Range Rover. Land Rover engineers also designed a four-wheel-drive tractor with four-wheel steering some time around 1952; the idea was that it could be put into production quickly if Land Rover sales collapsed. This did not happen of course, and the prototype remained unique.

The Land Rover was launched at the Amsterdam Motor Show on 30 April 1948, displaying some of the pre-production batch, and in the sales department, the flood gates opened to greet orders from all over the world. Extraordinarily, there are no known photographs of the débutant Land Rover stand at the 1948 Amsterdam Show. But clearly the durability provided

Using the power-take-off from a protype Land Rover to evaluate its agricultral potential. The Jeep-based prototype had rounded front wings, Jeep-like door openings and central steering wheel.

One of the pilot build Land Rovers is put through its paces, prior to the launch at the Amsterdam show in April 1948.

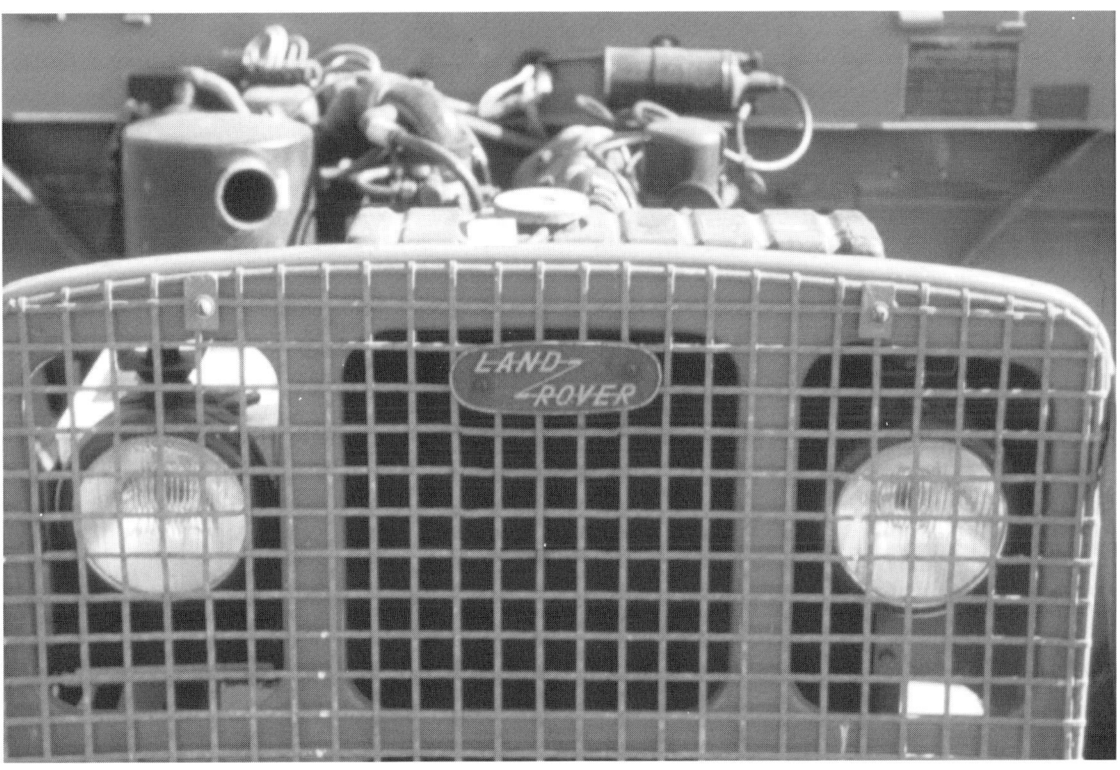

1948 Land Rover front panel and engine.

Instrumentation and ignition switch of a Series I. Dials are made by Jacger.

by its sturdy chassis and aluminium panels was a major attraction, combined with the high and low ratio gearbox for control and off-road ability.

Production commenced at the Solihull factory in the summer of 1948. It seemed that everyone wanted a Land Rover, from King George VI, who bought one for the Sandringham and Balmoral estates – the first of many royal Land Rovers – to farmers, foresters, police, and the armed forces. The greatest demand of all came from Africa and other parts of the developing world where a utilitarian go-anywhere vehicle was a bonus.

When the Land Rover was introduced in 1948, the Rover Company's intention was to use this new product to keep the production lines running until normal trading conditions returned to the car market. But in fact, normality never did return for Rover. The company had to take the export market seriously, and the success of the Land Rover turned Rover from a car manufacturer into a company which was first and foremost a maker of light commercial vehicles.

Keeping it in the Family

The Rover Company remained a family-run concern from the early 1930s to the late 1960s. Key figures were brothers Spencer and Maurice Wilks, and their nephews Peter Wilks and Spen King. As company chairman E. Ransome Harrison explained to Rover shareholders in December 1948, it was becoming clear that the Land Rover was destined to be far more than a stop-gap. With Robert Boyle in charge and Tom Barton as senior designer, the Land Rover underwent a constant process of development during the first five years of its life, which produced more variations than at any time in its subsequent history. Astonishingly, by 1951, the company was selling twice as many Land Rovers as Rover cars.

THE SERIES I

Detailing and Evolution

The first series Land Rovers were only referred to as Series Is retrospectively, when the concept was sufficiently updated to call new models the Series II. There are more variations in the Series I's evolution than subsequent models, simply because they were still trying to establish the best way of making it. The first Series I models built between 1948 and 1953 had a wheelbase of just 80in (2,032mm).

The 80 was superseded in 1953 by the 86in (2,184mm), and the 107 was the first long-wheelbase model. The 107in (2,717mm) prototype was built in mid-1950 and had a truck cab, using parts from the 80in Station Wagon.

Series I Station Wagons: the Woodies

From a very early stage in the genesis of Land Rover, its parent company planned a number of special vehicles. All of them were produced in small numbers, but the most popular version in 80in form was the Station Wagon. Conceived in the autumn of 1948, the Station Wagon was visualized as an upmarket multi-purpose vehicle. Its virtues were touted in the publicity brochures as follows: 'Conveniently adaptable to many passenger and transport needs. Station Wagon, estate car, shooting brake, service vehicle, family runabout, school or hotel bus, it fills all these and many other requirements.' There was little else around at the time to fulfil such a

LAND ROVER SERIES I

80in	1948–1954
86in	1954–1956
107in	1955–1958
88in	1957–1958
109in	1957–1958

Layout and Chassis

Two-door truck-cab pick-up, or three- or five-door Station Wagon
Box-section steel ladder chassis

Engine

Type	1948–1958, ioe petrol	
	1957–1958, ohv diesel	
Block material	cast iron	
Head material	cast iron	
Cylinders	four	
Cooling	water	
Bore × stroke	petrol	1948–1951: 69.5mm × 105mm
		1952–1958: 77.8mm × 105mm
	diesel	1957–1958: 85.7mm × 88.9mm
Capacity	petrol	1948–1951: 1,595cc
		1952–1954: 1,997cc
	diesel	1957–1958: 2,052cc
Compression ratio	petrol	6.8:1
	diesel	22.5:1
Carburettor	petrol	Solex
	diesel	CAV fuel injection
Max. power (DIN)	petrol	1948–1951: 50bhp @ 4,000rpm
		1951–1958: 52bhp @ 4,000rpm
	diesel	1957–1958: 51bhp @ 3,500rpm
Max. torque	petrol	1948–1951: 80lb/ft @ 2,000rpm
		1951–1958: 101lb/ft @ 1,500rpm
	diesel	1957–1958: 87lb/ft @ 2,000rpm

Transmission

1948–1950: permanent four-wheel drive with freewheel in front drivetrain
1950–1958: selectable two- or four-wheel drive in high-range, permanent four-wheel drive in low-range. Freewheel absent

Gearbox	four-speed plus reverse, syncromesh on third and fourth
Clutch	Single dry-plate
Ratios	3.00, 2.04, 1.47 (third: 1.38 from 1950), 1.1:1; reverse: 2.54:1
Transfer box	1.148:1 step-down in high range, 2.89:1 in low range
Final drive	front and rear: 4.7:1 from mid-1948 onwards

Suspension and Steering

Live axles front and back with semi-elliptic leaf-springs and hydraulic telescopic dampers all round

Steering	Recirculating ball, worm-and-nut, ratio 15:1

Tyres	6.00 × 16 or 7.00 × 16 109in model: 7.00 × 16 or 7.5 × 16
Wheels	16in pressed steel

Brakes

Type	hydraulic drums all round, mechanical hand brake operating on transmission
Size	1948–1954: 10in × 1.5in 1954–1958: 11in × 1.5in

Dimensions (in/mm)

80in model

Track	50/1,270 front and rear
Wheelbase	80/2,032
Overall length	132/3,352
Overall width	61/1,550
Overall height, tilt up	70.5/1,790 (1948–1952), 73.5/1,866 (1952–1954)
Unladen weight	2,594lb (1,174kg)
Maximum payload	1,000lb (453kg)
Turning circle	35ft (10.5m) 6.00 tyres, 40ft (12m) 7.00 tyres

86in model

Track	50/1,270 front and rear
Wheelbase	86/2,184
Overall length	140.7/3,574
Overall width	62.6/1,585
Overall height, tilt up	76in/1,928
Unladen weight	2,702lb (1,224kg)
Turning circle	37ft (11m)

107in model

Track	50/1,270 front and rear
Wheelbase	107/2,717
Overall length	173.5/4,406
Overall width	62.6/1,585
Overall height, tilt up	83.5/2,114; Station Wagon: 78/1,978
Unladen weight	2,740lb (1,241kg)
Maximum payload	1,500lb (679kg)
Turning circle	50ft (15m)

88in model

Track	50/1,270 front and rear
Wheelbase	88/2,235
Overall length	140.75/3,574
Overall width	62.6/1,585
Overall height, tilt up	76/1,928
Unladen weight	
petrol engine	2,740lb (1,241kg); diesel: 2,935lb (1,330kg)
Maximum legal payload	petrol 1,450lb (657kg); diesel 1,352lb (611kg)

Turning circle	38ft (11.5m)
109in model	
Track	50/1,270 front and rear
Wheelbase	109/2,768
Overall length	173.5/4,406
Overall width	62.6/1,585
Overall height, tilt up	83.5/2,114
Unladen weight	petrol engine 2,740lb (1,241kg); diesel 2,935lb (1,330kg)
Maximum legal payload	7 × 16 tyres: 1,500lb (679kg); 7.5 × 16 tyres: 2,000lb (906kg)
Turning circle	45ft (13.5m)

Performance

Top speed, 2.0-litre petrol	59.5mph (95.7km/h)
0–50mph	24.9secs
Fuel consumption	21mpg (13.5l/100km)

An early model with windscreen folded down and drop-down tail-gate lowered. The tilt hoops are stowed behind the seats.

diverse role. In the States they had car-based station wagons, better known as 'woodies'. These had ash-framed rear passenger and luggage compartments with alloy panels and twin rear doors, but as time went by, the half-timbered look was faked up with external woodwork. A few found their way to the British colonies, but in general something more robust was needed.

In Britain there were refurbished pre- and post-war shooting brakes – Ford V8 Pilots were most popular – and precious little else. A few companies converted army surplus Jeeps by lengthening the chassis and adding traditional timber-framed bodywork with comfortable seating. An upmarket version was offered by John Burleigh Automobiles of Kensington in 1947 at £550, while similar, but more basic

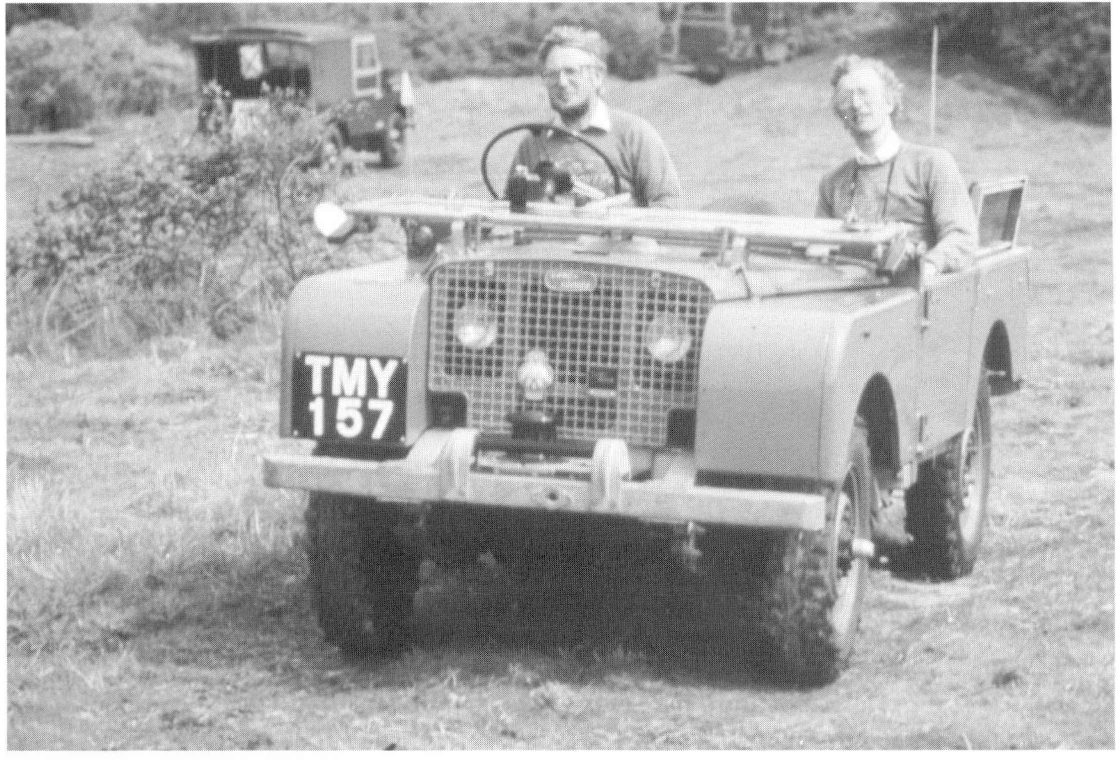

Land Rovers are vehicles with a distinct personality and, perhaps predictably, this 1948 Land Rover is known as Tommy.

versions were being produced by the London company Metamet. Others were created from small delivery vans, with seating and side windows.

The 80in Station Wagon had a single-piece windscreen, thirty-five years before the 110, while Santana-built Land Rovers had one-piece screens during the 1970s. The Rover Company did not build the 80in Land Rover Station Wagon body itself, and there is still confusion about who did: the prototype was built by Tickford, but the production ones may well have been built by Abbey Panels and Mulliners. Nobody is certain, but it was not uncommon for manufacturers to farm out special lines to more than one company; the subcontractors often lacked the capacity to take on the entire production run.

In any event, Rover supplied basic vehicles without rear bodywork, doors, seats and windscreen to the coachbuilding firm, either Abbey Panels, Mulliners or Tickfords at Newport Pagnell. The vehicles were driven there with the driver wearing goggles and sitting on a wooden box mounted above the petrol tank. It was a relatively common sight in the 1950s to see vehicles being transported in this way. A trimmer who used to work at Tickfords explained that although orders for Station Wagons were irregular, when an order for a batch was received, more than a dozen vehicles might be built and trimmed in a week. A total of 651 Station Wagons were built between May 1949 and January 1951, and these were preceded by two prototypes.

Restoring the Originals

Many elderly Land Rovers which survive today have fascinating tales to tell, and the story of the original Station Wagon is perhaps one of the most intriguing. Identified by its chassis plate as L20, it was a pre-production vehicle built in May 1948, and registered HAC 381. It was sent via Franco-Britannic Autos as a demonstration vehicle to the Paris Motor Show of October 1948. Photos indicate it was left-hand drive, although it was registered in Britain as right-hand drive. Its first road tax expired in December 1948, and it was not re-taxed until December 1960; its location during these missing years is not known. In 1960, HAC 381 was acquired by a young Rolls-Royce apprentice in Scotland, by now described as 'well worn' and having been fitted with a Perkins diesel engine.

According to Series I authorities, getting HAC 381 started was a rather bizarre procedure. It had a Ky-gas starter, consisting of a small paraffin reservoir mounted on the engine side of the bulkhead, and inside on the dashboard was a small chrome knob to pump paraffin into the inlet manifold. To start her up, you would first turn on the ignition to heat up the glow plugs. Next, a few furious pumps on the Ky-gas, and with any luck a strange glugging sound would be heard, indicating that the paraffin was alight in the inlet manifold. Pressing the starter would, with luck, then bring the old Perkins to life.

The Scottish apprentice used HAC 381 until early 1961, when the bodywork began to fall apart; in fact his fiancée fell out when the passenger door flew open – although despite this impediment, the marriage still took place. Due to bodywork and mechanical problems, the vehicle was left to stand until the offer of a job abroad forced a decision, and the old prototype made its last trip to Charlie Waters' scrap yard at Elderslie, Renfrewshire. Lest anyone get excited at the prospect of finding it, sad to say this yard was cleared some years later to make way for a roundabout opposite the old Linwood car factory.

Before production of Station Wagons could get under way, Rover had found itself in need of another prototype. To build this, a standard pick-up, No 71 production, was dispatched from Rover's Seagrave Road works in London to Tickford's. This vehicle was shown at the London Motor Show, Olympia, in October 1948 while the other Station Wagon was being exhibited in Paris. Number 71 was reputedly ordered at the show stand by the Marquis of Cholmondeley, and was delivered to the Houghton estate near King's Lynn in early 1949 where it remained in continuous use, mostly chauffeur driven, until damaged in an accident with an estate lorry in the 1980s.

There may well be a happier ending to this story. After several years' storage it was sold off at a farm auction and bought by an enthusiast who subsequently offered it to its present owner John Beeken, who was set to undertake a potentially difficult restoration.

There are still a few Series I production vehicles around, although rotten wood has probably put paid to the majority by now. Some have been painstakingly restored, though most are still languishing. An 80in Station Wagon makes a very difficult and expensive restoration: parts are practically impossible to find, and one or two have actually had to be broken for spares.

One or two restorations are in the pipeline. Laurie Pack has been working on his Station Wagon for several years, and it is now nearing completion; it had to be stripped, and needed repairs to the bulkhead and other areas. 'Down under' in Australia Keith Cree had an unbelievable find when he acquired an 80in Station Wagon in pieces without a chassis, and then, separately, an 80in pick-up, which on closer examination proved to be a 'bitzer', rebuilt on a Station Wagon chassis. Amazingly, the body plate number and stamped chassis number were just four digits apart. John Smith owns the oldest production vehicle, EPN 262, which originally belonged to relatives of the Churchill family, and it is in excellent unrestored condition. A vehicle spotted in 1995 in a scrap yard at Ilkley, Yorkshire, is not an abandoned derelict but a future restoration project for its owner, John, at Jake Wright Land Rovers, although he might be persuaded to part with it. This one seems to have its original engine, but it also has a lot of rot. It was part-exchanged for a Lightweight many years ago.

The seven-seater Series I Station Wagon is a charming vehicle, and a practical concept too, but if considering buying one, do not be tempted unless you have a great deal of skill, very deep pockets and a stubborn streak. Vehicles which are apparently sound can hide rotten woodwork, while a completely stripped vehicle is a potential nightmare.

From a sales point of view, the 80in Station Wagon was hardly a success and was dropped from the catalogue in mid-1951. When launched, it was hideously expensive at £949 – you could buy several houses for that sort of money then. Classified as a car, the Station Wagon attracted purchase tax of £207, but being multi-purpose and thus potentially a goods vehicle its speed was restricted to 30mph (50km/h). To circumvent this, some estate car users sealed up the back doors to declassify it as a van, which was hardly

An assortment of Series Is including soft-tops, a Station Wagon and safari-roof models, with semaphore arms prominent.

what Rover intended. Not surprisingly, home market sales were slow, while colonial customers had little need of such a fancy vehicle. Surprisingly, the largest single order was from UNICEF who sent the Station Wagons to Poland. Four vehicles have materialized there in recent years, and there may yet be more.

Towards a Longer Wheelbase

The only problem about the Series I was that the load space was not that big, especially when compared with descendants such as a 109 or an FC which could almost accommodate a SWB in the back. The logical progression was towards a longer-wheelbase model, but for the moment the company's hands were tied. The drawing office and engineering staff were fully occupied with getting the new P4 saloon into production for its eventual unveiling in September 1949, and the production side of the company was working flat-out to satisfy demand for the Land Rover. By 1950 the pressure had eased a little, and technical boss Maurice Wilks was given the green light for some further development work on the Land Rover.

Customers had already declared they wanted improvement in the load-carrying capacity, and Rover's initial reaction was not simply to enlarge the existing vehicle but to think in terms of a much larger companion model. It is likely that they were inspired by the Willys Jeep Truck, which had been announced in 1946 and was already doing well as a rural pick-up in the USA.

The earliest known record of a long-wheelbase Land Rover is a series of photographs taken in August 1950, sometime after the trial batch of 2.0-litre models had been built. It was in all probability an 80in chassis with an extension inserted behind the second crossmember to give a wheelbase similar to the 107 model introduced three years later.

The first long-wheelbase Land Rover was perhaps more of a feasibility study than a

Six of the best line up outside South Works – the building still in wartime camouflage – circa 1949.

A 107in Series I with pick-up back section and aluminium hard top.

prototype. It was recorded simply as the 'Long Buss', complete with mis-spelling. Apparently no records survive to explain why a wheelbase of 107in should have been chosen. However, according to Land Rover historian James Taylor, the Solihull engineers probably started with the dimensions of the load-bed they wanted, and then arranged the other measurements around it. The production 107 had a 6ft (1.8m) load-bed, and it seems likely that this first try-out would have had the same, because a round measurement would have been the most obvious starting-point.

Size-wise, Rover obviously did not copy the Jeep Truck, which had a much longer 118in wheelbase; this made for a large and unwieldy vehicle. In addition, the Jeep's rear wheelboxes were placed outside the load-bed. Rover elected to make their vehicle's load-bed a full-width one, to enclose the wheelboxes under its sides, and to fit lockers ahead and behind the wheelboxes on each side.

Land Rover also capitalized on the size of the load-bed by moving the spare wheel from its position behind the seats of the standard 80in model and mounting it on the vehicle's bonnet. On this score, the Jeep design was unsuitable, and its spare wheel was mounted outside the load-bed, ahead of the left-hand wheelbox.

Until now, all production Land Rovers except for the Station Wagon had open tops. The crude metal roof and rear panel of Land Rover's truck cab model had yet to

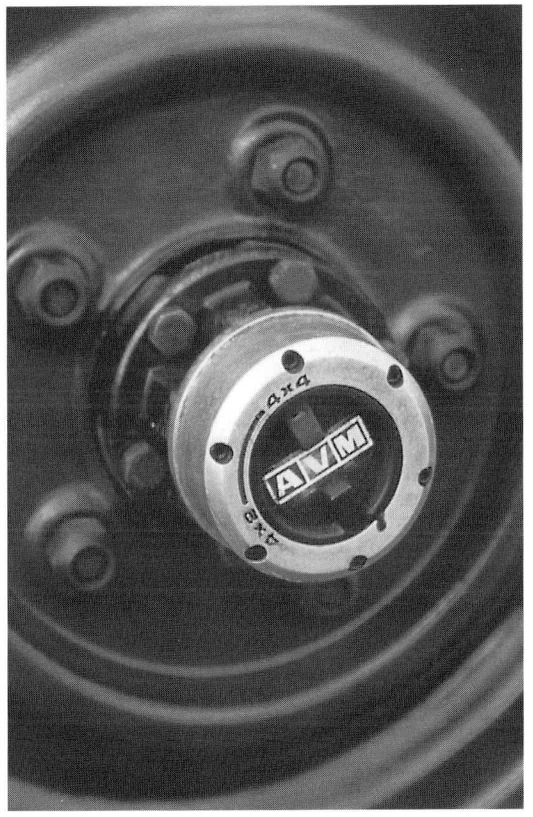

appear on the options list, but it was clear that the new long-wheelbase vehicle needed a fully enclosed cab. On this point, there is a good case for assuming that they were inspired by the example of the Jeep Truck, which featured just such a cab as standard.

The only full-height Land Rover doors in production in mid-1950 were those on the Station Wagon, making them a sound basis for the new model. Solihull engineers would have noted that their Jeep counterparts had employed the doors from their Station Wagon for the cab of the Jeep Truck. Because the Station Wagon doors were hung on a bulkhead which was unique to that model, the truck cab model was fitted with the same bulkhead, together with the one-piece windscreen which went with it. From there on, however, new components were needed. A rear panel for the cab had to be fabricated specially, and a new roof panel was also made up, which

Freewheel hubs are an aftermarket extra, but well worth fitting for improved economy.

Regular Series I soft-top in profile; there are more varieties of Series I than any other Land Rover, and 218,327 units were produced between 1948 and 1958.

A very rare 80in coachbuilt Station Wagon, as yet unregistered. Bodies were aluminium over ash frames, made by Abbey Panels of Coventry and Mulliners of Birmingham, and possibly Tickfords of Newport Pagnell.

was rather flatter in profile than the Station Wagon's. The tops of the doors were also modified to suit this flatter roof line. Twin bulkhead ventilators were fitted, which were absent from the 80in and Station Wagon specification. Thus the long-wheelbase prototype was the earliest Land Rover to be equipped with ventilators.

Cab ventilation was certainly a problem on the contemporary production 80in models, as there was no alternative to the two extremes of open or closed. Bulkhead ventilators did not appear on production models until 1953, with the introduction of the 86in and 107in, in spite of the fact that their ventilators were different from those on the prototype.

The cost of building a truck cab on the 107 prototype was a serious consideration, because to put it into production would have meant either modifying the already expensive coachbuilt doors and bulkhead of the Station Wagon, or setting up new machine tools to manufacture the new panels.

As things turned out, it was another two years before a long-wheelbase Land Rover was built, and in the meantime they compromised by stretching the wheelbase of the 80in model to make a larger SWB Land Rover. The prototype chassis for the 86in model was probably the experimental army staff car of June 1951.

The solution to the truck cab design was the crude roof-and-back-panel assembly, productionized in August 1951 as the optional metal cab for the 80. This was a lot cheaper than the cab design which had been proposed during 1950, and it was logical to amalgamate it with the flatbed feasibility study of 1950.

Work began again on the long-wheelbase models during 1952, and the first official prototype – rather than feasibility study – was up and running before the end of the year. The production 107 was launched a year and a half later; the chassis of early 107in models was painted blue.

Variations on a Theme

Several landmarks in the vehicle's evolution centre on the 86in model. The first one was probably the experimental army staff car built in 1951, two years before 86in production began, while the first State Review Land Rover was built in 1953 on an early 86in chassis. It remained in service until 1975 and is now in the Heritage Collection. The first long-range desert patrol Land Rovers used by the Special Air Service Regiment were also unit-converted 86in models. In 1953 Land Rover bowed to customer pressure for better load-carrying capacity by introducing the 86in model, featuring a 6in longer wheelbase and additional overhang at the rear. The 107in wheelbase model was conceived as a pick-up, which would really keep the farmers happy. In 1954, another seven-seater Station Wagon appeared, but this time it was constructed not around a wooden frame, but utilizing parts from existing models like the hard top. It was thus an affordable proposition, and was followed in 1957 by a ten-seater version built on the long-wheelbase chassis.

This Red Cross ambulance is based on a 107in Series I, built from 1954 onwards.

This Series I ambulance was made by Pilcher Greene and finished to a very high standard.

For some time the bureaucrats had some difficulty in deciding what niche the Land Rover should occupy. It was legally a commercial vehicle until 1956, when an historic judgement gave it the right to be considered a dual-purpose type.

From 1956 the wheelbases were tweaked again, by another couple of inches to 88in and 109in, but without any tangible benefit to load-carrying capacity. The extra length was in order to accommodate the physically larger diesel engine which was scheduled for the following year.

Engine Development

Rover had to wait until they had completed tank engine contracts for the British army before they could find the factory space to build a diesel engine for the Land Rover. Meanwhile, the original petrol-fuelled 1,595cc four-cylinder power units were bored out to 1,997cc in 1951, largely in response to customer demand. Feedback had suggested that road performance needed improving, and the engine section of the drawing office under Jack Swaine drew up the larger 2.0-litre version of the existing engine.

The British army evaluated a batch of thirty-three Land Rovers equipped with Rolls-Royce B40 2.8-litre engines in 1949, and the taller Rolls-Royce engine in the experimental batch meant that rubber buffers had to be provided on the front panel to raise the bonnet slightly. Then in the first few months of 1950, a batch of fifty 2.0-litre Land Rovers was built to test the new Rover engine. At the same time, the six-cylinder saloon car engine was enlarged from 2.1-litres to 2.6-litres, and the new engine was tried in a batch of thirty P4 saloons. The car engine proved unsatisfactory and had to be redesigned for

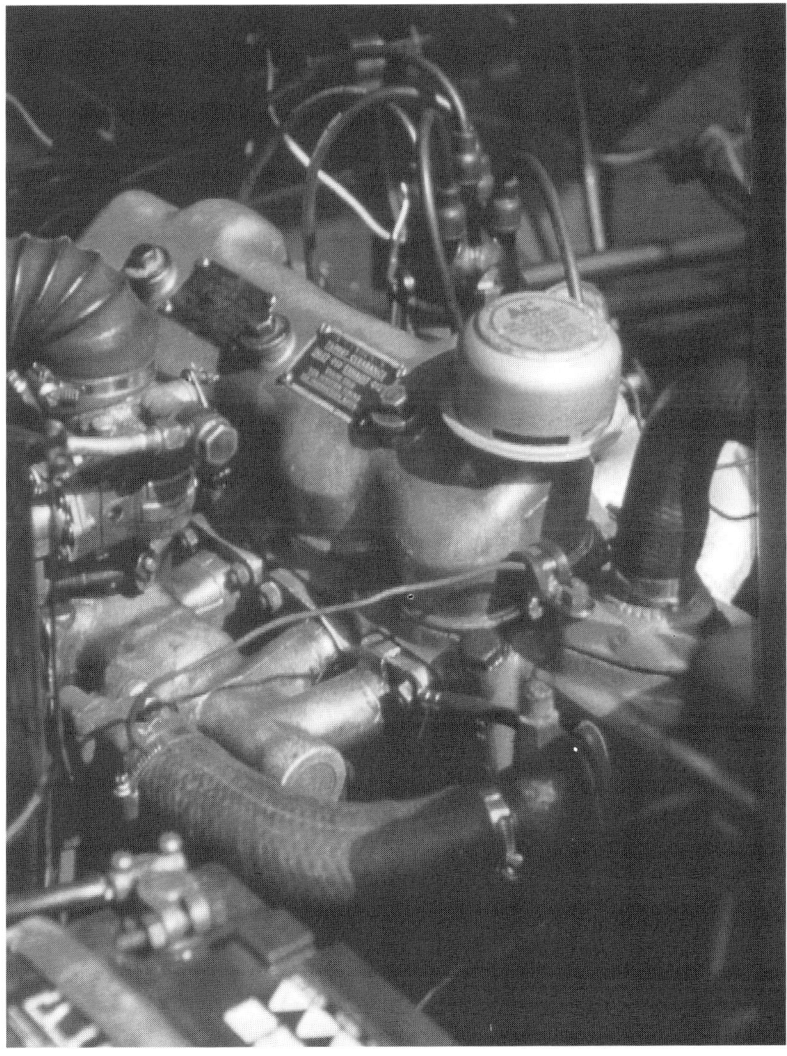

2.0-litre Series I petrol engine developed 52bhp at 4,000rpm and 101lb/ft torque at 1,500rpm.

production, while the Land Rover engine was deemed to be satisfactory. Although the spacing of the bores was changed with the 86in and 107in models in 1953, this engine remained fundamentally unaltered until 1958 and beyond.

Land Rovers were selling to customers who also ran diesel-fuelled lorries, so it was logical to install such an engine in the Land Rover. Development started in the mid-1950s, and the first diesel engine was introduced in 1957, a 2,052cc overhead valve type unit. Because it was physically larger than the regular petrol unit, it was necessary to enlarge the engine bay behind the front axle by a couple of inches (50mm)to accommodate it. Thus the 86in became the 88in, and the 107in became the 109in model. The change was made in mid-1956, some six months ahead of the diesel models' launch in order to help spread the cost of the entire project. Land Rover was experimenting with a five-bearing 2.5-litre turbocharged diesel engine as early as 1962. It did not go into production until 1986, however.

A Good Grilling

The early 80in vehicles are characterized by their distinctive, but basic grille and headlight arrangements. First came the style with small headlights completely covered by wire. Cleaning the lights in this arrangement was difficult, to say the least, so after more than a year's production this grille was superseded by the variation which had the 7in (178mm) headlights protruding through the wire mesh. These continued until mid-1951, while the sidelights were small units mounted in the corners of the bulkhead. From mid-1951, all Series Is had the familiar upside-down, T-shaped grille, and sidelights in the wings.

After the middle of 1951, wings with pressed and punched sidelight apertures produced a raised-eyebrow look. From mid-1951 to mid-1953, wings were of one-piece construction, with inner and outer combined. All top and front inner wings up to mid-1953 were made from a single sheet of metal. After that, the top and front were formed from two sections with an evident join above the sidelight. Only 88in and 109in wings have a spot-welded stiffening plate behind the wind door buffer. Restorers have to note that wings from 86in and 107in models are not interchangeable with 88in and 109in wings, as the wheel apertures are further forward on the later models.

Series Is had four basic types of bulkhead. Those of the first vehicles were constructed from flat steel sheet, followed by one with curved, pressed footwells. Occasionally bulkheads were made of steel angle, clad in sheet aluminium. All these were fabricated for the 80in Land Rover, and contained lozenge-shaped instrument panels containing three small dials. All later Series Is had a bulkhead made from flat sheet steel with a rectangular instrument panel containing two large dials, and a pair of opening air vents in the top.

Doors are easy to identify, since all later Series Is have doors with a vertical rear shut line, and a recessed handle. Although there are differences in detail, they are interchangeable. Early 80in doors do not have door handles, just a triangular canvas flap which has to be lifted to access the inner handle. This was still state-of-the-art for sports cars at the time, but from mid-1951 protruding external door handles were fitted to the 80in, with the door tops losing the canvas triangle.

When you open the door you see that 80in seatboxes have horizontal tops and wedge-shaped cushions, while later Series Is have raked boxes and flat cushions. If the seat back is folded down, you find that later Series Is have a large space behind for tool stowage.

Early seats were hinged by vertical brackets up the seat back, while the early 80in vehicles had a seat which tapered at the top and was bolted on sprung loops to the rear body capping. A few early production vehicles had seat backs consisting simply of an upholstered 5in deep strip. From the middle of 1951 to mid-1953, seats were simply hinged at the corners. One way of telling if a Series I is the later type is if the rear body has the tool storage space behind the seats. 80in vehicles had a 3in wide galvanized capping behind the seats until early 1950. Thereafter, in an attempt to gain leg-room, it was very much narrower.

There were many differences in chassis design. Later Series Is had five brackets supporting the rear body, while the 80in

Pleasing simplicity of a Series Land Rover's internal door handle.

Close-up of Series I door hinges.

Soft-top Series I. Note the single wiper, and the solitary sidelights in the wing fronts.

made do with four. The difference between 86/107in and 88/109in models is most easily seen in the difference in the position of the spring hangers on the front dumb-irons. You can also tell an 86in from an 88in by the position of the front wing retaining bolt, slightly further back on the later model, while the grille panel simply has one aperture rather than three.

Chassis Detailing

By 1958 some chassis details were pretty much as they would be for the forthcoming Series II vehicles. The most obvious change on the 80in chassis is the upgrading from narrow 1¾in springs with swinging shackles at the front, to wider 2½in springs shackled at the rear. This was done to nullify steering shimmy. Early 80in chassis had an extension to the front dumb-irons for attaching the bumper.

The rear axle had semi-floating halfshafts, identifiable by a slight recess in the centre of the wheel, although from April 1957 the LWB and the 107in Station Wagon received the new, protruding and fully floating halfshafts, which were also optional on 88in models. Halfshafts were not interchangeable with those of the Series II, being slightly longer. On the front axle, the steering lever was fixed to the top of the swivel housing, an arrangement that passed over onto Series II models. Only later was it positioned below the swivel housing.

Gearboxes remained much the same throughout, but early 80in models used a

A mobile workshop made for Castrol by Pilcher Greene on a long-wheelbase Series II chassis.

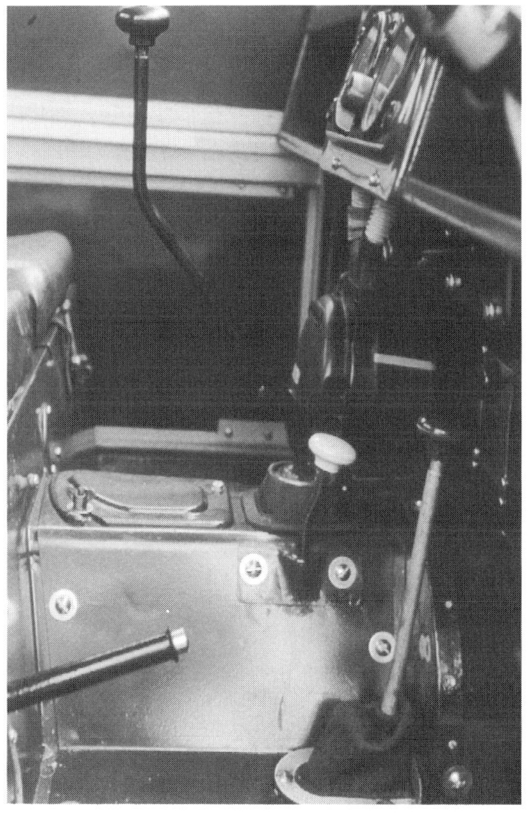

Driving position of a Series I, with the three transfer box gear levers.

Instruction plate on Series I transfer box also gives the vehicle's number.

Series I belonging to Nigel Weller, fitted with a safari-top Station Wagon body. The spare wheel is mounted on the bonnet.

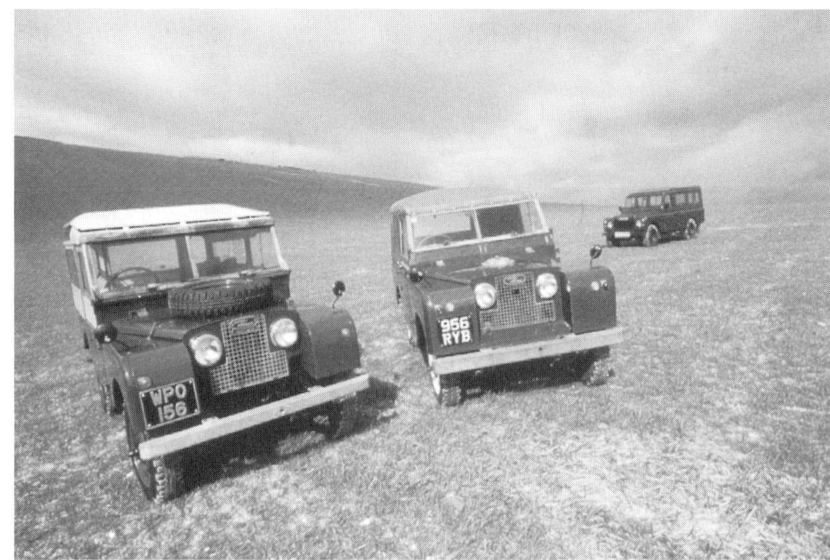

A Series I and Series II, with a 110 Station Wagon at the rear. The Series II shows a narrower screen, indicators in the wing fronts, a deeper front panel, a bonnet catch, and vents in the scuttle.

permanent four-wheel drive system with a freewheel in the front drive line. The freewheel is recognizable as the second of two casings forward of the transfer box, whereas the more usual selectable four-wheel drive system is a single casing. A ring pull mounted on the off-side floorpan will lock the freewheel, but freewheel units continued to be fitted for some time to vehicles with three gear levers.

Except for the diesels, all Series I engines were of overhead-inlet, side-exhaust layout. Later, post-1954, spread-bore 2.0-litre models had the oil filter on the right-hand side. An oil filter located on the left-hand side indicates an early Siamese-bore 1,595cc unit. On the 2.0-litre engines a water dispersion tube entered the rear of the block, and was secured with a cover plate with two bolts. The 1,595cc engine had a water pipe entering the front of the engine.

2 Series II to the Present

Land Rover evolution had slowed down by the late 1950s, and the following Series models merged almost seamlessly into one another. The Series II was the first Land Rover to pass through the hands of the recently established Rover Styling Department. Working with the engineers, they made such a good job of it that the basic lines of their 1958 design are still highly attractive today. The Series II was introduced in April 1958. Differences were largely in the appearance – you could hardly call the changes 'cosmetic'; it is not that sort of vehicle. Station Wagon and truck-cab styling was cleaned up, and Series IIs now featured barrel sides instead of plain, and there were side valences to cover the chassis rails.

There were mechanical differences too, with a wider track, and a larger and more powerful 2.25-litre petrol engine replacing the Series I's 2.0-litre unit. It was virtually the same configuration as the 2.25-litre diesel. When the diesel power-plant was updated in 1961 to match the petrol engine's dimensions, the Series II became the IIA. The Series IIA was produced from 1961 to 1971, and Series IIA diesel Land Rovers had a distinctive plastic grille badge proclaiming 'Rover Diesel'. In 1968, new US Federal regulations called for headlamps to be repositioned, but before

The Land Rover stand at the 1958 Amsterdam show, featuring an 88in Series I and the first of the Series IIs, with snow plough, ambulance, and safari top Station Wagon.

Station Wagons could be supplied with safari tops, like this 1965 twelve-seater Series IIA. The gap between 'lids' allowed air to circulate and made for a cooler interior.

A late Series IIA, with headlights in the wing fronts like the Series III, but still with the wire-mesh radiator grille.

LAND ROVER SERIES II

88in	1958–1961
109in	1958–1961

Layout and Chassis

Two-door truck-cab pick-up, three- or five-door soft- or hard-top and Station Wagon
Box-section steel ladder chassis

Engine

Type	ioe petrol optional ohv diesel
Block material	cast iron
Head material	cast iron
Cylinders	four, three-bearing crank
Cooling	water
Bore x stroke	petrol 90.47mm × 88.9mm diesel 85.7mm × 88.9mm
Capacity	petrol 2,286cc diesel 2,052cc
Valves	eight
Compression ratio	petrol 7.0:1 diesel 22.5:1
Carburettor	petrol Solex diesel CAV fuel injection
Max. power (DIN)	petrol 77bhp @ 4,250rpm diesel 51bhp @ 3,500rpm
Max. torque	petrol 124lb/ft @ 2,500rpm diesel 87lb/ft @ 2,000rpm

Transmission

Selectable two- or four-wheel drive in high range, permanent four-wheel drive in low range

Gearbox	four-speed plus reverse, syncromesh on third and fourth
Clutch	single dry-plate
Ratios	3.00, 2.04, 1.38, 1.1:1; reverse: 2.54:1
Transfer box	1.148:1 step-down in high range, 2.89:1 in low range
Final drive, front and rear	4.7:1

Suspension and Steering

Live axles front and back with semi-elliptic leaf-springs and hydraulic telescopic dampers all round
Steering: Recirculating ball, worm-and-nut, ratio 15:1

Tyres	6.00 × 16 109in (2,768mm) model: 7.50 × 16
Wheels	16in pressed steel

Brakes

Type	hydraulic drums all round, mechanical hand brake operating on transmission
Size	11in × 1.5in 109in model: 11in × 2.25in

Dimensions (in/mm)

88in model

Track	51.5/1,307 front and rear
Wheelbase	88/2,235
Overall length	142.4/3,617
Overall width	64/1,625
Overall height, tilt up	77.5/1,966
Unladen weight, petrol engine	2,900lb (1,314kg); diesel 3,095lb (1,402kg)
Maximum weight limit	4,453lb (2,017kg)
Turning circle 3	8ft (11.5m)

109in model

Track	51.5/1,307 front and rear
Wheelbase	109/2,235
Overall length	175/4,443
Overall width	64/1,625
Overall height, tilt up	83.5/2,114
Unladen weight, petrol engine	3,294lb (1494kg); diesel 3,489lb (1,580kg)
Maximum weight limit	5,905lb (2,675kg)
Turning circle	45ft (13.5m)

Performance

Top speed, 2.28-litre petrol	68mph (109.5km/h)
0–50mph	16.8secs
Fuel consumption	18mpg (15.7l/100km)

Series II 88in Lightweight emerges from the mire.

Over 110,000 Series IIs were produced between 1958 and 1961.

the restyled wings – which incorporated the headlamps – were actually fitted, a small number of vehicles were built with the lights simply screwed onto the wing fronts. Understandably, these vehicles are now very rare.

Owners of early Series Land Rovers today might be dissatisfied with performance, but a top speed of 50mph (80km/h) is not necessarily the limit. Retro-fitted with a 2.25-litre engine, overdrive and free-wheel hubs, an early Series Land Rover is light enough to reach a top speed of over 70mph (110km/h), and will cruise at 55–60mph (90–100km/h) quite happily. Purists will say why bother, and if the vehicle is in original condition, they would be quite right.

Land Rovers were going from strength to strength. By the late 1950s and early 1960s the reliability and durability of leaf-sprung Series Is and IIs were legendary where they led a hard life, and on this basis many a farmer would probably be more than happy to purchase a new leaf-sprung vehicle today if one were still available, not only because of their ruggedness, but also because of ease of maintenance and repair. The British army was very much at home with Land Rover products for these reasons, having used them since 1948. By 1956, Land Rovers were standard issue for general purpose, light and medium utility work, and a number of special derivatives were produced.

Special Derivatives

The Forestry Commission was one of the first to require a special model, a Land Rover converted from standard and fitted with four sets of twin bogie wheels driving caterpillar tracks. It was allegedly somewhat unwieldy, and its ground clearance was considerable, making it capable of crossing inundated forestry land. Some slightly less unconventional anomalies crept in from time to time. A small number of left-hand drive CKD 88s and 109s were created in 1960 and shipped overseas with Perkins diesel engines, while Land Rover was also preparing to build a light 4 × 4 as a joint venture with Willys in 1958; a Land Rover-Willys hybrid prototype was actually assembled. And when fitted with flanged wheels, a diesel-powered 109in Land Rover was pressed into service on the railway, where it was capable of hauling trains weighing 50–60 tons. Bringing them to a halt was an entirely different matter, though.

A few military specials were given field trials, including the special-bodied 109s built in 1962 for stacking three high in transport aircraft. They were also amphibious, with a fibreglass propeller on the rear propshaft, waterproofed controls and foam-filled chassis rails, and fitted with rubber pontoons which were suspended from brackets either side of the body and inflated via the exhaust pipe.

Another mid-1960s oddball was the

Military Series II Lightweight and 101 – or One Tonne – Ambulance.

LAND ROVER SERIES IIA

88in	1962–1971
109in	1962–1971
109in One Tonne	1968–1971
109in Forward Control	1963–1966
110in Forward Control	
Series IIB	1967–1972

Layout and Chassis

Two-door truck-cab pick-up, three- or five-door soft or hard top and Station Wagon
Box-section steel ladder chassis

Engine

Type		ioe petrol
		ohv diesel
Block material		cast iron
Head material		cast iron
Cylinders		four, three-bearing crank; 109in model available with six-cylinder petrol engine from 1967, seven-bearing crankshaft
Cooling		water
Bore × stroke	petrol four	90.47mm × 88.9mm
	petrol six	77.8mm × 92.1mm
	diesel	90.47mm × 88.9mm
Capacity	petrol four	2,286cc
	petrol six	2,625cc
	diesel	2,052cc

(109in) FC only available with petrol four; 109in. One Ton only available with petrol six; SIIB FC available with all three engine options)

Compression ratio	petrol four	7.0:1
	petrol six	7.8:1
	diesel	23:1
Carburettor, petrol four		Solex until 1967, then Zenith onwards
	petrol six	SU on early models, replaced by Zenith
	diesel	CAV fuel injection
Max. power (DIN)	petrol four	77bhp @ 4,250rpm
	petrol six	83bhp @ 4,500rpm
	diesel	62bhp @ 4,000rpm
Max. torque	petrol four	124lb/ft @ 2,500rpm
	petrol six	128lb/ft @ 1,500rpm
	diesel	103lb/ft @1,800rpm

Transmission

Selectable two- or four-wheel drive in high range, permanent four-wheel drive in low range

Gearbox		four-speed plus reverse, syncromesh on third and fourth
Clutch		Single dry-plate
Ratios,	1962–1967	3.00, 2.04, 1.38, 1.1:1; reverse: 2.54:1
	1967 onwards	3.60, 2.22, 1.50, 1.1:1; reverse 3.02:1

Transfer box	1.148:1 step-down in high range, 2.89:1 in low-range until 1967, then 2.35:1
109in One Tonne and FC models	1.53:1 step-down in high-range; 109in (2,768mm) One Tonne: 3.27:1, and 109in (2,768mm) FC: 2.92:1 step-down in low-range
Final drive, front and rear	4.7:1

Suspension and Steering

Live axles front and rear, with semi-elliptic leaf-springs and hydraulic telescopic dampers all round. SIIB FC has front anti-rollbar

Steering	Recirculating ball, worm-and-nut, ratio 15:1. 109in (2,768mm) FC is lower geared
Tyres	6.00 × 16 109in model: 7.50 × 16 109in One Ton and FC model: 9.00 × 16
Wheels	16in pressed steel

Brakes

Type	hydraulic drums all round, mechanical hand brake operating on transmission
Size	11in × 1.5in 109in model: 11in × 2.25in 109in six-cylinder models: 11in × 3in drums at front. FC has servo assistance

Dimensions (in/mm)

88in model

Track	51.5/1,307 front and rear
Wheelbase	88/2,235
Overall length	1.42.4/3,617
Overall width	64/1,625
Overall height, tilt up	77.5/1,966
Unladen weight, petrol engine	2,953lb (1,338kg); diesel 3,097lb (1,403kg)
Maximum weight limit	4,453lb (2,017kg)
Turning circle	38ft (11.5m)

109in model

Track	51.5/1,307 front and rear; FC model 53/1,350; SIIB FC 57.5/1,451
Wheelbase	109/2,768; SIIB FC 110/2,793
Overall length	175/4,443; FC: 193/4,900
Overall width	64/1,625
Overall height, tilt up	83.5/2,114
Unladen weight, petrol four	3,301lb (1,496kg); petrol six 3,459lb 1,566kg); 109in One Tonne 3,886lb (1,762kg); 109in FC 4,200lb (1,902kg); diesel 3,445lb (1,560kg); SIIB FC diesel 4,505lb (2,041kg)
Maximum weight limit	5,905lb (2,675kg); One Ton payload 2,240lb (1,015kg); 109in FC payload 3,380lb (1,531kg)
Turning circle	45ft (13.5m)

Performance

Top speed, 2.28-litre petrol	68mph (109.5km/h)
0–50mph	16.8secs
Fuel consumption	18mpg (15.7l/100km)

special transporter for the Rover-BRM gas turbine Le Mans racing car, created by Land Rover Special Projects. Based on prototype Land Rover components, it had a special rear suspension system which could lower the load-bed to the ground, enabling the sports-racer to be driven on and off without ramps.

Of more dramatic value were the SAS's Long-Range Desert Group patrol vehicles of the late 1960s, based on the 109 Series IIA chassis. A reminder of the LRDG Rommel-baiters in North Africa during World War II, they were equipped with all the accoutrements of desert warfare, including a light machine gun or two, and were usually painted pink, an unlikely but effective camouflage colour (see chapter 5).

The Half-Tonne or Military Lightweight was far more numerous, and was driven regularly by civilian off-roaders. It was actually heavier than the normal 88 on which it was based, although it was lighter if the demountable body panels were removed. The army's requirement was for a vehicle which could be slung beneath military helicopters, and the bulkhead of the 88 Lightweight was narrower than standard so that the vehicle could be loaded two abreast into the Argosy transport aircraft. The Lightweight entered service in 1968, and was produced until 1983. You can see the very last one in the Heritage Collection, but since they are regularly decommissioned, more and more find their way into private hands.

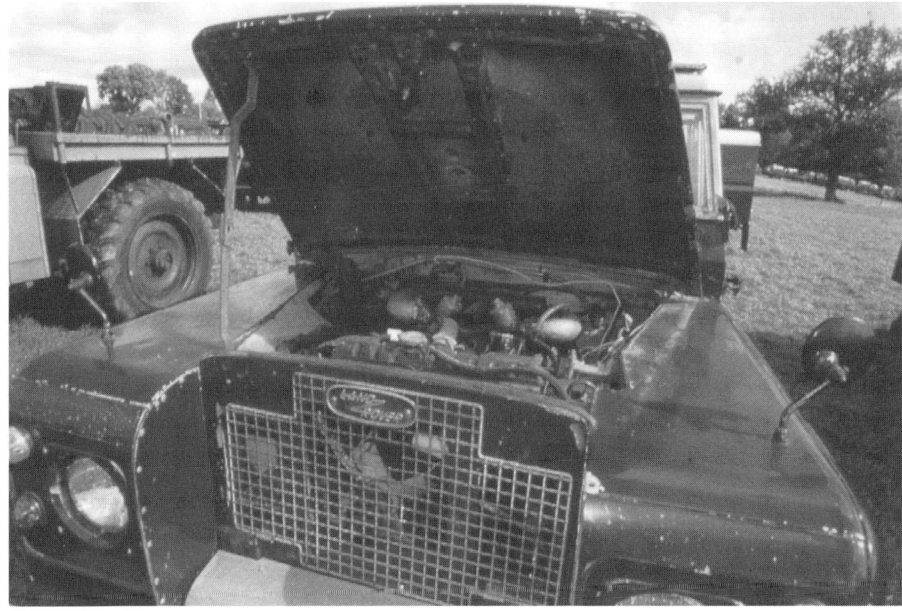

The prototype Series IIA V8; this was the first-ever short-wheelbase Land Rover to be fitted with a 3.5-litre Rover V8.

Camper conversion by Pilcher Greene on a 109in SIIA Forward Control model.

109in Forward Control Series IIA pick-up, with tilt fitted.

The Forward Control

Most notable and numerous of the Land Rover derivatives was the Forward Control model. This was based on a long-wheelbase chassis, and the cab was moved to the front of the vehicle over the engine, producing a long load-carrying platform behind. The legacy of siting the cab at the front of the vehicle was that it had to be higher to clear the engine, and it was thus somewhat less stable than the normal configuration Land Rover. Nevertheless, they were certainly the only small 'lorries' which could venture off-road.

The Forward Control model IIA was made from 1962, and was replaced by the IIB Forward Control in 1966. This had its rear axle relocated to give a 110in wheelbase. It was originally planned to build an 88in Forward Control Land Rover as well as a 109in version, but they seem to have scrapped the idea when it became obvious that the vehicle would compete directly with the regular 109in Pick-up. The Spanish Santana company's equivalent of the 109 Forward Control was called the 1300, and it had no sub-frame above its chassis.

In spite of its odd looks and layout, plenty of enthusiasts swear by their IIA/B Forward Control Land Rovers as everyday transport, as well as their off-road ability. Because you sit on top of the engine, there is a case for wearing ear-defenders in order to make the journey bearable. But with its

The Series IIB Forward Control Land Rover has a 110in chassis, and this one has a flatbed cargo deck. Only 2,305 Series IIB FCs were built.

Chassis of the Forward Control Series IIA, demonstrating that the engine was amidships in relation to the cab and driving position. The girder frame rests above a normal long-wheelbase chassis.

great flexibility, the six-cylinder engine is a pleasure to drive. Engine access is via a clipped-on box directly behind the cab section.

When off-roading, the rear suspension does not start working unless there is at least half a ton in the back, and this can lead to being cross-axled at the least obstacle. But with some weight in the back, it really comes into its own, and the ride can even be described as comfortable – better, in fact, off-road than on. In the wet, the FC has been known to keep going through the mud where other supposedly more capable coil-sprung vehicles have had to be towed out. However, since the last Forward Control models were made in 1972, they

The 101 was also known as the One Tonne because that was its payload. Most were soft-top general service vehicles, built between 1972 and 1978. Only 2,669 units were made; this is an ambulance version

are by now a little long in the tooth, and have to be viewed as classics.

The 101 Forward Control

Rather more aggressive in appearance was the magnificent One Tonne or 101 Forward Control Land Rover, usually seen as a soft top, and growling along cross-axled on its leaf-spring chassis, powered by its rumbling V8. It was allegedly designed by the British army, and put together using a variety of existing Land Rover components. It entered service in the mid-1970s and the final ones were made in 1978. They are gradually being decommissioned now, and like the Lightweight, examples of 101s trickle onto the enthusiast off-roading market, when they are sometimes converted into campers.

The 101in Forward Controls were assembled on the same Solihull factory lines which had previously turned out the stately Rover P5 saloons and coupés. Land Rover intended to use the 101 Forward Control as the basis for a civilian model, but it always remained a military vehicle because they were unable to satisfy the Construction and Use Regulations without having to resort to expensive modifications. However, Spanish associates Santana had no such trouble, and turned it into the S-2000, fitted with their own six-cylinder engines – effectively one-and-a-half of Solihull's 2.25-litre fours – and distinctive bodywork. The UK prototype 101s had six-cylinder engines, and one was also fitted with an Australian Ford Falcon V8 engine, supposedly to tempt the Australian army into placing an order. In fact, the largest user of 101s outside Britain was, somewhat bizarrely, the Luxembourg army.

There was never any doubt that the concept of the Forward Control vehicles was sound. A production line had already been set up at Solihull in the mid-1980s for the Llama FC model, but the project was axed because it failed to win a military contract.

THE RANGE ROVER

The six-cylinder models marked a trend towards Land Rovers which were at once more capable than the fours, as well as being easier to drive – more of a leisure vehicle, in fact. In the mid-1960s Land Rover commissioned a survey to establish what made the leisure market tick in North America. The result was the Range Rover, launched to wide acclaim in 1970. It

Six Pack

There is nothing quite the equal of a six-cylinder engine on full song, and in the days of cheap petrol during the mid-1960s, it was an obvious avenue for Land Rover to explore. The first production six-cylinder Land Rover was the 109in (2,768mm) Forward Control, which was offered with the 2.6-litre engine from autumn 1963. The 3.0-litre six-cylinder engine was used in experimental 109 Station Wagons as well as various military prototypes in the mid-1960s, and it also figured in proposals for the Range Rover. The first regular Land Rover to acquire the six-cylinder motor was a 1965 Station Wagon, NLT 9, belonging to the Queen Mother. The model was not offered to the general public until two years later in 1967, when it was fitted in the 109in ((2,768mm) models. The so-called NADA (North American Dollar Area) 109 Station Wagon had a high-compression version of the 2.6-litre six, as well as a limited-slip differential in the rear axle. The LSD proved so problematic that many were replaced by standard differentials.

Prototype six-cylinder 101 with soft top in use as a gun tractor, made in 1972.

A special-bodied shooting brake Series I specially made for an African safari for HM the Queen Mother.

was an instant success, and in such demand in Europe that the US market simply could not be satisfied; it was seventeen years before sales in the USA finally began. Original Range Rovers had selectable four-wheel drive, because the permanent four-wheel drive components which designer Spen King wanted were not then available.

It is such a different animal from the regular Land Rover that it does not bear more than a passing mention here (the full story is told in James Taylor's and Nick Dimbleby's excellent book in the Crowood series). Suffice it to say that the marvellous 3.5-litre V8 engine, combined with the coil sprung chassis, pointed the way towards Land Rovers of the future. Not only did the V8 motor give you the feeling that it would get you out of anything, it provided effortless on-road cruising, while the suspension gave a more comfortable ride as well as better axle articulation in the rough. Rover's North American subsidiary tried to persuade Solihull to put a V8 into the 88 Land Rover back in 1966; they even created a prototype called the Golden Rod and shipped it over to the UK, but the management was not amused. A few V8-powered 88s were built in the early 1980s, but the model was never offered for sale to the general public.

Meanwhile, to keep abreast of the corporate side, Land Rover Engineering had not been formally separated from saloon car engineering until 1956, eight years after the first Land Rover went on sale. In 1969, Rover was absorbed into the British Leyland conglomerate, and the disgraceful consequence was that profits from Land Rover sales were used to fund loss-making Austin and Morris family saloons of very little merit. Rover finally lost its independence in 1972, when its engineering department was merged with that of Triumph.

Because the Land Rover was originally supposed to be a stop-gap product to see Rover through a difficult period when they had nothing else which could be exported in large volumes, the company took twenty years to adjust to the Land Rover's success. By the time of the Land Rover's 25th anniversary in 1973, the vehicle had earned Britain over £475 million in foreign currency. But right up to the 1970s, Rover still thought of itself primarily as a car manufacturer, even though Land Rovers paid the bills. There is a powerful school of thought which believes this to be still the

Dunsfold Collections

Fans of Series Land Rovers should consider a visit to the Dunsfold Land Rover Trust. It is run by Brian Bashall and Richard Beddall, and is a collection of classic Land Rovers, unrivalled by any other in the world.

The Trust is keen for them to be seen by everyone, and in addition, they are happy for garages to use vehicles for promotional purposes, provided they make a donation to the Trust and pay for delivery to and from the display venue.

Among the Land Rover memorabilia they have a copy of the first Land Rover Owners' Club magazine – volume 1, number 1 – dated September 1957. Featured on the cover is HRH the Duke of Edinburgh driving a Series 1.

All Land Rover owners are invited to join the Dunsfold Trust, and there is a minimum donation of £20 a year. The Trust can be contacted on 01483 200 058.

case today: that Land Rover Defenders fund expansion and production on the company's car lines at the expense of Land Rover build quality.

The regular increases in production volumes for today's Discovery are reminiscent of the early 1950s, when Rover was constantly obliged to increase Land Rover production to meet demand. Land Rovers have always shared a number of components with Rover cars, and even the most recent Range Rover is no exception.

Back in 1969, BL had committed so much to the Range Rover launch that there was very little available to fund development of the new Land Rover. Thus the Series III which came out in 1971 was not all that different from the Series IIA. The wheelbases were identical, the SIII inherited the 2.6-litre six and the 2.25-litre petrol and diesel engines, and the late IIA's repositioned headlights were carried over. The

The 88in Series III used either a 2.25-litre petrol or a diesel engine. This is a 1972 model.

County spec Series III Station Wagon had de luxe *trim and side decals from 1982.*

Lightweight Series III had a one-piece screen and the headlights in its wings.

all-synchromesh gearbox of the Series III models had already been fitted to the final run of UK market Series IIA Station Wagons. Perhaps the only significant new option for the Series III was fitment of an overdrive. Externally it had flatter door hinges and a new plastic radiator grille, not a thing of beauty. Inside, the instrument panel was revised.

The millionth Land Rover was a 1976 Series III, originally to be painted gold, but the paint proved so troublesome that it was finished in metallic green instead. Although cosmetically different, it was not so different from the Series I. Had things worked out differently, there might have been a Series III Land Rover rather more like a miniature Range Rover. Stylist Tony Poole worked on renderings for such a vehicle in the mid-1960s, and its key feature was 45° cut off front wings with niches in the corners for the headlights. Known as the SD5 project, it was to be a 111in, with almost no overhang, allowing much steeper angles of approach and departure. There were similarities between its envisaged manufacturing process and that of Japanese 4 × 4s, and it could have been the Land Rover of the 1980s.

In 1978, British Leyland announced an investment programme for Land Rover products, and at the same time Land Rover Ltd became a separate operating company. By 1981, Rover car production had left the Solihull site completely, and Lode Lane was exclusively the province of the Land Rover.

Top Brass

Tom Barton, who helped design the original Land Rover in the late 1940s and later became Land Rover chief engineer, was awarded an OBE for his services to trade and industry. The most influential figure at Land Rover since Tom Barton's days was probably Tony Gilroy, managing director from 1983–1988, whose reforms saved the company from going under. At least three key Land Rover people have gone on to work at Rolls-Royce. Frank Shaw, who has since retired, was once in charge of Land Rover transmission design. Mike Donovan was the leader of the 'Project Jay' Discovery team, and Chris Woodwark was Land Rover's commercial director in the early 1990s.

LAND ROVER SERIES III

88in	1972–1984
109in	1972–1985
109in	One Tonne: 1972–1980
109in	Stage 1 V8: 1979–1985
101in	Forward Control One Tonne: 1975-1978

Layout and Chassis

Two-door truck-cab pick-up, three- or five-door soft or hard top and Station Wagon
Box-section steel ladder chassis

Engine

Type		ioe petrol four, ohv V8 ohv diesel
Block material	fours, six	cast iron; V8: alloy
Head material	fours, six	cast iron; V8: alloy
Cylinders		in-line four (three-bearing crank replaced by five in 1980); straight-six, seven-bearing crank (engine discontinued in 1980); V8, five-bearing crank
Cooling	water	
Bore x stroke	petrol four	90.47mm × 88.9mm
	petrol six	77.8mm × 92.1mm
	petrol eight	88.9mm × 71.1mm
	diesel	90.47mm × 88.9mm
Capacity	petrol four	2,286cc
	petrol six	2,625cc
	petrol eight	3,528cc
	diesel	2,052cc

(109 One Tonne only available with petrol six; military 101 One Tonne only available with V8)

Compression ratio	petrol four	7.0:1
	petrol six	7.8:1
	petrol V8	8.1:1
	diesel	23:1
Carburettor	petrol four	Zenith 361V
	petrol six	Zenith 175 CD25
	petrol V8	two Zenith-Stromberg
	diesel	CAV Pintaux fuel injection
Max. power (DIN)	petrol four	77bhp @ 4,250rpm
	petrol six	83bhp @ 4,500rpm
	petrol V8	91bhp @ 3,500rpm
	diesel	62bhp @ 4,000rpm
Max. torque	petrol four	124lb/ft @ 2,500rpm
	petrol six	128lb/ft @ 1,500rpm
	petrol V8	166lb/ft @ 2,000rpm
	diesel	103lb/ft @1,800rpm

Transmission

All SIII models apart from V8: selectable two- or four-wheel drive in high-range, permanent four-wheel drive in low range

Gearbox	four-speed plus reverse, all syncromesh.

Clutch	Single dry-plate
Ratios	3.68, (3.73 later models), 2.22, 1.50, 1.1:1; reverse 4.02:1
Transfer box	1.148:1 step-down in high range, 2.35:1 in low range
Overdrive ratio of 0.782	1 optional from August 1974
Final drive, front and rear	4.7:1

109in Stage 1 V8 model

permanent four-wheel drive	Ratios
	4.069, 2.448, 1.505, 1.0:1; reverse: 3.664:1. Transfer box high range: 1.336:1; low range: 3.321:1
Final drive, front and rear	3.54:1, lockable centre diff

101in One Tonne

as above, except for: Ratios	
	4.05, 2.41, 1.61, 1.0:1; reverse: 4.22:1
Transfer box high range	1.174:1; low range: 3.321:1
Final drive, front and rear	5.57:1

Suspension and Steering

Live axles front and rear, with semi-elliptic leaf-springs and hydraulic telescopic dampers all round. 101 FC has double-acting hydraulic telescopic dampers all round

Steering	recirculating ball, worm-and-nut, ratio 15:1
Tyres	6.00 × 16
	109in mode 7.50 × 16
	109in One Tonne 9.00 × 16
	101in One Tonne FC 9.00 × 15
Wheels	16in pressed steel
	101in (2,565mm) FC 15in pressed steel

Brakes

Type	hydraulic drums all round, mechanical handbrake operating on transmission. Optional vacuum servo assistance on 88in models, standard on Station Wagons, 109in and V8 models; 101 FC has hydraulic servo
Size	11in × 1.5in; 109in model: 11in × 2.25in; 109in six-cylinder model 11in × 3in drums at front

Dimensions (in/mm)

88in model

Track	51.5/1,307 front and rear
Wheelbase	88/2,235
Overall length	142.6/(3,612
Overall width	66/1,675
Overall height, tilt up	77/1,954
Unladen weight	petrol engine 2,953lb (1,338kg); diesel 3,097lb (1,403kg)
Maximum weight limit	petrol 4,453lb (2,017kg); diesel 4,765lb (2,159kg)
Turning circle	38ft (11.5m)

109in model

Track	52.5/1,332 front and rear; 101 FC model 60/1,524 front, 61/1,550 rear

Wheelbase	109/2,768; 101 FC 101/2,565
Overall length	175/4,443; V8 177/4,496; 101 FC 162.5/4,122
Overall width	64/1,625
Overall height	79/2,003
Unladen weight	petrol four 3,301lb (1,496kg); diesel four 3,445lb (1,560kg); petrol six 3,459lb (1,566kg); petrol V8 3,396lb (1,538kg); 101in One Tonne FC 3,886lb (1,762kg)
Maximum weight limit	petrol four 5,905lb (2,675kg); petrol six 5,905lb (2,675kg); diesel 6,217lb (2,819kg); V8 5,976lb (2,707kg); 101 One Tonne FC 8,048lb (3,650kg) gross, payload 2,204lb (998kg)
Turning circle	45ft (13.5m), all except 101 37ft (11.2m)
Performance	
Top speed	2.28-litre petrol four-cylinder 88in: 68mph (109.5km/h) 2.62-litre six-cylinder 109in: 73mph (116km/h) 3.5-litre V8 109in: 76mph (122km/h)
0–50mph	2.28-litre petrol 88in: 16.8secs 2.62-litre 109in: 17secs 3.5-litre V8: 16.9secs
Fuel consumption	2.28-litre: 18mpg (15.7l/100km) 2.62-litre: 16mpg (17.6l/100km) 3.5-litre: 17mpg (6.7l/100km)

Next phase in the Land Rover saga was the introduction in 1982 of the up-market County versions, driven largely by the need to keep abreast of the competition in the expanding leisure-vehicle market. Externally, the vehicles were treated to frankly less-than-appealing side-stripe graphics proclaiming the higher specification.

Land Rover performance made a quantum leap on- and off-road when the 3.5-litre Range Rover V8 was fitted in long-wheelbase models, replacing the six-cylinder option. The 109in V8 was in production from 1979 to 1988, and can be readily identified by the more extended bonnet, which comes right to the vehicle's front line. One of the more overt benefits of corporate ownership meant that three of the new colours for the 109 V8 came from the Triumph sports car range.

The 109 Safari V8 was known as the Stage 1, and it used the Range Rover's four-speed LT95 gearbox with integral permanent four-wheel-drive transfer case and vacuum-operated centre differential lock. It also had the 3.54:1 final drive ratio instead of the SIII's 4.7:1 unit, and retained the SIII's drum brakes and leaf-spring suspension. The output of the V8 was curbed by restricting the intake manifolds, though actually, it is a simple matter to pull out these restrictors from behind the carbs, and retune it. Again, the increase in power attracted all sorts of other possibilities. For instance, the Laird Centaur was a half-track derivative of the V8-powered long-wheelbase Land Rover. The rear bogies were sourced from the Scorpion light tank, and the vehicle had a payload of three tonnes. It was not a success in the military marketplace, however.

The next major evolution for the Land Rover was the adoption of the Range Rover's coil spring suspension system. In fact, the first prototypes of the coil-sprung Land Rovers used Range Rover chassis with 100in (2,540mm) wheelbases. There were several military 100in Land Rover prototypes as well.

It would have been commercial suicide for Land Rover to have replaced the Series III with coil-sprung models in one go, because of the workings of the fleet market. Fleet buyers often take three years to evaluate new vehicles before placing an order, while their rolling replacement programme means they still order new vehicles every year. It was clearly vital for Land Rover to keep the leaf-sprung models in production during the three-year evaluation period, otherwise customers might easily have looked elsewhere.

The switch-over involved three models being built together: the 88 and 109 Series IIIs, and the 110 coil-sprung model, selected on the basis that 70 per cent of Land Rover's world-wide market was taken up by long-wheelbase variants.

ENTER THE ONE-TEN

The UK launch of the 110 was at Eastnor, near Ledbury, in February 1983. Land Rover enthusiasts were invited to attend through the clubs, and the event marked the company's 35th anniversary celebrations.

The 110's international launch was at the Geneva motor show in March 1983. It was available only in the UK and Switzerland to start with, entering other markets during the next few months. It was known as the One-Ten, as this was a

The anatomy of a 110, showing coil springs and transmission

snappy sort of name, and partly to avoid confusion with the Series IIB Forward Control 110. The One-Ten was available in the familiar range of five body types: the soft-top, hard top, pick-up, high-capacity pick-up and Station Wagon. It could also be supplied in chassis-cab form if aftermarket special bodywork was required.

The major difference was a taller single-piece windscreen in place of the split screen fitted to all Series Land Rovers. The One-Ten also had a new flush front panel, black slatted plastic grille, and matching black plastic headlamp surrounds. The heater air intake was relocated to the top of the left wing instead of in its side, and was matched by a dummy intake on the right wing. The neat bonnet panel featured a shallow depression at its centre.

The rear lights were mounted on the lower corners instead of at waist level on the Series III. Station Wagons now had a third hinge on the rear door, and the spare wheel had a higher mounting position, which made it possible to fit a tow hitch to the rear crossmember.

While the Series III Land Rover interiors were uncompromisingly utilitarian, the One-Ten was luxurious by comparison, and the new County cloth seats were the first fully adjustable seats in a Land Rover, with both fore-and-aft and backrest rake

Dashboard evolution: Series I.

Series II dash.

Series III dash.

Defender 90 dash.

adjustment. The driver's seat on 109 models had been adjustable fore-and-aft to a limited extent since 1961.

The dash was completely new, and the instrument panel was a lot neater than the Series III's had been. A four-spoke steering wheel with the Land Rover logo at the boss replaced the old three-spoke design. The gear levers and handbrake were smartened up and clad with robust rubber gaiters.

There was a transformation in ride quality: coil-sprung suspension meant that One-Tens rode more like a Range Rover, being altogether softer and more comfortable. The only downside was that the long-travel springs allowed more body roll when cornering than leaf-springs. However, there was no doubt that the One-Ten was more able than Series Land Rovers because of the increased suspension travel. It was actually 50 per cent greater at the front and 25 per cent at the rear, enabling better axle articulation in extreme circumstances so the wheels stood a better chance of remaining in contact with the ground. Braking had never been a strong point in a laden Series III, and it was vastly improved by the fitment of discs at the front, aided by a vacuum servo.

Prospective One-Ten owners could specify one of three engines, all carried over from the Series III Land Rovers. Least powerful was the 2,286cc four-cylinder indirect-injection diesel, producing 60bhp at 4,000rpm and 103lb/ft torque at 1,800rpm. This engine had last been improved in 1980 when it was given a five-bearing crankshaft, but it actually dated from 1961 in its original three-bearing form. It could be traced back to the very first 2.0-litre Land Rover diesel engine of 1957. Now in the One-Ten, it was fitted for the first time with a key-operated cut-out.

The smaller 2,286cc petrol engine had the same basic layout as the diesel, and was introduced as a three-bearing unit in 1958. Like the diesel, it received a five-bearing crankshaft in 1980. Installed in the One-Ten, it had revised inlet and exhaust manifolds, reprofiled cam, and a Weber 32/34 DMTL carburettor instead of the old Solex. Low-speed torque was improved, and the 2.3-litre petrol engine improved matters further with its 74bhp at 4,000rpm and 163lb/ft torque at 2,000rpm. The 3.5-litre V8 petrol engine was some 25 per cent better than the version used in the 109 Series IIIs, developing 114bhp at 4,000rpm, and 185lb/ft torque at 2,500rpm. When it came to refinement, flexibility and at-the-speed limit cruising potential, this engine had no peers. It was thirsty, however, having only the four-speed Range Rover LT95 gearbox with permanent four-wheel drive. The V8 had to wait until 1985 before it got the extra cog. The two four-cylinder models had LT77 five-speed gearboxes, originally made for Rover and Jaguar saloons and the TR7, with permanent four-wheel drive, or with the selectable four-wheel drive used in earlier Land Rovers. The main gearbox drove through a two-speed LT230R-type transfer 'box, first used in the automatic Range Rover of 1982.

The One-Ten was an immediate success, accounting for nearly a third of Land Rover sales in the UK in 1983; not only had it usurped the 109in models, but 110 Station Wagons were selling outside traditional Land Rover markets. Their higher levels of refinement now made them a serious alternative to regular estate cars. The top-of-the-range County Station Wagons came with halogen headlights, front and rear mud-flaps, reversing light, side repeater flashers on the front wings, a hazard warning system, a spare wheel cover and a bonnet lock. There was tinted glass, brown cloth upholstery, rubber pedal pads, dipping interior mirror, clock, ammeter and

LAND ROVER 90 AND 110

90	1984–1990
110	1983–1990
127	1983–1990

Layout and Chassis

Two-door truck-cab pick-up, or three- or five-door hard-top, and Station Wagon. Ultra-LWB 127in (3,225mm) Crew Cab model has extra 17 in (431mm) in the wheelbase
Steel box-section ladder frame chassis

Engine

Type	ohv petrol four, ohv petrol V8	
	ohv diesel, ohv turbodiesel	
Block material fours	cast iron	V8: aluminium alloy
Head material fours	cast iron	V8: aluminium alloy
Cylinders		in-line four, V8
Cooling	water	
Bore × stroke,	petrol four	1983–1985: 90.47mm x 88.9mm
	petrol four	1985–1990: 90.47mm x 97.0mm
	petrol V8	1983–1990 (from 1985 in 90 models): 88.9mm × 71.1mm
	diesel	1983–1984: 90.47mm x 88.9mm
	diesel	1984–1986: 90.47mm x 97.0mm
	turbodiesel	1986–1990: 90.47mm x 97.0mm
Capacity,	old petrol four	2,286cc
	new petrol four	2,494 (five-bearing crank)
	petrol V8	3,528cc
	old diesel four	2,286cc
	new diesel four, turbodiesel	2,494cc (five bearing crank)
Valves, fours	eight, V8	sixteen
Compression ratio	old and new petrol	8:1
		V8 8.13:1
	diesel	23:1
Carburettor,	petrol fours	twin-choke Weber 32/34DMTL
	V8	Zenith Strombergs replaced by two SUs in October 1986
	diesel	DPS fuel injection;
	turbodiesel	DPS fuel injection, Garrett AiResearch T2 turbo
Max. power (DIN),	old petrol four	74bhp @ 4,000rpm
	new petrol four	83bhp @ 4,000rpm
	V8	114bhp @ 4,000rpm; 134bhp @ 5,000rpm from October 1986
	old diesel	62bhp @ 4,000rpm
	new diesel	67bhp @ 4,000rpm
	turbodiesel	85bhp @ 4,000rpm
Max. torque,	old petrol four	120lb/ft @ 2,000rpm
	new petrol four	133lb/ft @ 2,000rpm
	old diesel	103lb/ft @1,800rpm

	new diesel	114lb/ft @ 1,800rpm
	turbodiesel	150lb/ft @ 1,800rpm

Transmission

Permanent four-wheel drive, with selectable two- or four-wheel drive available only in four-cylinder models

Gearbox	four-cylinder models: four-speed plus reverse, all syncromesh. Five-speed LT77 box optional in 110, standard in 90
Clutch	single dry-plate
	V8: four-speed LT95 replaced by five-speed LT85 Santana-built box, May 1985; all 90s have later five-speed box
Ratios	four-cylinder models: 3.585, 2.301, 1.507, 1:1; reverse: 3.701:1
	V8 from 1985: 3.65, 2.18, 1.43, 1.1, 0.79:1; reverse: 3.82:1
Transfer box	four-cylinder models (new LT230R unit): 1.667:1 step-down in high range, 3.320:1 in low range
	V8 and turbodiesel from October 1986: 1.41:1 high range, 3.32:1 low range
Final drive	front and rear: 3.54:1 with lockable centre diff

Suspension and Steering

Live axles front and rear with coil springs – uprated at front – and dual-action, hydraulic telescopic dampers all round. Rear A-frame, 110s have automatic self-levelling option at rear, standard on County models. 90s have uprated high-load option

Steering	Power-assisted recirculating ball, worm-and-nut, ratio 20.55:1
Tyres	90: 6.00 × 16 or 205 × 16
	110: 7.50 × 16 or 205 × 16
	All County models: 205 × 16
Wheels	16in pressed steel

Brakes

Type	dual-circuit hydraulic system, discs front, drums rear, mechanical hand brake operating on transmission
Size, 90 front	11.75in discs
	90 rear: 10in drums
	110 front: 11.8in discs
	110 rear: 11in drums

Dimensions (in/mm)

90 model

Track	58.5/1,486 front and rear
Wheelbase	92.2/2,342
Overall length	146.5/3,710
Overall width	70.5/1,788
Overall height	77.6/1,969
Unladen weight	petrol fours 3,533lb (1,601kg); V8 3,524lb (1,596kg); diesels 3,614lb (1,637kg)
Maximum payload	petrol fours 1,747lb ((792kg); diesels 1,665lb (754kg)
Turning circle	38ft (11.5m)

110 model

Track	58.5/1,486 front and rear
Wheelbase	110/2,793

Overall length	175/4,443; Station Wagon: 180.3/4,579; high-capacity pick-up 184/4,673
Overall width	70.5/1,788
Overall height	80.1/2,034
Unladen weight	petrol four 3,501lb (1,586kg); V8 3,446lb (1,561kg); diesel and turbodiesel 3,525lb (1,597kg)
Gross weight	6,724lb (3,049kg)
Maximum payload	petrol fours 3,221lb (1,459kg); V8 3,276lb (1,484kg); diesels 3,197lb (1,448kg)
Turning circle	42ft (12.7m)
Performance	
Top speed,	110 2.5-litre petrol: 78.5mph (126.2km/h) 90 V8: 82mph (131.9km/h) 110 2.5-litre turbodiesel: 76mph (122km/h)
0–50mph	110 2.5-litre petrol: 16.9secs 90 V8: 10.0secs 110 2.5-litre turbodiesel: 14.2secs
Overall fuel consumption	110 2.5-litre petrol: 19mpg (14.8l/100km) 90 V8: 15mpg (18.8l/100km)

sun visors. Because the headlining consisted of resin-impregnated felt with good insulation properties it was unnecessary to fit the tropical roof of earlier Safari Station Wagons.

In addition, the One-Ten had self-levelling rear suspension, power-assisted steering and radial tyres instead of the cross-plies of other models. A wide range of optional equipment was available, such as winches and power take-offs. They could be specified individually or in option packs such as electrical gear, protection, towing and interior fittings. More comprehensive specialist vehicles were produced by the Special Projects Department, including fire tenders, ambulances and other special-bodied derivatives.

The old Series III range soldiered on in low-volume production until 1986, by which time more than 250,000 Series IIIs had been built. It was not before time, as the Series III, excellent though it was, was lagging seriously behind Japanese competition through under-investment in its development. The new 90 and 110 redressed the balance to a great extent, although the damage had been done in some foreign markets.

The 'One-Ten' nomenclature referred accurately to the length of the wheelbase, but the 90's wheelbase was actually 92.9in (2,359mm) in length: 'Ninety' was more convenient from the marketing point of view. With the new models came a redesigned and more purposeful frontal treatment, as well as the distinctive rubber spats or 'eye-brows' over the wheelarches. They had more physical presence than their predecessors, helped in part by still wider track.

This was a period of considerable upward revision in terms of power units, particularly so when compared with the rate of change during the previous two decades. Between 1983 and 1985, production of the Series III leaf-sprung Land Rovers was run down, and the build programme switched over entirely to coil-sprung models. Solihull was now operating under the businesslike guidance of its new managing director Tony

The Land Rover Llama Forward Control truck of 1986 was destined never to go into production.

Gilroy. He instigated a major reorganization of Land Rover's production facilities, with more manufacturing and assembly work brought into the Lode Lane site with the consequence that several outlying plants became redundant. In July 1985, the new Special Vehicle Operations division was set up, absorbing the work of the old Special Projects Department, and taking on conversion work which had previously been done by specialists.

Shortly after the introduction of the five-bearing engine, its capacity was increased. With the abandonment of a turbodiesel V8 project, the One-Ten's new engine was announced at the 1984 Amsterdam show. The old 2.3-litre four-cylinder diesel was replaced by a new, longer stroke 2.5-litre 67bhp version, translating as a 12 per cent power increase and a 10 per cent rise in torque to 113lb/ft at 1,800rpm. It was still below par for many overseas markets, but an improvement nevertheless, certainly as far as acceleration and fuel consumption were concerned.

The new 2.5-litre unit had a more modern, toothed rubber timing belt instead of roller timing chains, which also drove the new DPS injector pump. One benefit was more accurate fuel metering, which minimized fuel consumption. There was also a self-priming system, rather than the earlier hand primer, while cold starting was also improved by more efficient sheathed-element glow plugs. The alloy castings used for its water pump housing and front cover also saved weight.

Not surprisingly, the selectable four-wheel-drive option on the first four-cylinder One-Tens was virtually ignored, and when the forthcoming new models were announced in June 1984, permanent four-wheel drive became standard. The facelifted One-Tens had single-piece front door windows. Earlier models had been fitted with the same detachable door tops and sliding windows as their Series III counterparts, but Land Rover finally recognized that these were somewhat crude on a vehicle of the County Station Wagon's aspirations, and for the first time the 1985 Land Rovers had wind-up windows. In order to keep costs down, the doors continued to be made in two pieces, with a galvanized garnish rail disguising the joint. The new door trims incorporated locking buttons on the sills. Station Wagon bodies also had revised sliding windows in the rear, while soft tops and three-quarter tilts were now supplied in the much lighter 'matt stone' shade instead of khaki, although soft tops of dark-green hue were still fitted to military vehicles.

Levels of standard equipment now reached what would have been considered the height of luxury for Land Rovers not many years earlier, a trend driven by customer expectations in this sector of the market. Thus from mid-1984, all One-Tens had a cigarette lighter, a steering column lock, bonnet lock and locking fuel cap, and Station Wagons had a heated rear window and rear wash-wipe as standard kit.

County Station Wagons still topped the range, and the list of standard equipment extended to twin radio speakers and an aerial, although you had to buy your own radio/cassette player. There was now carpeting in the passenger area. Refreshed two-tone side decals were co-ordinated with the vehicle's body colour and proclaimed its County status.

THE CREW CAB

Utility companies such as electricity boards with personnel to move about were catered for by the 127in (3,175mm) model, logically known as the Land Rover Crew Cab when it was introduced in 1983. In 1990 it became the Defender 130. The Crew Cab was based on a shortened high-capacity pick-up load-bed, together with a four-door, six-seater cab which was constructed from a mixture of Station Wagon and truck-cab parts. At first the Crew Cab was individually converted from the One-Ten chassis by Special Projects, and only later did it become a line-built product in its own right. All the componentry used in its construction was already available, so manufacturing costs were reduced and the sales cost was also relatively low. Specialist converters could not hope to match Land Rover factory prices.

The Crew Cab had the same 6,724lb (3,050kg) gross vehicle weight as a standard 110, and could be built with any of that model's three engine options. Until 1989 it always wore the silver grille badge of the old V8 Stage I model, saying simply 'Land-Rover', including anachronistic hyphen.

The pick-up area was normally covered with a tilt or fibreglass Truckman Top. The 127/130 was such a useful device that a few owners extended the chassis even further, creating a variety of different load platforms in the process.

THE NINETY

The 90 had been on the stocks since 1977, although no progress was made between 1978 and 1981. The wheelbase was extended from 90in (2,286mm) to 92.9in (2,359mm) soon after work began again, and it was pretty much an open secret that a short-wheelbase coil-sprung Land Rover was not far behind the 110; the 90 was eventually launched in June 1984, at the same time as the facelifted 110. It was timed to include all the updating and uprating of the 110 spec, including permanent four-wheel drive. There was no 3.5-litre V8 petrol engine, and the 2.3-litre four-cylinder petrol and 2.5-litre four-cylinder diesel units were scant consolation for some. The turbodiesel engine came on

The prototype Land Rover 90 had a true wheelbase of 90in, rather than the 92.5in of production vehicles.

stream in 1986 and was a huge improvement, but it was not a wholly new item. Land Rover had turned the old diesel engine into a turbodiesel for budgetary reasons: they could not afford the VM turbodiesel for the Land Rover as well as the Range Rover.

The 90 had disc brakes up front, and the five-speed LT77 gearbox and the LT230R transfer box were standard, although the 90's lighter weight permitted a taller and more economical high ratio in the transfer box than was possible in the 110's.

Visually, the 90 was a shortened 110, imitating the relationship between Series III 88 and 109. The 90 was 4.4in (112mm) longer overall than the 88, with a shorter rear overhang than its long-wheelbase sibling. The departure angle for off-roading was therefore excellent, and the wheels were located almost exactly at each corner of the vehicle. The additional 4.9in (124mm) wheelbase increased load-carrying capacity and allowed more front seat travel.

The 90's payload was increased by between 14 and 33 per cent, depending on which type of the four possible body variants was fitted. Predictably, these were soft-top, hard-top, pick-up and seven-seater Station Wagon, with the latter in optional County trim spec. The 90 was also available as a chassis-cab unit for special bodywork to be fitted.

In 1987, Land Rover displayed a new 'sunshine concept' vehicle called the Cariba, based on the soft-top 90. A similar project vehicle was built by Special Vehicles Operations that year, and the concept finally entered production in 1995: lucky old USA got the 3.9-litre V8-powered NAS 90, while Britain got the Tdi-powered SV90.

Meanwhile the new Land Rover Discovery was launched in 1989, pitched at the dual-purpose leisure market worldwide, and targeted fair and square at the German, Japanese and US rivals. It was based on the Range Rover chassis and running gear, with an optional new direct-injection turbodiesel engine. More ergonomically up-to-date, yet notionally less up-market than the Range Rover, the Discovery's cabin also offered a seven-seater capability. The Discovery quickly proved itself on the supremely arduous Camel Trophy. My father-in-law had both Range Rover and Discovery at different times and, having driven various models as a journalist, I have to say that while the Discovery is a fine vehicle, you cannot beat the cosseting provided by the latest Range Rover. But I digress. In the real world of utilitarian transport, the traditional Land Rover is undisputed king.

DEFENDER

The 90 and 110 ranges were given a name in 1991, and the apt title, Defender, was allegedly coined in a bar in downtown

Left-hand drive Defender 130 Tdi with pick-up rear body and tilt.

The current 110 County Station Wagon. The Defender range was announced in 1990, and legend has it the name was thought up in a Boston bar.

New meets old: a 1994 Defender 90 County Station Wagon and its Series I counterpart. Different generations but still conceptually similar.

Boston, when representatives from Solihull were socializing with their American colleagues. Whatever, the model was just as successful as its predecessors, consolidating the backbone of the company.

The Defender was given the latest version of the turbocharged direct injection diesel engine, the 300Tdi, as well as the

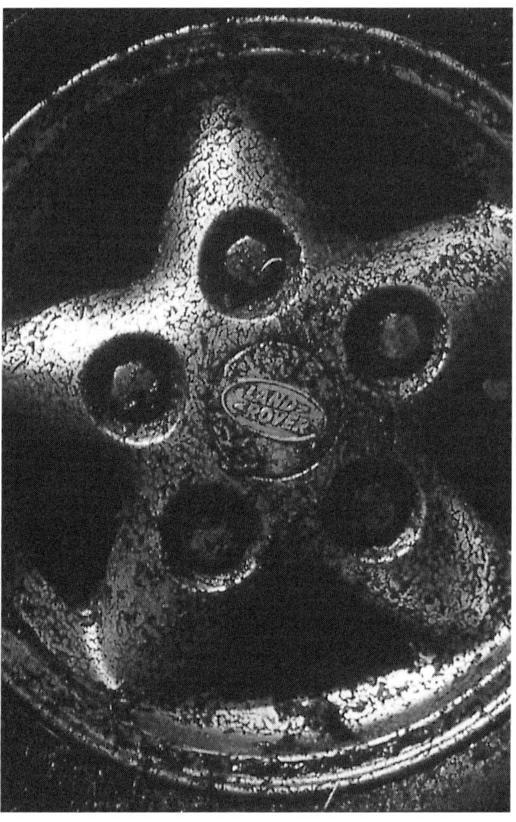

Freestyle alloy wheels became an optional extra on Defender 90s in 1995.

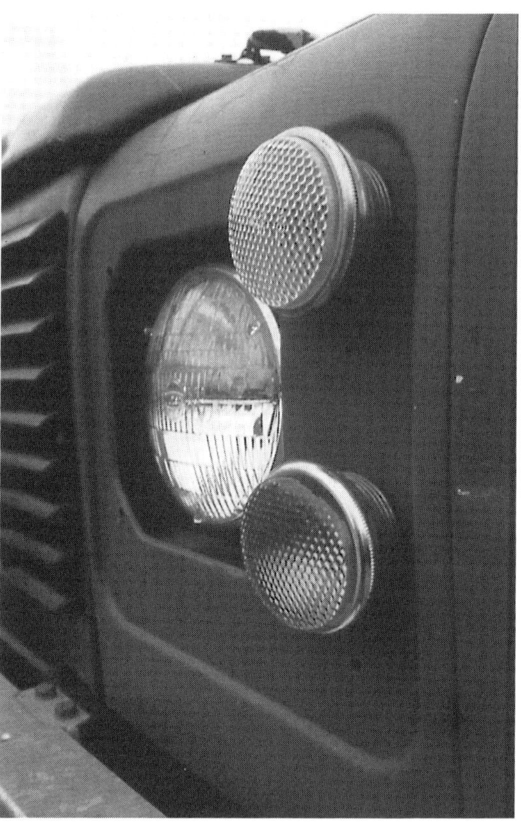

These are the front lights of an RAF Defender.

LAND ROVER DEFENDER

Defender 90	1991–
Defender 110	1991–
Defender 130	1991–

Layout and Chassis

Two-door truck-cab pick-up, high-capacity pick-up, soft top or three- or five-door hard top, and Station Wagon. Ultra-LWB 130 model retains 127in (3,175mm) chassis
Steel box-section ladder frame chassis

Engine

Type	1991–1994: petrol four	
	1991: petrol V8	
	1995: Rover T16 twin-cam petrol four optional for certain markets	
	1991: 1994 200Tdi turbodiesel (normally aspirated diesel available for fleet orders only)	
	1994–300Tdi turbodiesel	
Block material	fours: cast iron; V8: aluminium alloy	
Head material	Tdi, V8: aluminium alloy	
Cooling	water	
Bore × stroke,	petrol four	90.47mm × 97.0mm
	V8	1991–1994: 88.9mm × 71.1mm
	V8	1994–: 94.0mm × 71.12mm
	diesel	1983–1984: 90.47mm × 88.9mm
	diesel	1984–1986: 90.47mm × 97.0mm
	turbodiesel	1986–1990: 90.47mm × 97.0mm
Capacity,	petrol four	2,494cc
	old V8	3,528cc
	new V8	3,946cc
	diesel, turbodiesel	2,495cc
Valves, fours	eight, V8, T16	sixteen
Compression ratio	petrol	8:1, 3.5 V8: 8.13:1, 3.9 V8: 9.34:1
	diesel	23:1, Tdi turbodiesel: 19.5:1
Carburettor	petrol four	twin-choke Weber 32/34DMTL
	V8	two SUs
	NAS Defender 90 V8	Lucas fuel injection
	normally aspirated diesel	DPS fuel injection;
	Tdi turbodiesel	DPS fuel injection, Garrett AiResearch T2 turbo
Max. power (DIN)	petrol four	83bhp @ 4,000rpm
	3.5 V8	134bhp @ 5,000rpm
	3.9 V8	183bhp @ 4,750rpm
	normally aspirated diesel	67bhp @ 4,000rpm
	turbodiesel	111bhp @ 4,000rpm
Max. torque	petrol four	133lb/ft @ 2,000rpm
	3.5 V8	187lb/ft @ 2,500rpm
	3.9 V8	230lb/ft @ 3,100rpm
	normally aspirated diesel	114lb/ft @ 1,800rpm
	Tdi turbodiesel	195lb/ft @ 1,800rpm

Transmission

Permanent four-wheel drive

Gearbox	five-speed R380 unit standard in all Defenders from 1994
Clutch	single dry-plate
Ratios	90: 3.692, 2.132, 1.397, 1.0:1, 0.77:1; reverse: 3.536:1
	110: 3.692, 2.130, 1.397, 1.0:1, 0.77:1; reverse: 3.429:1
Transfer box	LT230T, all models: 1.411:1 step-down in high range, 3.320:1 in low-range
Final drive	front and rear: 3.54:1 with centre lock diff. Defender 110 and 130 have Salisbury rear axles

Suspension and steering

Suspension	Live axles front and rear with coil springs and dual action hydraulic telescopic dampers all round. Rear A-frame; Defender 110s have automatic self-levelling option at rear, standard on all County models. Defender 130s have coaxial coil springs on the rear, plus anti-roll bars front and rear Anti-rollbars fitted on rear only of Defender 110 County, and optional on rear of other 110. Defender 90s have uprated high-load option, plus front and rear anti-roll bars optional
Steering	Power-assisted recirculating ball, worm-and-nut, ratio 20.55:1. Export orders can be specified without power steering
Tyres	Defender 90: 205 × 16 Michelin XM + S Freestyle alloy wheels on BF Goodrich 265/75 mud terrain tyres optional in 1995 Defender 110: 750 × 16 Avon Ranger (P4 & NA) V8: 750 × 16 Avon Range Master All County Station Wagons: 205 × 16 Defender 130: Michelin XZY
Wheels	5.50F × 16 pressed steel

Brakes

Type	Girling dual-circuit hydraulic system, servo-assisted, discs all round. Ventilated on heavy duty specification, cable-operated handbrake drum on transfer box output
Size	90: 11.75in discs all round 110: 11.8in discs all round

Dimensions (in/mm)

Defender 90 model

Track	58.5/1,486 front and rear
Wheelbase	92.9/2,359
Overall length	152.9/3,872
Overall width	70.5/(1,788
Overall height	77.3/1,967
Ground clearance	7.5/189
Luggage capacity	1.6m^3
Unladen weight	petrol fours 3533lb (1,601kg); V8 3,524lb (1,596kg); Tdi 3,579lb (1,621kg)
Gross weight	Tdi 5,290lb (2400kg)
Turning circle	38ft (11.5m)

Defender 110 model

Track	58.5/1,486 front and rear
Wheelbase	110/2,793
Overall length	175/4,443; Station Wagon: 180.3/4,579; high-capacity pick-up: 184/4,673
Overall width	70.5/1,788
Overall height:	80.1/2,034
Luggage capacity	2.3m^3
Unladen weight	petrol fours 3,501lb (1,586kg); V8 3,446lb (1,561kg); Tdi 4,002lb (1,813kg)
Gross weight	6,724lb (3,050kg)
Turning circle	42ft (12.7m)

Performance

Top speed,	Defender 110 2.5-litre petrol: 78.5mph (126.2km/h)
	NAS 90 V8: 99mph (159.2km/h)
	Defender 110 Tdi: 80mph (128.7km/h)
0–60mph	Defender 110 2.5-litre petrol: 16.9secs
	NAS 90 V8: 9.6secs
	Defender 110 Tdi: 17.4secs
Overall fuel consumption	Defender 110 2.5-litre petrol: 19mpg (14.8l/100km) (unleaded compatible)
	NAS 90 V8: 18mpg (unleaded compatible)
	Defender 110 Tdi: 28mpg (10.1l/100km)
Tank capacity:	Defender 90: 12 gallons (54.4l)
	Defender 110: 17.5 gallons (79.4l)

The 90 hard-top is almost without question the best utility vehicle in the world.

County-spec seat upholstery and trim in a Defender, palatial compared with Series model Land Rovers.

Instrument panel of the 1996 Defender – just 19 miles (30km) on the clock.

Hard-top 90 emblazoned with County graphics and Tdi logo.

NAS DEFENDER

It is bold and brassy, and is enough to bring on pangs of jealousy. While the rest of the world has to content itself with the Tdi, the US market gets the 3.9-litre North American spec NAS 90 V8, with petrol injection and 9.35:1 compression, developing 182bhp and 232lb/ft of torque. It sports huge BF Goodrich Mud Terrain T/A 265/75 R16 tyres on shiny 7 × 16 Freestyle wheels, rows of extra lights and a beefy roll cage. Not surprisingly, the NAS 90 caused a stir in the US by upstaging the native Jeep in off-road magazine back-to-back tests.

Launched in 1994 with the old-pattern LT77 gearbox, the North American spec Defender acquired the new R380 unit in 1995. Although the six-leg roll cage and canvas top are similar to the UK-spec SV90 Tdi, the NAS 90 is quite different, a legacy of selling vehicles in the world's biggest market. The spare wheel carrier is a specially made tubular unit, opening via a nifty parallelogram linkage beside the tailgate, which is itself side-hinged rather than drop-down. The spare wheel carrier also doubles as a mount for the hoop that supports the high-mounted brake light. The sturdy tube-frame rear step and bumper is bolted to the crossmember, which is fitted with a US-style hitch mount. The tail lights are square-section, and the fog light is absent, while on either side behind the rear wheels are small red warning lights, with similar ones in orange on the front wings.

A pair of catalytic converters lurks beneath the chassis, while the exhaust itself has the proportions of a drainpipe. There are anti-rollbars front and rear, as well as rear disc brakes, which no other Defenders get. Also, the petrol tank is located behind the rear axle as a safety measure, instead of side-mounted ahead of the right rear wheel as in the regular Defender 90. Logically then, the NAS's filler cap is behind the wheel instead of in front of it.

Other visual differences extend to small stick-on V8 badges behind the front wheelarches, while the grille badge states 'Land Rover' instead of 'Defender'. There are four sidelights and rectangular orange indicators in niches within the front bumper.

Curiously, the NAS Defender uses Series III doors, so that when the hood is removed, the occupants can also detach the door tops, which of course they could not do with the one-piece Defender doors. The familiar pull-up handles let you in, and sliding windows and an inner door handle at

The NAS Defender 90 came out in 1994, and was powered by the 3.9-litre Rover V8. Lucky old US!.

hip level complete the door furniture.

The NAS is a left-hooker, obviously, and the familiar dashboard is laid out appropriately. The steering wheel is like that of a Classic Range Rover with extra padding on the boss. Instead of where you would find a clock in a new County, there is a diminutive rev-counter alongside the temperature and fuel gauges. There is a cubby box and pair of cup holders between the seats, unique to the NAS 90, while the radio-cassette player can be hidden by a locking flap along with the cubby box lid. Waterproof speakers are mounted in the doors and rear section.

Here, the steel tubes of the roll cage would not disgrace a Titan. They are specially made for Land Rover and encased in tough yet malleable plastic, which is just as well when being bounced around in the back as I was in the Scottish Highlands. The back section can be unbolted, allowing greater front seat travel.

Performance-wise, the NAS 90 is no slouch on the road. The 0–60mph time is around ten seconds, which is close to that of the 4.6-litre Range Rover and just about halves the 90 Tdi's time. However, the V8 is somewhat over-geared, especially for its tall tyres. It does 29mph (46.5km/h) for every 1,000rpm in high-box fifth gear, and at 70mph (110km/h) it is cruising along at a relaxed and economical 2,400rpm, but at the expense of throttle response. Floor the accelerator in second, and it leaps into orbit, not so much NAS as NASA. Its power band extends from 1,500rpm right up to 5,000, whereas the Tdi's useful power spread is between about 1,700 and 3,500rpm.

The standard US soft top for the NAS 90 consists of a tilt which ignores the rear part of the roll cage and slopes straight down to the rear panel. Also sometimes seen is a 'bimini' top, which is simply a rectangle of canvas tied above the driver and passenger's heads, next to useless in the rain, and more of a sunshade really. The full soft-top tilt is an optional extra in the USA. It is an extraordinarily complex canopy with zips, poppers and Velcro to lash it into weather-defeating shape. The downside is massive wind roar at motorway speed, although in its native habitat there is no such problem. However, since putting it on is a ten-minute job for two people, it pays to have an eye on the weather. A dousing does not matter too much, as there is no cloth or carpet in the cabin to get soaked. For winter use, owners can get snug in an optional glass-fibre top.

new R380 manual gearbox. Reverse gear now had synchromesh, and clutch control was improved. Other refinements were the long-overdue fitting of seatbelts for inward-facing rear seat passengers in the Station Wagon models, better interior lighting and stereo. Innovations for the Defender 90 midway through 1995 were the 'Freestyle Choice' option of five-spoke alloy wheels on BF Goodrich 265/75 Mud Terrain tyres, plus front and rear anti-rollbars. County models got removable radios and new body colours.

In Britain, the 1,500,000th Land Rover was a Defender 90SV, and driven off the assembly lines by Land Rover-owning North American spec rock star, Bryan Adams. And the conveyors roll steadily on: there is no sign whatever that the BMW take-over has impinged at all on the company. While the media speculates about the new model scheduled to arrive in mid-1997, we can look forward with some certainty to the two millionth Land Rover.

3 The Factory

Middle class, middle England, Solihull lies on the south side of the Birmingham conurbation, well served by the M42 motorway yet equally within easy reach of some of England's choicest countryside. The Land Rover factory is well signposted in the town, and is located on the main road on its outskirts, in an area of middle-class housing estates.

Perhaps the most surprising thing about the Land Rover production line is that virtually every vehicle going down it is different. You might see a right-hand-drive truck cab followed by a County Station Wagon followed by a left-drive military staff car, with a 130 in there as well. This is because most Defenders are single orders. The only time you see a batch of vehicles all the same is if they push through a consignment of army Land Rovers. In the event of an order from the MoD for, say, a thousand Defenders, they would probably be filtered through in batches of a hundred; production would be wound up a bit and turn matt green for a while.

Normally, the line will inevitably be a mix of vehicles because the company is supplying so many markets at the same time. It would not work if they worked in batches of one particular model, because delivery times would be horrendously long. The reason it is possible at all is because Land Rovers are made by hand, not by robots. Unlike programmed machines, the

The Defender line is a hive of activity as different vehicles are fettled according to their specification. Normally, no two Land Rovers are the same.

Defender workforce is flexible, and the variety of models makes it a more interesting environment to work in.

Production went up in March 1996 to 600 units a week. All Defenders are built in the original South Works factory, with the Discovery line in the same building. Classic Range Rovers were also built here until their demise, and now the model is made entirely in North Works on the opposite side of the Lode Lane site. Originally built in 1936, South Works has been extended over the years, in particular the inspection areas and to accommodate Discovery bodies; but to all intents and purposes it is still the single storey 'hangar' used to make aircraft engines during World War II. The nature of South Works will change over the next few years, as Land Rover sinks some £150 million into new buildings and plant. A new paint shop comes on stream in 1997, satisfying EU solvent legislation, improving paint quality, and increasing potential capacity to 300,000 units. It will service all production lines, Defender as well as Discovery and Range Rover, so that access will be direct – no trailering of painted panels and shells around the factory site.

Land Rover's Defender line is something of a hybrid, since it is both volume and specialist manufacture: some 27,000 units were produced in 1995, so they come into a mass-handbuilt category. A forest of hoists and pulleys hangs down like creepers in the jungle from overhead gantries, and electric forklift trucks speed from one area to another in the kind of dangerous chaos associated with trams in Amsterdam. You need to watch your back if venturing from the line into the internal roadways.

The factory operates on a 'just-in-time' basis, a system invented in highly efficient Japanese car plants, where components are delivered to the relevant point on the work-station or 'cell' as they are known, exactly when needed. Hence the frantic ongoing forklift activity.

There is no particular smell about the Land Rover plant, unlike some more specialized factories, and there is a marked absence of Radio One-style pop music blaring out. Some cells elect to have the radio on, but they seem to be in the minority. So the noise you hear is of the general cacophony of metal on metal as the parts are assembled, the shrill high-pitched whine of a multitude of compressed-air tools and hoists, and frequent hammering. At breaktimes the factory klaxon hoots, the line stops, and the workforce retires to the canteen on the mezzanine floor or to the subsidized restaurant – itself something of a production line.

Something like 400 people work on Defender production; most cells function with fifty fitters, while there are a few floating operatives, as well as clip-board-carrying personnel from Logistics or Audit who check on schedules and ensure that components arrive on time and are of satisfactory quality. Cells are divided up into teams, and the number of people working within each team is unequal, although there are usually six. In general, employees – or associates as they are called – stay in their own cell, performing specific jobs according to their work station, but there is a degree of interchangeability. On the Defender line, 90 per cent of the workforce is male; this is because by its very nature it is a more physically demanding build process. I saw only three young women on the actual production line, involved at the very end in minor fixings, although other women were active alongside the line in door, trim and bulkhead preparation. Camaraderie in general seems excellent throughout the Defender line. A team leader covers two or three cells; his is not the same role as a foreman, and employees and associates can, and do, make constructive suggestions about streamlining the assembly procedure. There are actually more people involved in Defender production than either of the other two ranges because of all the different elements which make up the vehicle. A Discovery body simply drops onto its chassis and is fastened in eight places by two people, but a Defender has separate wings, bulkhead and floorpans, according to whichever model it is.

There are six cells on the Defender line, and in effect there are two lines, the first being where the chassis, fresh from GKN Sankey Engineering in their dull black powdercoat finish, begin their journey. Land Rover has every facility apart from a foundry, and to justify having one would mean making large quantities of everything, not merely the chassis.

During the manufacturing process, every vehicle has a docket or build sheet, made out by Logistics, which identifies what model it will be, colour, mechanical specification and any special features ordered by the customer or dealer. So the chassis are either 90, 110, or 130in wheelbase. It takes sixty hours to build a Land Rover from scratch, and that includes chassis and panel manufacture, engine and transmission assembly, painting, and time on the assembly lines. Certain models take longer than others to assemble; clearly there are more items of trim in a County Station Wagon than a pick-up, but the line evidently proceeds without coming to a standstill. Occasional hiccoughs are inevitable, if for instance a part is wrong or missing, but the delay is brief.

The factory works two shifts, both day and night, so the process is an on-going one. However, it is feasible that if you stood at the start of the first line at the beginning of the day, you would see the first chassis emerging at the end of it as fully fledged operational vehicles. Roughly the same number of vehicles is built during the night as during the day. For Land Rover, the main considerations of operating shifts – that there is no time for doing maintenance work on the equipment, demands on suppliers are higher, and pay rates for night-shift workers are higher – have to be bal-

Bare chassis are lowered into place by overhead gantry and made ready for the suspension to be fitted.

anced against improved volumes and better turnover. Also, if they need to move workers from one line to another, it is difficult to implement training if they are working 24-hour shifts.

The methodology is such that a collection of panels is produced for each individual Defender in the body-in-white panel shop at East Works, according to the docket made out by Logistics, and each set of panels stays together on a jig as they go across via a gantry into the paint shop. It is not just a question of a fitter on the line taking, say, a green door or bonnet out of stock. Everything is bespoke, and that way all the panels have a better chance of fitting properly, nor is there any colour variation, which could happen according to slight changes in temperature. So even if there is a small variation in the paint shade, all panels will still match. Although there is a standard range of twelve colours, customers can choose virtually whatever colour they like, and panels can either be

Axle and differential units, complete with brake assemblies, ready for fitting.

Fitting driveshaft couplings, torsion bars and dampers to a rear axle.

painted 'in the system', or go on to Special Vehicles to be done there. Traditional colours such as dark green, white and dark blue are still the favourites, but in and around the factory you do see one or two striking hues. Metallic cherry red, and metallic green looked especially attractive. The factory very occasionally does one-offs; the 500,000th Land Rover was finished in yellow with a red chassis, although no-one can remember what shade it was.

After painting, the jig carrying what looks like an exploded Land Rover skeleton is towed into South Works and delivered to the trimming assembly cell, where doors, roofs and bonnets are carefully stacked until their chassis arrives. There is a long way to go yet, though.

Unlike a factory dealing with monocoque unit-construction saloon cars, all Land Rover products have a chassis assembly area. Defender was always thus. Meanwhile, the bare chassis starts its journey at Cell One. Having been selected from a waiting pile, it is first prepared by a team of four, then a rectangular cradle hoist transports it a few yards to the first work station where the suspension components are fitted by four men. The individual springs, torsion bars, dampers and so on have been bought-in from specialist manufacturers, and they wait ready for selection in dump bins at the edge of the cell, effectively dividing it from the internal roadways.

The second stage merges with the first, and this is fitment of brake and hub assemblies, complete with the plastic fluid reservoir which for the moment waves around vaguely. The brake and hub assemblies are made up beforehand elsewhere in the factory from bought-in components, and are fastened to the chassis pick-up points with compressed-air torque tools. Again, there are four men at this work station, and the chassis is now swung round through 180° onto the first conveyor belt.

Next comes the installation of the engine and gearbox units. These rest on stands on pallets beside the line, and virtually all are the Tdi engine. A few customers order V8s, and they make around 800 North American-spec Defenders a year, which have the 3.9-litre Rover V8 engine. A recent contract with the Italian *carabinieri* calls for Rover 2.0-litre T-series 16-valve twin-

A chassis is lowered onto the jig to have the complete axles and suspension married up. The build docket is rolled up in the crossmember mounting.

A 300Tdi engine and gearbox is suspended over the conveyor prior to lowering into its chassis.

Attaching the front suspension turret housing.

Chassis and drivetrain assembly is now virtually complete. The next chassis along is just receiving its engine and gearbox.

cam petrol engines, and they had taken 1,500 or so up to 1996. In theory a customer could order one of these engines, but it would be a one-off. Almost all Defenders have the Land Rover 380 manual transmission, but if automatic is specified, these are sourced from ZF. Automatic transmissions tend to be favoured by the electricity companies for operational reasons. All Land Rover engines are built on site, apart from the 2.5-litre BMW unit powering certain Range Rovers. The Tdi units are made in the diesel facility round the back of North Works, and gearboxes are made next door to that.

From a PR point of view, Land Rover loves high-profile contracts like the *carabinieri*, the Italian army, not to mention our own police and MoD, because its vehicles are seen as protectors of the people. Such publicity can only be good for sales.

As the designated chassis arrives next to the waiting engine units, a fitter hooks up the hoist, and with a deft swing, takes it across to the chassis and lowers it into place. Four colleagues then swoop on it to do up the mounting bolts, and another busies himself with connecting ancillaries.

The Land Rover chassis has now transferred over to the second conveyor, and has been fitted with its bulkhead.

The radiator and fuel tank have been fitted and the wiring loom is being installed.

They are completely focused about their tasks, while appearing quite relaxed at the same time. There are frequent pauses in the natural progression of things, and some light up a cigarette or exchange a joke.

The contents of the dump bins change as the vehicle begins to take shape. After the engine and transmission are installed, you notice the bins are full of radiators, hoses, exhaust pipes, silencers and shrouds. As the chassis moves along at something marginally faster than snail's pace, these elements are installed. The fitters make it look deceptively easy.

Now the chassis leaves the first conveyor, hoisted away by chains attached to its hubs via another overhead cradle onto the main assembly conveyor. From here it is built up rather like a Meccano set. First installation is the steel bulkhead, already equipped with instrument wiring loom. Apart from the chassis, the front bulkhead is the only major steel component in the whole vehicle. Then the pedal box is fitted, enabling the brake system to be connected up.

Brackets are pop-riveted in place on the rear body section. The build docket is constantly referred to so that the specification is exactly right.

The first piece of recognizable bodywork to go on is the back end. The bottom half of the rear is always the same: for example, the lower back section of a 90 will be the same for a pick-up as for a hard-top or Station Wagon. A 110 County requires central door pillars, of course, so its rear section is different to the 110 pick-up. The top half is lowered into place and the transformation takes place.

Fifty yards on, and the dump bins' contents are different again, now full of bits of bodywork, and smaller bins contain thousands of screws and fasteners of one sort and another. There are hundreds of batteries, and larger sections such as doors stand in special racks, while different roof panels also wait their turn. The wiring loom is an early fitment, because of the complexity of the vehicle. Certain special additions such as side steps are attached as the chassis goes down the line. Sometimes a foreign market demands a different rear lamp configuration from standard, and variations like this have to be incorporated. Such details are all on the build docket.

About halfway down the line, the chassis starts to look like a Land Rover. The floorpan is fitted, and the bulky seat mounting base mounted. Front wings are brought to the chassis, having had their galvanized

By now the Land Rover is beginning to look like one, with front wings fitted. They are clad in plastic shields to guard the paintwork, and the bumper is similarly protected.

The roof section of a 110 Station Wagon is hoisted into position.

A vehicle's panels are all painted at the same time, but its doors are prepared separately; glazing and fitting locks and handles is done to one side of the production line.

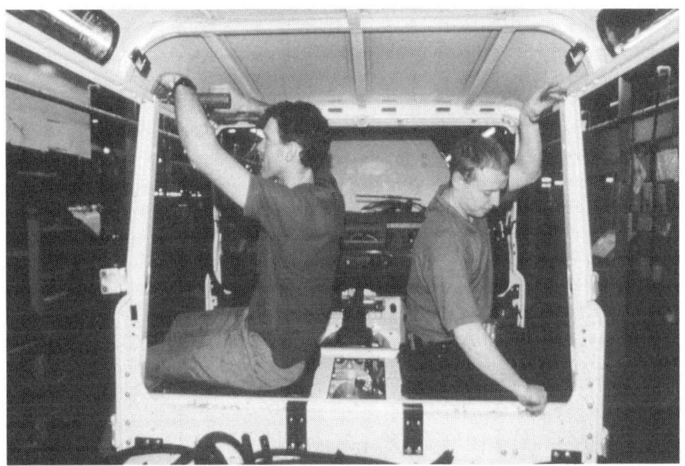

The Station Wagon's roof is secured in position with pop-rivets.

Trimming and carpeting the rear of a 110 Station Wagon interior. Seat belts have already been fitted.

inner panels fitted, headlights installed and washer bottle kits screwed on.

The wings and doors have thick, custom-made plastic covers over them to protect them from knocks and accidental blemish from the fitters' apparel, which may be impregnated with oil or grease. Bumpers come wrapped in polythene, which protects them from pre-delivery parking scrapes. The panel-fitting process sometimes overlaps, as vehicles further back have to wait while a more complex County station wagon is worked on. Very often a roof section performs a feat of aerial ballet as it is swung overhead on a hoist by a fitter and taken to a vehicle a bit further back up the line. The fitters below seem unconcerned, not even bothering to duck despite the part above their heads behaving like some guided missile.

The soft-top models such as 130s and pick-ups have galvanized tilt hoops fitted at this point. At any given time, ten rear door skins and frames lie flat on work benches while their glazing is put in and they are equipped with hinges, handles and spare-wheel mounts.

Defender trim starts to go in now, and

while the County Station Wagon has more than most, there is little variation. Unlike the posher siblings with a wide range of upholstery, fabric and colour options, the Defender gets rubber mats and grey trim, with only a couple of variations. But in a utilitarian vehicle, it hardly matters. Again, like the majority of componentry, seats and trim items are sourced from manufacturers outside the company. Sixty per cent comes from specialist firms in the Midlands, and contrary to speculation when BMW came on the scene, nothing is sourced in Germany. Wheels and tyres are Defender standard issue, unless otherwise specified by customer or dealer.

As they get to the end of the line – an area known in factory speak as 'Defender Final Buy-Off' – small details such as the wing tread plates are screwed in place, and the interiors vacuumed. A quality control inspection then takes place, before the Land Rovers are driven to an assembly point. As they travel under their own power in the factory, stacker pipes are fitted to the exhaust to direct fumes up

Doing the Defender's wheelnuts up all in one go with a multiple air hammer.

The end of the line known as 'Final Buy-Off', and a completed Defender is given a once-over before being driven off for testing.

towards the plant's extractor system. Later they will be driven around the factory roads to confirm that all systems are fully functional, and thence to the despatch depot. Those requiring registration will have that done. Some vehicles do not get that far to start with, but are taken to one side because some part was not available as it passed along the line, or perhaps a door does not fit, and the particular problem will be rectified. At the end of the day, the line stops, but then the night shift takes over.

The Defender may be a very labour intensive vehicle to produce during all phases of its construction, but that is what makes it such a characterful machine. It is a truly fascinating process.

NOW FOR SOMETHING SPECIAL

Land Rover's Special Vehicles Operation building is tucked away behind the main production lines at Solihull, but you realize you've arrived at somewhere out of the ordinary because of the oddballs and specially liveried vehicles parked outside. Here stand some recently finished examples, like those RAC special recovery vehicles or Northern Electricity Board's extending hydraulic lift platforms, along with a number of candidates waiting their turn for modification. This is where all Defenders, Discoveries and Range Rovers requiring factory-fitted options or specialized bodies come to be finished off, and they might be in for just a couple of hours or over a week.

The vehicles concerned come straight off the line, and instead of massing in the main compounds, they go directly to SVO, where everything from fitting accessories to undertaking serious rebuilds is done. The jobs may be one-offs, or replicated several or many times over. A Discovery having a set of 'eyebrows' above its wheel-arches takes only an hour or so, while a full-blown 110 mobile workshop bound for Tanzania takes at least a week to build.

Team leader Larry Court, aged fifty-eight, has worked at Land Rover for thirty years. He started in 1966 in the main assembly shop, building 88s and 109s, and worked on the first lightweights in 1968.

Larry is Solihull born and bred, and talks about his job and the SVO with a typical Brummy drawl. He is characteristically modest, yet clearly proud of his job and accomplishments. After a brief stint on the Rover P6 line, he joined the long-running Special Installations department. 'Then four years ago Special Vehicle Operations took us over,' he says. 'They were doing much the same sort of work as us, so it was a logical move.' Now Larry's expertise is 'right across the board' – and it has to be because he has to have an answer if one of his colleagues comes up with a problem. A host of different specifications brings a variety of different problems. He leads a team of twenty-five fitters in the modern single-storey workshop, and to an extent he is the figurehead, 'but we have to find an answer to every problem we come up against,' he says. Thus one of the things they look for when recruiting new fitters is a problem-solving ability.

Modifications are many and varied, ranging from the cosmetic to the full treatment – the Camel Trophy vehicles are all kitted out here – and the recovery and service vehicles are legion. A typical conversion might include the fitting of a mechanical drum winch, galvanized plates on wings and bonnet, full-length roof-rack, eight-spoke alloy wheels, interior cabinets for tools and equipment – and this would represent a week's work for two fitters.

At the other end of the scale are more everyday items such as tow-bars, dog-guards, roof-racks, alarms and bull-bars, a combination of which would take a day and a half to fit. They do police vehicles as well, mostly to a standard format, which individual police forces then customize to their own requirements. But sometimes they do have to fit the enormous blue lights and sirens for motorway patrol cars, and this applies to ambulance conversions, too.

'Every day we've got something different to do,' says Larry. 'Anything the customer wants, we can do.' In a way, Larry and his team are at the cutting edge of Land Rover development, as they create vehicles to new specifications and overcome the difficulties of incorporating them. Several of the components fitted at SVO are sourced outside the factory, such as roll cages and winches, and they have full Land Rover approval. 'SVO is a one-stop shop,' says Larry; 'if the requirement is too specialized, such as hydraulic jacks on these hoist platforms – in this case for Northern Electric – we source them and fit them, or have them fitted for the customer if it's something highly detailed like a mobile kitchen or surgical unit.'

Probably the most glamorous Land Rovers to pass the factory gates are the sand-glow Camel Trophy vehicles, which have been Larry's province for the last fifteen years – for as long as Land Rover have been supplying them in fact – and it's left to me to get them built from start to finish, from the moment they come off the line to the moment they go into the packing case,' he says. 'We built fifty-four this year, including all the support vehicles, and we're starting on next year's vehicles shortly.' Extra kit installed at SVO includes racks, ladders, winches, jacks, radios and aerials, roll cages, sump and tank guards, and bull-bars. SVO also packs up all the tools and spares , plus shovels, sand-ladders, fuel and jerrycans.

Naturally Larry and his team have been instrumental in developing some of the equipment for the Camel vehicles, especially the Discoveries when they were first used. As everyone knows, these vehicles take more of a battering than at almost any other event. Says Larry: 'The support vehicles come back here, but the competition vehicles go to Belgium to be refurbished, and they're probably sold on from there.'

Recent US tax increases brought more work SVO's way. NAS 90s bound for the States now have extra rear seats, belts and rear roll-over bars fitted at SVO, rather than 'over there', which means Larry and his team are required to process fifty of the stocky V8s a week.

The Special Vehicles Operations has recently been relaunched because the nature of the business has changed, in that there is much more repetitive work – such as the NAS 90s – and fitting of accessories, rather than the more specialized tasks the department is capable of.

4 Land Rovers Produced Under Licence

MINERVA

Before World War II, the long-established Belgian motor manufacturer Minerva built rather conservative but high-quality luxury cars, and in the wake of hostilities had planned to return to this market, making cars based on the Armstrong-Siddeley Sapphire. Minerva was also set to make a small Italian car, the Cemsa-Caproni under licence, but when the Belgian army ordered 10,000 Land Rovers in 1950, Minerva made an arrangement with Solihull to manufacture them.

Drivetrains including engines and gearboxes were shipped to the Minerva plant in Antwerp's Mortsel suburb, and everything else, including body panels, was handmade to Land Rover patterns in Belgium. The 1,997cc engine was used for the vehicle's entire production life, and there were obvious differences in the front wings, which were raked forwards at an angle from the front panel. Grille treatment and lighting arrangements were quite different, and there was a Minerva grille badge

Belgian-built Minerva Land Rover, 1954. All panels were in steel.

featuring the helmeted Roman goddess of war. But the fundamental difference between Belgian and British models was that the Minerva had steel panels.

The Minerva Land Rover was available to the general public from October 1953, and was popular in all walks of life, from the Belgian armed forces to agriculture. Up in the hilly Ardennes forests, one of the most picturesque areas in Europe, the Minerva was in its element.

Production ended in 1956, when Minerva brought out its own Continental-powered jeep. A year later, the company collapsed. Meanwhile, the Belgian military had stockpiled large quantities of Minerva Land Rovers and components because they held them in such high esteem. Many are still going strong, having only been in service for a relatively short time.

Over the border in France, there might also have been a Land-Talbot if the Talbot company had acquired manufacturing rights to the Land Rover. At one time, Renault was equally interested in cashing in on Solihull's success. Meanwhile in Hamburg, the German Tempo company produced Land Rovers under licence, based on the Series I 86in chassis. Before the war, Tempo had specialized in three-wheelers, and a twin-engined military car which had a 600cc two-cylinder Ilo engine at either end of the vehicle. As well as the Land Rovers, Tempo continued to produce their three-wheelers up to 1956, when truck manufacturers Hanomag took a 50 per cent stake. By 1970 Tempo-Hanomag had become part of Daimler Benz; but by then the Land Rover connection was long gone.

The Land Rover in Spain

When travelling in northern Spain, I noted there were plenty of what appeared to be Series IIIs about. They were of course Santanas of one kind and another, most common being the 109 hard-top, followed by LWB Station Wagon bodies. Short-wheelbase 88s and 90s are less common, and are mostly seen in workhorse situations – although up in the mountains the farmers do literally use horses still, for ploughing and pulling hay carts. Quite a few Series IIIs are sign-written, and occasionally you see outlandish colour schemes. The most bizarre Land Rover sighting was a charabanc, a 109 minus its roof, with a seating arrangement like that of a coach.

These may look the same as home-grown Land Rovers, but there are a great many differences. In fact, no other Land Rover derivative has established such a strong identity for itself as the Spanish Santana vehicles. Interestingly, neighbouring Portugal has virtually no Santanas, while Series Land Rovers are plentiful. There are some real gems tucked away at the backs of barns as well.

Santana – Metallurgica de Santa Ana SA – began assembling Land Rovers from CKD kits sent over from Solihull in 1959. The firm was under an obligation to increase the proportion of their local content to 100 per cent, and although the earliest Santana Land Rovers had very few Spanish-made parts, by the mid-1970s every single part on a Santana Land Rover was made in Spain.

By the mid-1960s, Land Rovers were being assembled in no fewer than twenty-nine overseas countries, so foreign production lines were not exactly uncommon. However, Santana was probably the most significant. Land Rover and Santana parted company in the early 1980s. By this time, Solihull had already done the development work on the coil-sprung 110 and was all set for its early 1983 introduction

– but Santana had other ideas. It decided against using coil springs and permanent four-wheel drive because it was likely that its traditional South American markets would reject such a relatively sophisticated concept.

If this was the first major policy rift between Solihull and Santana, it was not the first time that Santana-built Land Rovers had been at variance with the standard product. As well as sourcing all components on native soil, Santana developed its own vehicles and mechanical componentry. These included the 88 and 109 Militar types for the Spanish Army, the civilian Ligero derivative of the 88 Militar, the 1300 and 2000 Forward Controls, and the six-cylinder derivatives of Solihull's petrol and diesel fours. By the early 1980s Santana was developing its own moulded GRP roof panels for Series III Santana Station Wagons, hard tops and winding windows, which in the case of the long-wheelbase Station Wagons produced a neater side view, with the front door handle located at the same height as the rear. This styling improvement predated Solihull by some four years.

Cazorla

In 1981, Santana introduced the Cazorla, a name which has similar connotations as the County. It was a 109in Station Wagon, with higher levels of equipment than the workhorse models. A year later, the rejuvenated Santana Land Rover range was split into two distinct segments: utility models and de luxe Station Wagons.

The new models introduced in October 1982 were known as Series IIIA types. Their galvanized chassis were identical to the superseded 88in and 109in Series III, but they were equipped with new parabolic leaf-springs with just two leaves per side, which produced a better ride and allowed longer axle travel. At the front, disc brakes replaced the drums of the previous Series IIIs, while power-assisted steering was optional.

This development work resulted in some benefit for the British range. Four-cylinder Santana Series IIIAs were available with a new five-speed LT85 gearbox, which was later exported to Solihull and from 1985 to 1990 fitted in 110 V8 models. When fitted to Santana vehicles, the LT85 came with a new transfer box which had a single-plane operating lever similar to some Japanese vehicles. The variety of positions available

It may be badged a Defender, but this Santana is an 88in leaf-sprung model. It is competing in the 1994 Warn Adventure in Morocco.

was two-wheel drive, neutral, four-wheel drive high range and four-wheel drive low range.

The 109 models continued to be equipped with the six-cylinder 3,429cc ohv engines, and the majority were the 94bhp diesel units. A few 103bhp petrol engines were built for export. The well tried 2,286cc ohv petrol and diesel fours were still being built, both running five main bearings like the Solihull-made equivalents. The only difference was that they used timing gears instead of a roller chain.

Another area where Santana was ahead of the game was turbocharging. It fitted the old diesel four-cylinder with a turbocharger and a modern timing belt, so it could produce 75bhp. While Lode Lane engineers would undoubtedly have considered turbocharging already, financial constraints prevented them from productionizing engines with timing belts before 1984, and Solihull's own turbodiesel was not launched until 1986.

Scuttle Change

Perhaps the most distinctive visual characteristic of the Series IIIA models is in the front bulkhead. There are no scuttle ventilators, and the windscreen is a single span with three wipers. When the revamp took place in 1982 the screen was enlarged and expanded downwards into the area the scuttle had occupied on earlier models. That meant ventilation now came via a black plastic air intake mounted at the rear of the bonnet, and also through louvres cut in the right-hand rear of the bonnet.

These ventilation arrangements were the same for both utility and *de luxe* models, although there were differences between the front end panels of the two types. The *de luxe* four-cylinder and six-cylinder Station Wagons had a new flush front, with a black plastic grille similar to that which was scheduled for the 110. The Santana badge was fixed at the bottom right-hand side, with the Land-Rover name – hyphenated – above it. The matching black headlamp panels were smaller than the 110s, and they had rectangular side-light-and-indicator units below them. The new bonnet panel was similar to the forthcoming 110, incorporating the air intake louvres and plastic ventilation grille.

On the other hand, utility pick-up and hard-top versions of the Series IIIA, both long- and short-wheelbases, plus soft-top 88s, retained the old Series III front end panels. Four-cylinder Santana models were the same as Solihull-built Series IIIs, apart from the black plastic grille with its Santana badge, while six-cylinder models retained the front panel and grille unique to Santana since 1977.

Model Range

The utility short-wheelbase model was known as the 88 Normal, and the long-wheelbases were called 109 4-Cil and 109 6-Cil according to engine size. There were three versions of the *de luxe* Station Wagon: these were the Super (four-cylinder petrol or diesel), the Super Turbo (turbocharged four-cylinder diesel) and the Cazorla (six-cylinder 109 petrol or diesel).

The base model 88 Super and 109 Super had four-speed gearboxes, while the five-speed 'box with its new single-lever transfer box was an additional-cost option. All 109s and diesel 88s with the five-speed gearbox were equipped with power steering, and all five-gear 109s and the five-gear diesel 88 also had special perforated-disc wheels. The five-speed diesel 88 was fitted with a special front bumper with integral steps and overriders. Decals on the rear flanks of these models read 'Land Rover 88

Like this 109, the majority of Santana-built Land Rovers are strictly utility vehicles. All parts are manufactured in Spain.

Super' or 'Land Rover 109 Super', whatever was appropriate.

The 88 Super Turbo and 109 Super Turbo were basically Super models fitted with the turbodiesel engine and five-speed 'box, power-steering, perforated disc wheels and special front bumper as standard. Cosmetically they had Turbo side-stripes and a small Turbo decal on the bonnet.

The top of the range six-cylinder Cazorla Station Wagon was targeted at the Spanish luxury 4WD class, a niche where Land Rover had no representation as the Range Rover was not imported into Spain. Because the five-speed gearbox was not yet available with the six-cylinder engines, the Cazorla was fitted with the four-speed gearbox plus overdrive and freewheel hubs. Power-steering was also standard, and the model could be identified by its rear badge proclaiming it as the Cazorla 6-Cil.

Gran Capacidad

Quite logically, the utility range also included a long-wheelbase model which was available either as a chassis/cab unit to accommodate special bodywork, or with a wide pick-up body along the lines of Solihull's high-capacity pick-up. It was known as the 119 Gran Capacidad, or 119in high capacity, and special bodies could be bought from the Special Projects Department at the Linares factory.

The 119 was introduced soon after the other Series IIIA models came out. It bore the usual Series IIIA hallmarks, with the air-ventless bulkhead, single-section windscreen and Series III-style front panels. The four-cylinder diesel engine was the specified power-unit, and gross weight was 6,945lb (3,150kg), the same as a six-cylinder 109 and some 860lb (390kg) more than the four-cylinder model. The 119 Gran Capacidad was always a low-volume model within a limited range, even by Land Rover standards. Later on, its chassis would be used as the basis for the M-300 military prototype.

Apart from Santana's Series IIIA models, two other types were available. They were both introduced before the Series IIIAs appeared in 1982, and were known as the 88 Ligero and the 2000 Forward Control. Essentially, the Ligero was a sporting version of the 88 Militar, which in turn owed something to the Solihull-built Lightweight. It first appeared in 1980 and was invariably finished in orange, white or yellow, with a black soft top and Ligero badges on the front wings. All Ligeros had freewheel front hubs and the majority had diesel engines, although theoretically, the four-cylinder petrol version was also available. The arrival of the Series IIIA models in 1982 signalled the updating of the Ligero, which was now fitted with disc brakes on the front wheels and an anti-roll-bar on the front axle. The Series III bulkhead, windscreen, and black Series III grille with rectangular headlamps were retained.

The rare 2000 Forward Control model of 1979 was developed by Santana from the 101 military One-Tonner. It was powered by a six-cylinder engine, which could be either petrol or diesel, and could be specified with a variety of body styles. It was not affected by the introduction of the Series IIIA, and even retained its all-drum braking system. A mere 923 units were built, up to 1990.

With the Series IIIA models up and running, Santana began to explore other possibilities. Since Land Rover sales were unlikely to increase markedly on the home front because of competition from Japanese 4WDs, and because the company was excluded from selling to countries where the Solihull-built product was available due to its agreement with Land Rover, diversification was the obvious move. Thus early in 1984 Santana reached an agreement with Suzuki to build their light-weight SJ-series 4x4s. Such joint ventures were becoming fashionable at the time, and this one clearly suited both parties, with Santana's projected output reaching some 10,000 SJs a year. This would give them the volume production they wanted, while it was a means for Suzuki of circumventing European import restrictions on Japanese vehicles. The first Santana-built and badged SJs reached Britain early in 1987.

While the joint venture with Suzuki looked good for Santana, it appeared less rosy for Solihull devotees, as the Spaniards set about simplifying their Land Rover range to reduce costs and rationalize production. Accordingly, several models were dropped during 1987, while engine and transmission options were simplified. The naturally aspirated, diesel four-cylinder engines and 2.5-litre petrol units were new in 1987. They were basically the same as their Solihull-made counterparts, and replaced the 2.25-litre types and the turbocharged diesel, while the diesel and petrol six-cylinder units remained in production. Petrol engines were no longer available in Spain, however, and were built purely for export.

When they stopped making the old four-speed gearbox, the six-cylinder models were available for the first time with five-speed LT85 transmission. This now had a two-part casing which made for easier assembly. Even now, Santana had still not entertained permanent four-wheel drive, and the second-generation Series IIIAs came equipped with a selectable system only.

When Ligero, Turbo and Cazorla production ceased, just the renamed successors to the utility and Super ranges remained. Utility variants were now called the 2.5 DC, 2.5 DL and 3.5 DL, while the *de luxe* models became the 2500 DC, 2500 DL and 3500 DL. In each case, the numbers identified the engine capacity, and the suffix 'D' meant 'diesel', the 'C' stood for *corto* meaning short, and the 'L' was for *largo*, or long. The new model was the 2.5 DLE, a 109 Station Wagon powered by the four-cylinder diesel engine, with utility standard specification. The 'E' stood for *Especial*, the name given previously to Series III Station Wagons. These vehicles just had Santana nameplates, with no Land Rover identification.

Utility models still had the bulkheads without ventilators, and instead of the black plastic grilles on their bonnets, there were air intakes in the trailing edges of the front wings. The de luxe range incorporated the 90/110 type bulkhead, with ventilator flaps below a raised windscreen; *de luxe* models also came with the stronger 90/110 type hinges and new roof panels with longitudinal ribbing. Both the utility and *de luxe* ranges featured flush-front panelling, two windscreen wipers rather than three, and all models had new rectangular rear-light clusters. *De luxe* Station Wagons had a new one-piece rear door, but the old two-piece door was still fitted to utility versions.

De luxe models also received restyled bumpers, and body-coloured deformable wheelarch eyebrows covering new wide-track axles, like Land Rover's coil-sprung 90 and 110 models. The 88in versions had anti-rollbars on the front axle, and 109s had them on both axles. The transformation was completed by 90/110 style façias, front seat adjustment for backrest and fore-and-aft movement, and carpet extending to the load area as well as the passenger compartment.

While it was prudent business strategy for Santana, this trend in the Spanish company's thinking called into question its future relationship with Solihull. As Land Rover expanded into Europe to compensate for sales lost to Japanese competition and

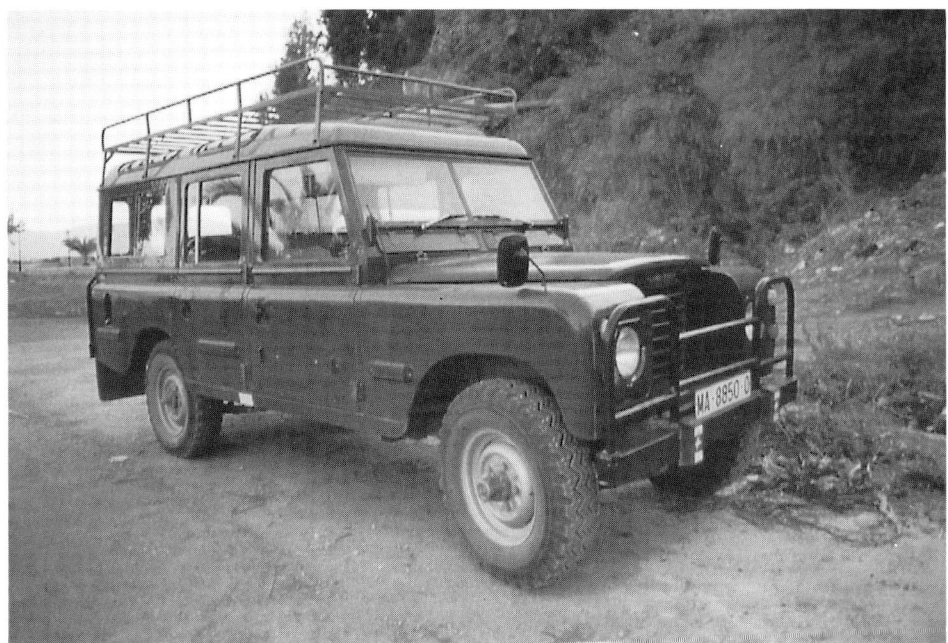

The main external differences are in the front end, although this Santana-built 109 has a standard Series III grille; seats, windows, roof and engine range are different.

the loss of traditional markets in Africa, it was logical for it to consider Spain as well. In order not to compromise Santana, Land Rover aimed further up-market with the Range Rover, and later, the Discovery. But while the coil-sprung 90 and 110 Defenders were sufficiently refined to slot in behind these two models, Santana's vehicles were too old-fashioned and down-market to fit into a coherent sales strategy. When the Spanish company introduced its Series IV models in 1989, they still had leaf-spring suspension.

In 1993 the Santana factory closed for a period due to financial and industrial relations problems; once operational again, the major part of vehicle production was devoted to the Suzuki Vitara.

Spares

Should you need to access spares for a Santana vehicle, Allmakes of Abingdon, Oxford, supplies items which are only available from Spain and listed in Santana catalogues and price lists. They deal with a company in Spain called Anglorecambios, C/Navales S/M, Manzana 15, Nave 31, Poligono Urtinsa 11, 28925 Alcorcon, Spain. Tel: 00 341 643 3655, Fax: 6439407.

The Santana parts operation is still running in Spain and while certain items are becoming scarce, most Santana parts are still available. More often than not, British-made items can be pressed into service.

THE SANTANA TURBODIESEL ENGINE, 1982–1987

Capacity	2,286cc
Bore	90.47mm
Stroke	88.9mm
Power	75bhp (55Kw) @ 4,000rpm
Torque	129.6lb/ft (176Nm) @ 2,000rpm

THE SANTANA SIX-CYLINDER ENGINES

Diesel engine

Capacity	3,429cc
Bore	90.47mm
Stroke	88.9mm
Power	94bhp (70Kw) @ 4,000rpm
Torque	152.4lb/ft (207Nm) @ 1,800rpm

Petrol engine

Capacity	3,429cc
Bore	90.47mm
Stroke	88.9mm
Power	103.25bhp (77Kw) @ 4,000rpm
Torque	176.7lb/ft @ 1,500rpm

THE 119 GRAN CAPACIDAD

Engine	2,286cc 4-cylinder diesel producing 61bhp (45Kw)
Transmission	Four-speed with selectable four-wheel drive
Wheelbase	118.97in (3,022mm)
Load capacity	3,130lb (1,420kg)
GVW	6,945lb (3,150kg)

A factory publicity shot from October 1986 of the 90 and 110 County Station Wagons.

5 Special Vehicles

There have been so many different specialized Land Rovers over the years that a full listing would make a book in its own right. These are some of the better known ones.

PINK PANTHERS

The Pink Panther, formally titled the FV18064 Truck, General Service, SAS, ¾-Tonne, Rover II, was designed to enable the Special Air Service Regiment (SAS) to carry out reconnaissance and raiding sorties in the desert. The Pink Panther nickname comes from the unusual colour scheme first seen in the SAS Rover IIs, a legacy of the North African campaign in World War II, when pink was found to be the best colour for aircraft camouflage. The Pink Panthers were originally painted bronze green, and in addition to desert use, they were also painted NATO green with black camouflage and sent to Belize for SAS jungle training. They usually operated in groups of three, each one carrying 100 gallons (455l) of fuel, 45 gallons (205l) of water and sufficient rations to maintain their three-man crews behind enemy lines for several days at a time.

The SAS used converted 86in and 88in Series I Land Rovers until the mid-sixties, and the long-wheelbase vehicles were more or less ignored until 1964 when they were used for training exercises. They were equipped with heavy-duty springs and extended spring hangers, and shod with 9.00 × 15 sand tyres; and despite being grossly overloaded, they created a sufficiently favourable impression for the engineers at FVRDE Chertsey to design a Pink Panther prototype. It was based on a 1961 109in (2,768mm) Series II, with doors, windscreen and tilt removed, heavy-duty suspension fitted, along with sand tyres and a bumper-mounted spare. Long-range fuel tanks were placed in the rear compartment, with a pintle-mounted machine gun with 360° travel. A second machine gun was mounted on the scuttle, operated by the commander, and there were smoke canisters front and rear. Sand channels were carried on both sides.

Other than uprating the suspension to cope with larger 9.00 × 15 sand tyres, the basic Series IIA military spec Land Rover needed few mechanical alterations. Ground clearance was improved by the larger tyres and extended spring hangers, but transmission guards were fitted front and rear for good measure.

For navigation and communications purposes, the Pink Panthers had an illuminated compass mounted by the driver, while two more basic compasses, three radios, plus a theodolite and tripod were also carried. Later on, the equipment inventory of each vehicle was extended to include three fire extinguishers, tyre lever, jack, recovery chain, shovels, first-aid packs, water

Everything was painted camouflage colour, including pedals, controls and switches.

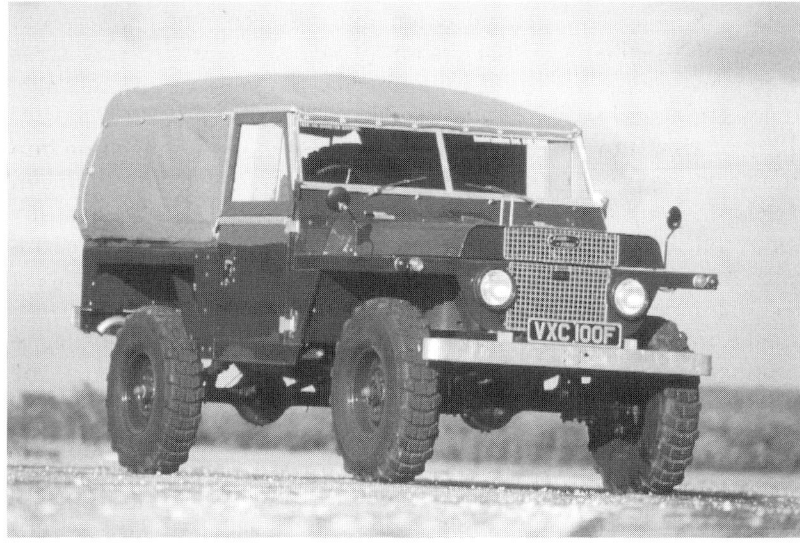

The prototype 'Middleweight' military Land Rover, now in the Dunsfold Trust Collection.

canisters, portible stove and cooking utensils.

In spring 1967, seventy-two Pink Panthers were ordered via Marshalls of Cambridge, and the first production vehicle entered service in October 1968, seeing action in the Yemen and other desert theatres. The Pink Panthers were officially retired in the mid-1980s when the 110 Desert Patrol vehicles appeared. Six Pink Panthers survive in museums, and a further ten or so are owned privately. The REME museum fleet is maintained by its curator Roger Jones, who restored his own Pink Panther – 10FG59 – in the early 1980s. He was responsible for much of the work done on the REME museum vehicle – 10FG40 – which is on display at Gaydon.

Lightweight number one fully stripped down at the Dunsfold Trust.

PATHFINDER LRPV

The role of the forty-strong Pathfinder Platoon of Britain's 5 Airborne Brigade is to parachute deep behind enemy lines to undertake covert reconnaissance and intelligence gathering. The Pathfinders use a small number of dedicated RAF Hercules transport aircraft, and the vehicles they use are the specially modified Defender 90 Airdrop. These are usually known as piggy-back 90s, because they can be double-stacked in the aircraft before being parachuted into action. To enable one to be mounted on the back of another, the rear sides have special demountable sections, allowing the front wheels of the rear vehicle to rest on the wheel boxes of the other. For regular service they have their windscreen, doors and standard soft top, but for airborne operations they are usually stripped down.

The Pathfinder Platoon also operates as part of the 3rd (UK) Division, and in this role its fleet of twelve Land Rovers undertakes long-range patrols with a three-man crew plus the necessary fuel, ammunition and supplies, while underbody protection and recovery equipment is also carried. It amounts to an SAS-style patrol vehicle based on the standard 90 and using standard components drawn from NATO stocks or fabricated in-house. Fittings not needed for airdrop operations have to be quickly removable without using special tools.

The first Pathfinder prototype Land

Series I with truck-cab body (JSK 737).

County spec 1995 Defender 90 with Freestyle alloy wheels, with Series I at rear.

Pristine 107in Series I with truck-cab body (478 CMB).

A 110 V8 goes for a bath in Wales.

NAS 90 prepared by Rover France.

French 90 high in the Alps on the Croisière Blanche *– this driver is taking no chances of getting lost.*

A 90 Tdi on the Warn Adventure in Morocco.

Bo Slavin drives the NAS 90 in Mexico.

A feast of Land Rovers, part of the Nigel Weller collection. Leading away from the camera, they are SII, SI, Stage 1 V8s, 101, 90, SII, SIII and 110.

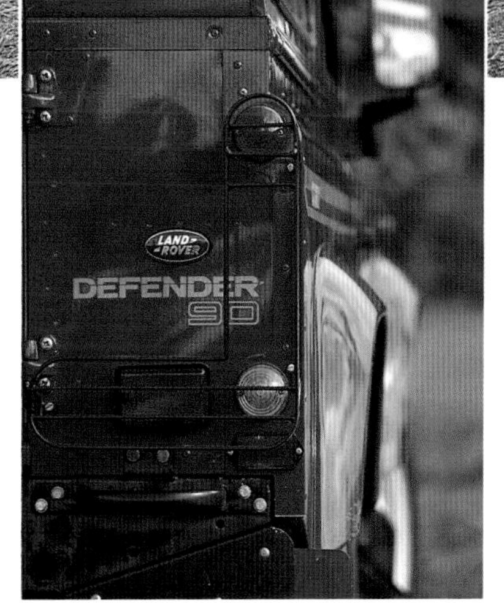

Rear badging of Defender 90 County Station Wagon, with lamp protector.

Rear badging of Series I Station Wagon.

Defender 110 Tdi in France.

The driver of this Defender wisely wears sunglasses to avoid snow-blindness.

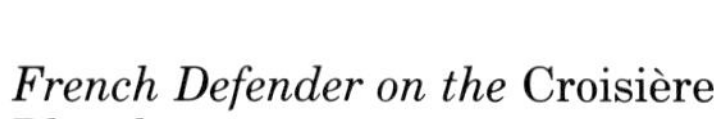

French Defender on the Croisière Blanche.

This Defender 90 is taking part in the Warn Adventure in Morocco.

The Hotspur 6×6 armoured 110, built by Penman Engineering.

Defender 110 earning its living for the National Grid.

Yellow Cab – or Dredd Shed – from the sci-fi movie Judge Dredd, *based on a 101 chassis and subsequently used for promotional work.*

Series III fire tender, used by the French sapeurs-pompiers.

A regular police Defender 110 TDi.

Rover 90 was known as Fastball, and was produced by 10 Airborne Workshop and 43 District Workshop, with input from Solihull, other military units and specialist equipment manufacturers. The Fastball 90 spec was quite comprehensive, with mounts for three machine guns, a raised command seat, external bins and panniers, a simple rollcage, underside protection, rear air locker, uprated suspension and a winch for self-recovery. Provision was made for a second spare wheel, high-lift jack and airbag. It was approved in 1993 and the rest of the fleet was gradually converted as funds permitted.

Mechanical conversion and overall weight was restricted to retain road-legal status for peacetime exercises. The Pathfinder Long Range Patrol Vehicles (LRPV) all have the following features fitted: rollcage, raised command seat, dashboard-mounted machine gun, rear-facing machine gun, storage bins and removable panniers either side, tailgate storage box, plus full Southdown underbody protection kits. Every other Land Rover has a bumper mounted drum winch, while minor additions include a slave start socket on the commander's seat base, lamp guards all round, a sand channel mounted on the tailgate and a compass on the A-post beside the driver.

Naturally, key elements of Pathfinder troop training are off-road driving, vehicle field repairs and maintenance, ensuring the LRPVs are kept in shape and used to best effect.

THE DEFENDER EXTRA DUTY RANGE

The Defender XD range was unveiled at the Royal Navy & British Army Equipment Exhibition in mid-1995. These specialized vehicles were developed for military and peacekeeping roles well into the twenty-first century; British army vehicles in these classes now have a minimum service life of twelve years. The Defender Extra Duty range was extensively re-engineered from the chassis rails up to match a large Ministry of Defence contract for no less than 6,000 light and medium utility trucks, and several hundred ambulances.

Land Rover's Project Wolf team, under chief engineer Paul Markwick, began redesigning the military Defender in mid-1992, using much of the CAD technology developed for the new Range Rover. The 90, 110 and 130 XD range then supplemented the standard military Defender, and were assembled on the main South Works production lines. Many detail differences were specified, and these were evolved in house at Lode Lane. They included some interesting chassis and running gear modifications. Additionally, Pioneer tool stowage brackets were provided on the wings and bonnet, with provision for a bonnet-mounted spare wheel; though both 90 and 110 carried theirs behind the passenger door.

Inside, the 90 had two substantial inward-facing double bench seats; in the 110 there were four, complete with lap belts for each passenger. A jerrycan could be carried in a holder between the rear seats and the bulkhead in the 90, but in the 110 it would be carried in the lockers behind the front doors.

The canopy frame on the soft tops was made of more substantial tubing than before, and even provided a degree of roll-over protection: the front bow, set in tubular sockets behind the bulkhead, was diagonally braced behind the cab, with large-diameter bracing struts running back to the body capping on both sides. The 110 had additional forward-facing struts to the rear bow. As before, the frame was easily removable, using a single spanner or key. The canopy was made of the same stretchable synthetic material as supplied to many foreign military users for over ten years, and the frame was slightly higher for better headroom.

The ambulance's rigid body extended over the cab area, and was designed to carry either four stretcher cases, six walking wounded, or a mix of two and three, plus attendant medic. The tinted windows could be kicked out for emergency evacuation, while Red Cross markings were painted on fold-away panels on either side, one rear door and roof. The spare wheel could be carried on the bonnet or the roof, accessed via a treadplate on the bonnet and a rung above the windscreen.

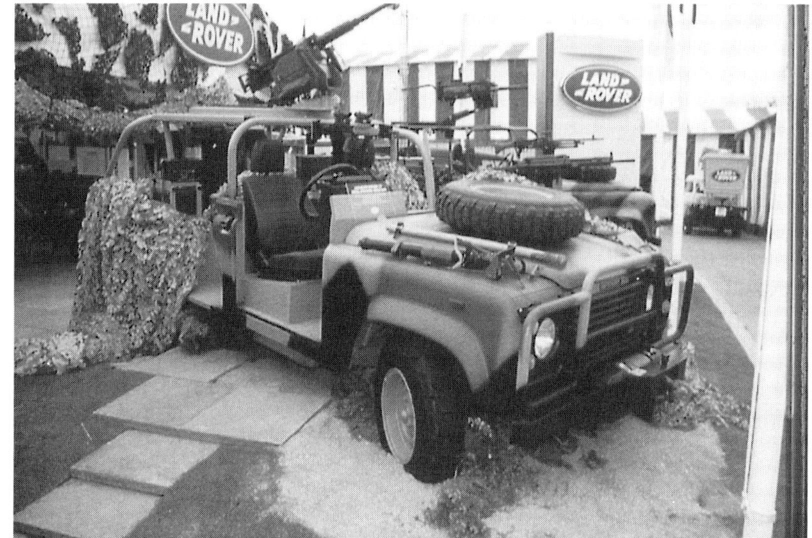

Armed to the teeth, these 110-based Special Operations Vehicles were designed for the US Rangers, with weaponry ranging from a .50-calibre machine gun on a ring-mount on the roll cage and a GPMG. As well as no doors, there was no bodywork ahead of the rear wheel box either.

This 1987 field ambulance has a body by Marshalls of Cambridge on a 127in chassis, and was used by the UN in Croatia in the early 1990s.

LAND ROVERS IN NORTHERN IRELAND

The intensive news coverage in Northern Ireland during the troubles brought with it almost daily contact with heavily armoured Land Rovers; they were always in evidence, and rather taken for granted. However, they were not the familiar green machines, but anonymous sinister-looking vehicles. In the hands of the security forces, their role was that of patrol vehicles, providing relatively secure transport for the army and the Royal Ulster Constabulary.

During the July 'marching season', the RUC Land Rovers formed a thin grey line between parading Loyalists and Nationalists, helping to control sectarian marches through residential areas. With a fleet of at least 350 vehicles, the RUC is one of the largest Land Rover users in the UK. But whereas mainland police forces use virtually standard models for all but the most specialist roles, those of the RUC are fully armoured.

The first armoured Land Rovers built for the RUC were 107in (2,717mm) chassis. This design was refined and eventually became the Shorland Armoured Car, made by Short Brothers of Belfast, with seating for three and a revolving machine gun turret on the roof. However, although the Shorland Armoured Car provided good mobility and protection for its crew, it was essentially a military patrol vehicle and was unsuitable for general police use. The gun turret was also seen as being too overtly warlike for daily use in urban environments. As the troubles escalated, the RUC perceived that it needed some form of armoured personnel carrier with a relatively unaggressive appearance: the Land Rover, with its heavy-duty chassis capable of accepting the weight of an armoured body, was the ideal vehicle.

The first armoured Land Rovers to enter service were actually designed by the RUC. Ernie Lusty of the Transport Services Branch is widely regarded as the instigator of the armoured Land Rover. His two companies in Wales and the West Midlands were given orders for batches of ten vehicles, but eventually it was decided that full production could be handled just as efficiently in the RUC's own workshops. At the height of production, two armoured Land Rovers were completed each week, as well as routine vehicle maintenance.

These Land Rovers were known as Hotspurs, after the brand of American armour plate originally used. Initially they were powered by the 2,625cc six-cylinder petrol engine, but once the V8 was available in the 109 chassis, it became standard RUC Land Rover fitment. The Hotspur had a simple armoured body which echoed the basic design of the hard-top LWB Series III, to make it as unpugnacious as possible. Whether they succeeded in creating such an image is debatable, however. Windscreen and door windows were in special armoured glass, and gun ports were provided in the rear body sides. Lights were protected from stone damage by steel mesh screens or plastic shields, and a pull-up windscreen grill was fitted to ward off missiles of one sort or another.

Based on their experience of manufacturing Shorland Armoured Cars, first for the RUC and later for foreign regimes, Short Brothers designed a range of armoured Land Rover patrol vehicles and personnel carriers. A small number of the SB401 model, based on the Series III 109, was bought by the RUC to serve alongside the Hotspurs. These vehicles were in service until at least the late 1980s, principally running between police stations and other establishments.

As Series III production drew to a close, the RUC design-engineers produced a batch of seventy-five vehicles as Hotspur replacements. These vehicles were nicknamed Simba and had a strengthened chassis, an extra 6in (152mm) of track width and were some 7.5in (190mm) wider and taller than the Hotspur. Headroom was thus significantly increased, and although the frontal aspect still resembled a Land Rover, from the A-pillar rearwards they were flat-sided.

With the introduction of the coil-sprung 110, redundant armoured bodies from the Series III Hotspur fleet were fitted to new rolling chassis, and the new model was christened Tangi, which means 'Tank' in Swaheli. Eventually, completely new bodies were fitted, and unlike the Simba, this model retained the standard Land Rover lines including the distinctive 110 wheel-arch eyebrows. Like the Simba, though, mesh guards were fitted below bumper level and rubber skirts were added all round to prevent missiles being rolled underneath.

There were six basic variations on the theme. The first major modifications

The modern Shorland armoured Land Rover, complete with revolving missile launcher.

An armoured 110 in service with the Metropolitan Police. It is not quite as well defended nor as sinister-looking as an RUC Tangi.

included raising the roof by about 4in (100mm) to give increased rear headroom, and enlargement of the observation slits in the sides for greater visibility. Sliding armoured glass blocks with cutouts were fitted to permit small-arms weapons to be used for self-defence should the vehicle come under fire. For increased protection in the rear compartment, armoured panels were added to the sides. A few of these Type Two vehicles were still in service in 1995. Another softer-edged, armoured version, classified as the Type Three, had the extended roof first seen on the Type Two, and in all other aspects, external fittings were virtually identical.

Very much in the minority and used mainly in Belfast, the Type Four had the same armour as the Type Three, but the roof was raised by a further 4in (100mm). It was initially presumed that these so-called ice-cream vans had additional overhead protection, but officially they were only built that way to get more headroom. Occasionally, high-top Tangis were used as command vehicles for four-Land Rover patrols.

The Type Five Tangi had hard-edged armour panels and lacked the higher roof of the Type Four. With the cease-fire in 1995, a number of Type Six Tangis had their additional side armour, mesh and rubber skirts, armoured radiator grille, window paint guards and much of the meshed light protection removed. The pull-up windscreen protection grille was retained, however. When stability returns, the majority of the Tangi fleet will be similarly disarmed, and might even be repainted in less sombre colours.

THE SANTANA 109 MILITAR

There have always been special requirements for battlefield Land Rovers, and they are sometimes very rare - like for example, the British one-ton APGP 109in military Land Rover, which was designed to be stacked three high in transport aircraft. It could also float when fitted with huge airbags. However, only twenty-eight units were built.

In the 1970s the Spanish military demanded something special, and Land Rover's Spanish associate Santana came up with the 109 Militar. It was a new, lightweight 4 × 4 utility with a 2,204lb (1,000kg) payload. The order was put out to tender in the military way, but only a very few companies would have been able to bid for it. The Spanish authorities insisted that their vehicles should be built in Spain, and at the time only two manufacturers had the chance to compete: Motor Iberica of Barcelona, whose under-licence Ford trucks were really too large for this new military role; and Metalurgica de Santa Ana, or Santana. Santana won the contract, and in liaison with the Spanish military, they designed a vehicle based on the 109in Land Rover. The earliest prototypes were running during the first half of 1973, and in service three years later.

There were a number of special features about the Santana 109 Militar, including its optional six-cylinder engines. If the laden vehicle was required to move quickly it needed more power than the 2.25-litre four-cylinder engine could muster. The Solihull-built 2.6-litre six-cylinder petrol engine was no use to the Spanish military because they wanted diesel power. Accordingly, Santana elected to build their own six-cylinder diesel engine using the existing Land Rover four-cylinder unit as a base. The new engines had the same bore and stroke as the four-cylinder versions and measured 3,429cc. They utilized as many common components as possible.

The diesel and petrol sixes were in production for military vehicles from 1976, but neither was available in civilian Santanas until the following year. The 109 Militar was built with the 2.25-litre petrol and diesel engines as well as the two new sixes, although by 1980 only the two larger engines were fitted. Transmission was via the standard Spanish-built four-speed 'box and two-speed transfer box.

The 109 Militar chassis was the same as the Spanish 109 pattern, and shod with 7.50 x 16 tyres. The six-cylinder models had twin fuel tanks, mounted between the axles and at the rear, providing 25.3 gallons (115l) capacity, and accessed by separate fillers. There was a 24-volt electrical system and 120 A/H alternator.

Bodywork was different from the standard Land Rover, with flat panels and angular wheelarches reminiscent of the mid-60s Solihull-built 110in gun tractor prototypes. There were also similarities with the Half-Ton or Military Lightweight. Like the 88 Militar, the front-end styling featured cutaway wing fronts, and diminutive, high-mounted headlights. Sidelights and indicators were located in oblong niches. Some examples had front bumpers mounted on extensions, which allowed jerrycans to be carried in the space between the wheels and bumper ends.

The majority of 109 Militars were soft top General Service vehicles. They were nine-seaters, potentially, with inward-facing seats for six in the back and a centre

The CAV 100, made by Courtaulds Aerospace with plastic composite armoured body, is used by the BBC and other news-gathering media organizations in the world's troublespots.

seat between driver and passenger. Door-tops were detachable and windscreens folded down, just like the Solihull product. Hard-top versions were kitted out as communications vehicles and four-stretcher ambulances, and a light recovery vehicle was equipped with a crane and electric winch.

Production of the 109 Militar ceased in about 1981 when more than 2,000 had been built. One vehicle fitted with the rare six-cylinder petrol engine was reputedly demonstrated to the British army, and that now resides at the Dunsfold Land Rover Trust. Meanwhile, the 109 Militar is still in service with the Spanish army, although numbers are dwindling as early models are replaced by locally built Nissan Patrols.

101 FC RAPIER TRACTOR

In its original guise, the Forward Control 101 or One-Tonne Land Rover of the mid-1970s was perhaps best known as a tractor for the 4in (105mm) light gun, and as a battlefield ambulance; but some were also used to tow the Rapier air defence system.

Made by British Aerospace, the Rapier is a low-level, surface-to-air missile system. Proven in the Falklands war, it is a second-line defensive weapon which can engage targets flying at up to 1,000mph

This 101 was used as a radio truck and is in Gulf camouflage colours. Production vehicles were only supplied to the military, and all were powered by the 3.5-litre V8.

(1,609km/h) at heights of up to 10,000ft (3,050m). Some Rapier systems are mounted on tracked vehicles to escort armoured formations, but the majority are towed behind specially modified Land Rovers.

The Royal Air Force Regiment and the Royal Artillery originally towed them behind 101s, but since the early 1990s the RAF has used the Defender 130, while army units ought to have had their 101 Land Rovers replaced by the troublesome Reynolds Boughton RB44 at about the same time. However, because of persistent technical faults with the RB44, a few 101s are still serving as Rapier tractors with the Royal Artillery in Germany. Veterans of the Gulf War, 58 Eyres Battery of 12 Regiment RA, is based in Dortmund, and is the last front-line Royal Artillery unit to use the 101 in its Rapier fire-truck and tracking radar-truck format.

These vehicles were very much state-of-the-art when they first entered service, with permanent four-wheel drive and excellent off-road ability. However, twenty-five years on, Eyres Battery will be going over to the Alvis Stormer, a tracked vehicle carrying the Short's high velocity missile system. The 101s are mechanically identical to standard service vehicles, but both variants have racks for four missile containers, as well as false floors to support and secure their equipment frames. The fire-unit truck and occasionally the tracking radar truck carry standard drum winches between the wheels on the near-side chassis rail.

The fire-unit truck also carries an optical tracking device on a large removable frame, which is secured to the false floor over the rear wheels. Associated electronic equipment is stowed ahead of the left wheelarch, accessed via the lower dropside panel, with personal kit and a jerrycan carried on the other side. Radio sets are fitted behind the front passenger seat, and the spare wheel occupies its usual position behind the driver. The tracking radar truck also carries four spare missiles in racks, as well as specialist equipment including the TVGU camera optical group and collimation unit electronic pack, located on a large removable handling frame secured to the false floor. A periscope, spare trailer wheel, fire extinguishers, tow rope, ground anchor, jerrycans, masts tripod, helmets and personal kit are strapped on top of the missile racks and under the dropsides.

An RA Rapier detachment consists of three vehicles: a fire unit truck towing a launcher, a tracking radar truck with the Blindfire radar fire control on tow, and an admin Land Rover which tows a trailer containing nine reload missiles. The admin Land Rover is a standard 110 Defender, but was originally a 109 Series III. In peacetime, each vehicle carries a crew of three, plus their immediate personal kit, while rations and other equipment are transported in the rear of the admin Land Rover. In wartime, the complement would increase to seven, when a third crew member would be carried in the fire-unit truck. When necessary, the launcher and radar tracker and assorted ancillaries can be deployed by the two 101s on their own, and an operational system could be transported in a Hercules aircraft.

The 101 fleet was manufactured between 1975 and 1978, so the vehicles are far from pristine. The Rapier tractors still in front-line service are a mixture of left- and right-hand drive, and their numbers have been swelled by a few ex-RAF vehicles, generally in better condition. Many former 101 Rapier tractors have passed into private hands, particularly ex-RAF issue, but the majority have had their missile racks and false floors removed before demobilization. In due course, these fittings may well turn up at auction where they will doubtless be snapped up by members of the Ex-Military Land Rover Association and FC101 Register.

THE AUSTRALIAN CONNECTION

When Australia was part of the Commonwealth, Land Rovers sold strongly, fostering a great deal of marque loyalty. However, the late 1970s and early 1980s were not a good period for Land Rover in Australia, because the Japanese motor industry made a determined onslaught on the Aussie 4 × 4 market. By the end of the 1970s, Toyota had achieved a position of total dominance, and as a consequence, Land Rover sales had sunk badly.

According to historian James Taylor, possibly the main reason for this was the Australian preference for diesel engines in their 4x4 vehicles, and Land Rover's puny 2.25-litre diesel was no match for the big six-cylinder Toyota units. Accordingly, Jaguar-Rover Australia, the company which took care of Land Rover sales and a certain amount of assembly 'down under', bought in Isuzu's big 3.9-litre 4BD1 diesel late in 1981, did a shoe-horn job and offered it in long-wheelbase Series III models.

When the 110 Land Rovers were introduced in Australia in November 1984 – just over a year after their announcement for other markets at the Geneva show – the Isuzu diesel unit remained available. However, the only model available in Australia was the 110 County Station Wagon, which came in ten-seater configuration with a choice of the 97bhp Isuzu engine or the petrol V8. But even in V8 form, these 110 Countys were not the same as the V8 Land Rovers sold in other markets: they all came with air conditioning as standard, with the benefit of an anti-roll-bar on the rear axle. The V8 engine was to Range Rover spec, with 9.35:1 compression ratio and developing 125bhp at 4,000rpm, in contrast to the 114bhp Land Rover V8 with 8.13:1 compression sold in most other markets. Since the high-compression engine had already been homologated under the Australian emissions regulations, there was not much point in going to the same trouble for the lower-powered version.

The V8-powered 110s were assembled back in Solihull, then transported to Australia as complete vehicles. However, the Isuzu diesel-powered models were actually assembled at Jaguar-Rover Australia's Moorebank plant in Sydney. They were essentially kits of parts dispatched in CKD form (Complete Knock-Down) from Solihull, which JRA then fitted with the Isuzu engines shipped over from Japan.

There is little doubt that the Isuzu diesel engine helped 110 sales in Australia, not least because it provided fuel consumption of around 25mpg (11.3l/100kg) instead of the petrol V8's low 16mpg (17.6l/100km). Prodigious amounts of torque were available, with a peak of 188lb.ft delivered at a modest 1,900rpm. If there was a downside, it was that the big, four-cylinder, direct-injection Isuzu unit was certainly not a refined engine. Its spiritual home was in Isuzu's own four-tonne trucks, and it was also used in tractors, road-rollers, excavators and other light industrial machinery. It could cruise satisfactorily at 60mph (100km/h), but above that, it became very noisy.

Probably the main reason why Jaguar-Rover Australia never imported any of Land Rover's utility models, and why the 110 V8 didn't last long there, was that it was developing its own model to match the country's particular conditions. The domestic model was announced in March 1985, and came as a chassis-cab unit ready for the fitting of locally made bodywork. It was no ordinary 110 chassis-cab, its wheelbase having been stretched to 119.6in (3,040mm) at the Moorebank plant by the simple expedient of inserting extra sections in the chassis side rails and installing a longer propshaft. For the sake of longevity, the chassis was galvanized, while heavy-duty suspension components permitted a payload of 1.3 tonnes, which was the same as the heavy-duty 110 HCPU sold in other markets. Unlike the regular Station Wagons, however, there was no anti-rollbar on the rear axle.

Although the vehicle was basically a heavy-duty Land Rover 110, JRA customers usually called it a 120, and the name stuck. You could only buy it with the Isuzu diesel engine, which was in a slightly different state of tune from the version in the 110 Station Wagon in order to give the heavier 120 more low-speed pulling power. Standard colour was glare-reflecting white, although some were painted in different colours to special order. The favoured body-style, available through JRA, was a large aluminium-alloy pick-up known as a 'tray-top', which suited the Australian 'ute' market. The tray-top was supplied by Alcan, and measured 98.4in (2,499mm) long and 78.7in (1,999mm) wide. The 120's extra-length wheelbase effectively reduced the rear overhang normally associated with pick-up bodies and consequently improved the vehicle's ability in the rough.

The specification of the Australian Land Rovers was uprated from time to time, and by the end of 1985, 110 V8s had the five-speed LT85 gearbox, and this was also fitted to the diesel-powered models from January or February 1986. Then, during 1986, the V8 engine was uprated to the same 134bhp tune as was found in V8 One-Tens for other markets.

The Ninety was never put on sale in Australia, and the One-Ten County and 120 chassis/cab models remained the only Land Rovers available in that market until June 1987, when JRA announced what it called the One-Ten County pick-up or Land Rover Dual-Cab – a strange hybrid which consisted of a four-door cab constructed mainly from Station Wagon parts and a shortened pick-up back body. The vehicle came with either five or six seats and could be had with either the petrol V8 or the Isuzu diesel engine. However, not many were made. The vehicle appears to have been designed originally for the Australian Bicentennial Authority, which took a batch, but there was only one dealer selling them to the public.

Project Perentie

In 1982 the Australian army declared it was interested in procuring a fleet of 3,000 all-terrain vehicles to replace its existing ones. The refit was known as Project Perentie. Of those 3,000 vehicles, 2,600 were to be one-tonne models to replace the army's existing Series III LWB 109 Land Rovers. With Solihull support, JRA was keen to keep the Land Rover flag flying 'down under', and three years on, was duly rewarded with the contract to provide all 2,600 vehicles.

The army announced its intentions in July 1986, the contract was formally signed in October, and the first of the new vehicles was completed at the Moorebank plant early in 1987. The initial batch of Perentie 110s joined the force in August the same year. Production continued at the rate of about 350 units a year, and the final batch of 110s fulfilling the original contract was delivered to the Australian army in 1994.

No less than six different versions of the Perentie 110 were delivered during that period. The basic general service soft-top model was supplemented by an FFR soft-top plus a soft-top surveillance vehicle. There were three closed-body versions as well, all made with safari roofs, which were never available on other 110s. These comprised a hard-top radio truck, Station Wagon, and senior officers' FFR Station Wagon.

BMC'S RIVAL: THE AUSTIN GIPSY

It was the popularity of the Land Rover which helped kill off the Austin Champ as a military vehicle, and it may well have done for their Gipsy, too. The army was not blind to the attractions of the Austin Gipsy, however. In the 1950s, British car production was dominated by the two major corporations of BMC and Leyland, with Land Rover just one of the minor brand names in the Leyland group. BMC came up with the Austin Champ, designated FV1801 Combat Truck, but the Land Rover edged out Austin's potentially superior vehicle.

In 1955 Austin tried to redress the balance and created a light utility vehicle to compete with the Land Rover. The Austin Gipsy was launched in February 1958 and was perceived as a civilian vehicle; however, a prototype was tried by the army in 1956. Subsequently, a high proportion of UK sales were for civil defence, emergency services and public utilities usage. By 1968, when the Mk4 Austin Gipsy was potentially good enough to win a large share of the market, Harold Wilson's Labour government had nationalized British Motor Holdings, which by then owned Austin, along with the Leyland group to form the unwieldy British

When compared with a Series IIA, the steel-bodied Austin Gipsy came out quite well; however nationalization of BLMC sank it.

SPECIFICATION

	90in Austin Gipsy	*88in Land Rover*
Wheelbase	90in (2,286mm)	88in (2,235mm)
Length	139in (3,531mm)	142in (3,617mm)
Width	67in (1,695mm)	65.5in (1,626mm)
Height	73.5in (1,867mm)	77.6in (1,969mm)
Gross weight	4,478lb (2,032kg)	4,453lb (2,020kg)
Army payload	1,120lb (508kg)	1,521lb (690kg)
Front track	55in (1,390mm)	52in (1320mm)
Rear track	52in (1,320mm)	51.5in (1,308mm)
Clearance	8½in (216mm)	8in (203mm)
Engine	Four cylinder ohv	Four cylinder ohv
Fuel	Petrol	Petrol
Power	62bhp @ 4,100rpm	70bhp @ 4,250rpm
Gearbox	4 forward and 1 reverse	4 forward and 1 reverse
Transfer box	2 speed	2 speed
Suspension	Semi-elliptical	Semi-elliptical
Tyres	7.50 × 16	7.50 × 16

Leyland Motor Corporation – and the low-volume Gipsy was history.

Its military potential was never fully explored, and remained unfulfilled. In 1963 two Gipsies of long- and short-wheelbase were subjected to 10,000 mile (16,093km) evaluation trials by the Fighting Vehicle Research and Development Establishment at Chertsey. A highly favourable report on their military suitability was published two years later, and subsequently, a batch of fifteen was acquired for military trials; but before the Gipsy could be ordered in quantity, its manufacturers were submerged in the Leyland conglomerate.

The Gipsy was powered by the 62bhp 2,199cc four cylinder BMC petrol engine, and its four-speed gearbox had synchromesh on second, third and fourth gears. Electrics were 24-volt, with waterproof wiring. To bring the vehicle up to military specification there were numerous factory modifications, including thicker chassis, underbody protection plates and split rims. External differences extended simply to bonnet-mounted spare wheel, military bumpers, tow eyes, and NATO tow hitch. All short-wheelbase 90in (2,286mm) Gipsies were equipped with the unique Flexitor independent torsion bar suspension, but when the 111in (2,818mm) long wheelbase model was introduced in 1960, Flexitor was fitted only on the front, with leaf-springs at the rear. It was basically a good system, but not a total success, and by late 1962, the suspension set-up had switched to beam axles on semi-elliptical springs all round on both models. Independent suspension remained an option until 1965. Military spec Gipsies were supplied with leaf-springs, and the trials vehicles also had heavy-duty springs at the rear, modified halfshafts, propshaft gaiters and strengthened rear crossmembers.

The Austin Gipsy had a box-section ladder chassis, but whereas the Land Rover's is a rectangular box-section, the Gipsy's was constructed from two U-sections welded horizontally, which produced an ovoid section. When the prototype Gipsy was built in 1955, it not only looked like an 86in (2,184mm) Series I, it even had rectangular chassis rails. But Austin's tests suggested the weld seams were over-stressed, so they went with the oval cross-section for production Gipsies. Although the Land Rover's chassis strength is legendary, that of the Gipsy is even stronger, and cracking is apparently rare.

Early Gipsies succumbed to damaged drivetrains and diffs in spite of, or perhaps because of the independent Flexitor suspension. Later Gipsies with leaf-springs were every bit as reliable as their Solihull equivalents, and if anything were slightly more comfortable; the Gipsy's ride quality was certainly more comfortable than that of Series II Land Rovers. The only area where the Land Rover had an advantage over the Gipsy was in its aluminium body, but the Austin's special factory body treatment endowed it with superior corrosion protection to any comparable steel-bodied contemporary.

By using pressed steel for the body, minor styling variations were possible, but it has to be said that the Gipsy looks very much like a Land Rover, even down to the radiator grille and inboard headlight arrangement. Although the transfer box arrangement was different, with high ratio only available initially in two-wheel drive at first, by 1963 both 4WD high and front-wheel drive only could be selected if required. They also made provision for front, central and rear power take-offs, although no aperture was provided in the rear crossmember. The Gipsy was supplied with a soft top, and a variety of fibreglass hard tops was available.

Had Gipsy manufacture continued for only a couple more years, maybe Austin could have won a large enough contract to assure the vehicle's future, and it is a matter of conjecture what would have happened to military Land Rover sales in the 1970s if the Gipsy had remained in production.

LAND ROVER ON FILM

Land Rovers have featured in many films, as diverse as *The Italian Job* and *Ace Ventura: Pet Detective.* Perhaps the most bizarre is the 1995 *Judge Dredd* movie. Judge Dredd is an American hero in the science fiction comic-strip film of 2000AD, a law enforcer in Mega-City One, formerly known as New York, in the dark days of the twenty-first century where society as we know it has collapsed. The only mode of transport to have survived in this anarchic world is the armoured utility vehicle, the yellow cab of the future which is built like a fortress on wheels to protect its occupants from the violent environment. However, it may be of some comfort to know that a Land Rover was perceived as the most likely survivor of this Armageddon scenario.

Late in 1993 it was rumoured that film company Cinergi Pictures Entertainment was on the look-out for vehicles. The film was to be set in a hostile future, and Land Rovers were on the shortlist. When the formal approach came to Land Rover's marketing department, Rover Group's Canley Design Centre was alerted. Rover Group designer David Woodhouse had already done some preliminary sketches for a Land Rover of the future, and he was entrusted with the job of designing the battlewagon.

He could have used a Defender chassis, but decided that the 101 Forward Control was a much better platform, being higher off the ground, as well as matching the taxi format of the film script, with the driver up front and the passengers in a protected cell behind. One of his drawings featured a yellow vehicle, just like the traditional Yellow Cab, and this was the one the film company wanted. They asked Land Rover to supply thirty like it, and were quite happy for the vehicles to wear Land Rover badges. It was suggested that the finished design should look as if it could actually have been made by Land Rover. Design influences ranged from American football helmets to the ambiguous angular shapes of the Stealth bomber, and the fibreglass wheel extensions designed to look like tyres when the vehicle is moving add to the aggressive pose. Around twenty members of the Rover Group design team were involved in the project at one time or another, and it was all accomplished very quickly indeed: whereas the Discovery went from drawing-board to production in three years, the Judge Dredd Land Rover took less than three months to get from drawing-board to film set.

After the basic sketches and final renderings came a quarter-scale model, followed by a full-size prototype, created on a left-hand drive 101 chassis. The original vehicle had been in service with the RAF, and was stripped to its chassis and bulkhead by Dunsfold Land Rover's Trust and delivered to Canley Design Studio to have its new body fitted. The moulds for the GRP bodies for the other thirty vehicles were taken from the prototype. This was the only vehicle to have a fully finished interior, and it was used for all shots featuring the inside of a Mega-City One Yellow Cab. The prototype also has a trick two-part side door, operated by the driver, and the sombre all-black cabin contains a rather bizarre seating arrangement for six.

Land Rover had to find thirty more 101 Forward Control chassis, which was no mean feat since the 101 has been out of production since 1978. In June 1994 the first of the 101s was acquired through a military auction in Germany, but the remainder were sourced by Philip Bashall of Dunsfold Land Rovers from private owners. Some were 12-volt, some 24-volt, there were radio trucks and ambulances as well as General Service vehicles. One was even a Gulf War veteran, and another was chassis number 13 of the right-hand drive 12-volt series. Such was the scarcity of left-hooker 101s, that several were right-hand drive. Authenticity in this respect was not crucial, as it is impossible to tell in the film where the driver is sitting.

The actual construction of the 'Dredd Sheds' passed rapidly through the premises of a well known coachbuilder to a company in Coventry, which specializes in making concept vehicles. They were delivered to Pinewood Studios on schedule in October when filming began – and the rest is history. Land Rover's contract with the film company stipulated that the 101s should be available for promotional use, and Dunsfold Land Rovers maintained and serviced them as necessary while the film was made. The Dredd Sheds are not road-legal, however, and the reversed-rim wheels and lack of windscreen wipers and a second headlamp would cancel out an MoT pass. Neither would they be a lot of fun to drive in practice. The 101 driving position is uncomfortable for anyone with long legs, and ventilation and heating is absent.

After filming was over, the Dredd Sheds went back to Lode Lane, and were to be seen parked forlornly by the test track to the north-east of the factory. The prototype was tidied up and used for promotional work in Britain and the USA. The rest have been retained in case they make a *Judge Dredd II*.

Lurking ominously in the back regions of Lode Lane are the Dredd Sheds which featured in the Sylvester Stallone film Judge Dredd.

SPECIAL PICTURES

Potential winner of the longest title in the universe is *Land Rover Conversions and Applications since 1948: The World's Most Versatile Vehicle at Work* by Richard de Roos. The book is soft back and in black and white only, but well worth looking at because its contents are a delightful mix of service vehicles, military and civil, based on the Land Rover platform. Any oddballs I have overlooked here can be found in pictorial form in the de Roos book.

The pictures come from a variety of sources, including Nick Dimbleby. There are also silhouette tables of different Land Rover configurations, as used by the company for publicity purposes. Predictably, there are fire engines,

The Defender 90 MRCV – Multi-Role Combat Vehicle – on a training exercise. The device in the rear is the MILAN anti-tank guided weapon launcher, with spare missiles in racks on either side.

This German 6 × 6 Defender 130 was built by Reynolds Boughton, and belongs to Dieter Sikorski.

A BBC Fast Response Unit, with Clark mast, used for transmitting live interviews and taped footage.

Ibex-bodied Land Rover, using V8-powered coil-sprung chassis. Minimal overhang means better angles of approach and departure.

police cars, SAS combat machines, personnel carriers and armoured cars, ambulances, campers, track-laying vehicles by J.A. Cuthbertson, snow ploughs, railway shunters, Forestry Commission Land Rovers with enormous wheels, and amphibious conversions. But there are lots of surprises too. Agricultural applications include a Series II 109 pick-up doubling as hovercraft, and a Forward Control chassis fitted with a detachable Luton-style wooden livestock container. There was the Pope-mobile of 1989, a 110 pick-up fitted with what looked like an air-conditioned goldfish tank. There was even a Series IIA and Series III refuse carrier with tipping body. Most astonishing military conversion is the Hussar armoured personnel carrier by Penman Engineering, an

Land Rover 130 chassis with tipper-truck body.

Carmichael 6 × 6 fire appliance, based on a Stage 1 V8, in service with Hereford and Worcester Fire Brigade, standing on top of the Malvern Hills.

armour-plated six-wheel drive vehicle which could carry fourteen men. Overall, it is a useful reference book, with an excellent cross section of specialized Land Rovers.

SPECIAL MODELS

More and more models are coming out of notable vehicles, and Land Rover is no exception. The vehicle's success has been mirrored by several model makers, one such being Hart Models in Hampshire. The series was started at the request of British Aerospace, and today is still actively encouraged by Solihull.

The forerunner of Hart Models was Denzil Skinner, a commercial model-making firm with a small number of employees. Development progressed on two fronts, making models for both the industrial and the collector's markets. When the owner retired in 1988, the firm closed, but two of the long-standing employees formed a partnership to continue as Hart Models.

The British Aerospace connection came about because they had previously been using converted 1:48 Corgi Toys to represent the Rapier Missile battery unit, complete with hand-built trailers. Something better was needed, and in due course a 1:48 scale Rapier IB missile system was commissioned from Hart. Although it was by no means the first model to this scale, it set new standards of detail for its size. The Rapier set consisted of the towed launching trailer, with fully traversing and elevating capability, and armed with four missiles. The radar trailer operated similarly, plus two small generator trolleys and a folding tripod-mounted optical tracker. Later on, something better was required to tow the coupled units and carry the generators, and the basic military Land Rover models were the result.

First came the 109 with full canvas tilt, with either Series IIA or Series III front, followed by the hard-top FFR and similar versions based on the 88in model. The forward area support trailer and the missile supply trailer with stowage for nine missiles complete the set. In due course the Lightweight GS Series III and 109 Series IIA and III ambulance were added.

Most basic Land Rover models have been available from Hart's as white metal kits, although many of the complex liveries are only produced as ready-mades. Kits are popular with owners wishing to reproduce their own vehicle. The castings are of excellent quality, but because the bodies are made of several castings, they can be quite time-consuming to assemble. More recently, high-density resin has become the medium for the main body shell, exemplified by the Shorland armoured car. This makes an ideal starter kit, with the additional benefit that camouflage paint finishes are also less demanding. All the fittings and chassis are metal, which gives the right feel and centre of gravity, and separate tyres, glass and decals are included.

The 90, 110 and Defenders which followed were initially only available in estate car form, featuring some interesting liveries. The British Telecom model with grey piper scheme is fitted with the final short-lived version of the front capstan winch. This, and the Royal Mail post bus, is manufactured for Roxley Models which specializes in Telecom and postal vehicle models. Military versions include the 110, finished in correct NATO and Territorial Army Royal Yeomanry gloss green, including roof and wheels. The 101 one-tonne Forward Control joined the line-up in 1994, and is available as the canvas-tilt GS version. It is in white metal with a resin canopy which imitates the texture of the fabric beautifully, and is a fairly complex kit. An ambulance with state-of-the-art resin body appeared as a ready-made in UN finish, and for showing fine detail, white or sand-coloured models are better than khaki.

Hart's original Lightweight takes the form of one of the Red Arrows' two hard-top Lightweights in its latest guise, as a one-piece body and including extra detailing. The display team's unique dye-replenishment trailer is an additional feature. This is carried aboard the Hercules support aircraft with the Lightweight, and is used to top up the coloured 'smoke' dyes used by the aircraft in their display. A donation goes to the Red Arrows Trust for every one sold.

The Series II Forward Control is a rare vehicle, and since detailed chassis are vital to model makers, the Forward Control, has two. Nevertheless, the model is built up virtually like the real thing. A 109in chassis has a front out-rigger added, with a complete subframe on top. Spacers in between allow a level top for mounting the cab and rear body, and the engine is visible within the cab.

The first model reproduces Dunsfold Collection's Series IIA, including the light grey paintwork unique to the Forward Control. The Series IIB model has revised headlamp locations, gear-lever positions and different rear wheel covers. Although still a Series II, it had a 110in (2,793mm) wheelbase. The ready-made model has a full-length canopy, and is finished as 21 BT 29, with prototype number 7140P on the doors. It was one of three vehicles used in military trials, despite the fact that the Forward Control was not a military success. However, commercial users included post office telephones, who employed them at the start of the yellow period with special bodies, as did a few security bullion-carriers. The HCB Angus Army Fire Service vehicle is quite well known, and a number of local authority fire services have used them in a variety of body styles.

The rare high capacity pick-up was introduced as a late Series III, but incorporated the wider axles and extra width of the 110. The HCPU was used by Hereford Special Air Service, whose vehicles feature unique alterations in the front crew area, and 24 KD 63 is a faithful reproduction in 1.48 scale, a little under 4in (100mm) long. There are 100 separate components.

LAND ROVER MODELS

Type	*WB*	*Model Details*	*Make*	*Scale*	*Makers No.*	*Price*
LR	90	Defender (kit) Station Wagon WM	Hart	1/48	HT39	£29.00
LR	110	Defender (kit) Station	Hart Wagon WM	1/48	HT38	£29.00
LR	109	SIII green Safari	Solido	1/43	1914	£8.50
LR	90	White 90 helicopter set	Majorette	1/56	961	£11.50
LR	109	SIII UN white and trailer	Verem	1/43	368	£12.50
LR	110	High-capacity red Marins-Pompiers Marseille	Verem	1/43	4004	£29.50
LR	90	Blue with horse trailer and four horses	Britains	1/32	9658	£15.99
LR	90	White and dumper truck	Majorette	1/56	MM4514	£11.50
RR	2-door	1978 Green	Solido	1/43	1817	£8.95
RR	2-door	1984 Paris-Dakar Rally Pacific light blue	Solido	1/43	1927	£8.95
LR	110	High capacity green military RAF (handbuilt resin and metal)	Verem/ Mondial	1/43	4007	£29.50
LR	110	Coastguard	Ertl	1/64		£1.50
LR		Shorland MkIII armoured patrol vehicle (N Ireland)	BWM	1/76	BW26	£6.50
LR		Shorts SB 301 armoured patrol vehicle (N Ireland)	BWM	1/76	BW31	£6.50
LR	110	Station Wagon	BWM	1/76	BW26	£6.50
LR	90	Forestry commission	Britains	1/32	5986	£8.50
RR		four-door and sea-green carvan	Majorette	1/56	MM3053	£8.20
LR	90	white with red, yellow & blue	Matchbox	1/96	MB16	£1.35
LR	90	Welsh mine Safari	Majorette	1/56	266	£3.50

All are available from Landcraft Model Shop, Plas-yn Dre, 23 High Street, Bala, Gwynedd, Wales

6 Living With Land Rovers

No other vehicle provides its owners with such camaraderie and opportunities for exploiting its potential as the Land Rover. As well as local clubs and owners' clubs devoted to specific models, there are national gatherings and off-road centres for practising your driving technique – and it isn't just special Land Rover events where the vehicles can be seen. For instance, a varied mix of new and unusual vehicles formed part of Land Rover's own display at the Royal Show: special vehicles, commercial Discoverys, a rare Series I and a Camel Trophy 110 were among the line-up of new spec Range Rovers and Defenders. The four-day event, held at the agricultural showground in Warwickshire, also featured an off-road course operated by the staff of Land Rover Experience, offering rides in new Range Rovers, Defenders and Discoverys.

Yet another important annual event is the Billing Show: in five years it has become the largest gathering of Land Rovers and Land Rover enthusiasts anywhere, and probably the largest get-together of national and single-marque Land Rover clubs. Virtually all the national and single-marque clubs are represented – Land Rover Register 47/51 club, the Series I, Series II and Series III clubs, Lightweight club, Range Rover Register, Club Discovery, Ex-Military L/R Association, the 101 Forward Control Register and the ARC (the Association of Rover Clubs). The All-Wheel Drive Club is not strictly a Land Rover club, but it plays a major role in the cross-country world both in competition and rights-of-way issues, as well as being the largest single 4 × 4 club in the UK. Billing also gives the clubs the best opportunity of the year to reunite members in one place. Some even hold their AGM over the weekend.

SPECIAL EQUIPMENT

To get the most out of Land Rover ownership, there are a number of accessories which make life easier when the going gets tough. For instance, before tackling anything serious, especially when climbing or descending steep hillsides, it is vitally important that not only does the engine run smoothly, but that the suspension, brakes and steering are in good order as well. And particularly in the wetter months of the year, off-roading is all down to traction, so the first consideration is tyres.

There is a lot more to a tyre than an impressively chunky tread. One of the leading manufacturers of specialized tyres is BF Goodrich whose 4 x 4 range includes five designs for all types of terrain – some are claimed to have a life expectancy of around 40–50,000 miles (65–80,000km). The Q-rated 'Commercial All-Weather' tyres are labelled 'M & S' for mud and snow, and these all-weather performers are

The right equipment and accessories are important. This long-wheelbase Series IIA has an excellent roof rack, plus additional illumination with spots and Series III-style wing front headlights.

basically road tyres suitable for occasional off-roading. They are constructed for comfort, economy and traction and the tread pattern is designed for even wear and longevity. Two durable steel belts help resist bruises, punctures and stone damage, while the polyester carcass radial construction provides a smooth ride at all speeds.

Radial Mud Terrains are also Q-rated, and as the name suggests, specifically designed for off-road use. The tread deals easily with deep mud, sand and snow, while providing reasonable on-road service. The self-cleaning tread has traction bars which penetrate deeply and shed the clods.

The **Trac Edge** is an excellent all-round tyre, built to function in mud, sand and snow, as well as having very good on-road qualities. The tread pattern is excellent for self-cleaning and quiet running, and the polyester carcass radial construction gives a smooth ride at all speeds.

Best seller in the BF Goodrich range is the **Radial All Terrain**, designed for on- and off-road use, providing a smooth ride as well as coping easily with rocky and hilly terrain. Its open shoulder grooves provide good traction on wet and slippery surfaces.

Although suitable for occasional off-road use, the **Trail** is an excellent on-road tyre. It has generally superior snow traction and is branded 'M & S' for mud and snow.

Tyres cost a small fortune at the best of times, so it's good to remind ourselves that remoulds for 4 × 4s are a practical proposition. Colway's range of all-wheel drive rubber tyres retail for around half the price of many original equipment ones, and a range known as the C-Trax 75 and 80 series off-road retreads has recently been introduced. The 75s are low-profile road-going tyres, while the 80s feature an open tread pattern more suitable for off-roading, with radial sizes 195/R15, 215/R15, 205/R16, and 31 × 10.5/R15, at which size these wide boots are Q-rated – that's 100mph (160km/h). There are also two cross-ply tyres, size 6.00 × 16 and 7.50 × 16, developed specifically for Land Rovers. Colway's remoulds are tested to European new car tyre spec.

Those looking for a less expensive deal

might check the classifieds in the back of the specialist magazines for a second-hand set of five 7.50 × 16 Mud Terrains, which at the time of writing might cost £100–150. But be sure your rims are wide enough to take them, as a 7.50 × 16 tyre requires a minimum of a 6in wide rim, as found on a LWB Land Rover. Alternatively, the 'Mud Pluggers' are remould versions of Firestone's Super All Terrain tyres, and provide good traction for about £40 each plus VAT (1996 prices).

ON-ROADERS

The science of tyre design is increasingly sophisticated, with tyre and car manufacturers liaising closely on new projects. Goodyear manufactures one in six of all tyres sold in the European 4 × 4 market, and the majority of its product development and testing is carried out at the vast US San Angelo facility and a large test complex at Colmerberg in Luxembourg. In 1984 Goodyear bought the hilly 2.1 mile (3.3km) race circuit at Mireval, west of Montpellier in south-west France, for high-performance testing. There is also a 1 mile (1.6km) off-road track and a mile (1.7km) wet section, as well as a 2 mile (3.2km) four-wheel drive test circuit in a stony valley alongside the main test track. This is where they evolve new rubber.

Some tyres clearly not intended as mud tyres, in fact cope adequately with the loose scree found on unmade tracks. Curiously enough, according to research, off-roaders are fashion victims, 51 per cent of customers preferring white outline lettering compared with 46 per cent who prefer black sidewalls, and a mere 3 per cent with no preference; based on these revelations, firms are now producing 235/70R × 16 tyres with both white lettering and black

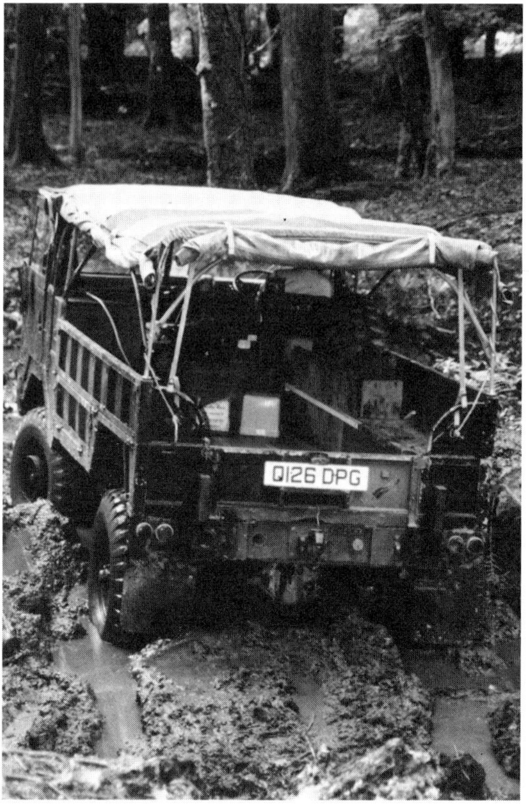

A 101 goes sure-footedly through the mud.

sidewalls. Research also suggests that the average Discovery owner confines his off-roading to grassy surfaces, so the 237/70R16 model is specifically produced with staggered shoulder blocks to give improved traction on grass.

Land Rovers are sometimes said to veer left or right under braking, and one explanation for this is different tyre pressures on the same axle, or a new tyre and a worn tyre on the same axle, which means the rolling radii of the wheels are different: one wheel will spin faster in a straight line than its opposite, causing the differential to be constantly compensating, and whining, and consequently cooking itself. Also, one brake would heat up more than its opposite number, and the faster rotating wheel would stop first.

TRAVELLING IN SNOW

On the subject of snow chains for winter work, the question of front or rear fitment depends on the circumstances. If you need to make a steep climb, the chains are best fitted on the rear axle because of weight transfer, thus giving maximum traction at the back, which is most important if the vehicle is heavily laden. However, getting up is not really the main problem: it is retaining control while coming down again, when it is easy to become over-confident. Hubris waits as you whizz smugly past all the grovelling, shovelling two-wheel drive owners, and you forget that going downhill the 4×4 has no real advantage over a regular car. In point of fact, low range and locked diffs can cause the lightly laden rear end to break away more easily, causing a 360° spin. It's as well to remember, too, that picturesque mountain scenery is usually punctuated by a vertical drop! On descent, the weight transfer will be at the front, and chains on the front wheels will give optimum steering and braking. A 4x4 or front-wheel drive car with chains on the front may have terrific traction and steering, but even a slight application of the brakes will cause the front end to stop and the rear end to overtake it.

There is a technique for cornering. When the vehicle refuses to co-operate, turn the wheel and stab the brakes on and off: as the front wheels lock the car slides, and as

When negotiating conditions like these, there is no substitute for snow chains.

they start to revolve it will go briefly in the direction of steering, until the next application of brakes. This only works below a certain speed, and requires practice where you won't run off the road. Also, practise fitting chains with the car stationary, because if you are already stuck, driving forwards to fit them is not an option. On icy roads, studded tyres could be a more cost-effective approach for some users.

On long-wheelbase models it is generally best to leave the chains on the rear to prevent it breaking away. Another reason for fitting chains on the rear is that you are less likely to cause damage to the vehicle. Remember to check that chains on front wheels are well clear of track rod ends and brake pipes, particularly if you have non-standard wheels and tyres fitted. But actually, you should fit chains to all driven wheels for maximum security, on the basis that if conditions are bad enough to stop a Land Rover from going up, they'll be far worse coming down. If you only need chains for your annual skiing holiday or whatever, then two will be perfectly adequate: the approach roads to resorts are bound to be well cleared because the vast majority of traffic is only two-wheel drive.

The price of chains generally reflects their quality, and the more expensive ones should last the life of the vehicle. Dealers often include a free repair service and they will adapt the chains if you change vehicles. The chains approved by Land Rover may be expensive, but the steel will be of good quality and they can be safely fitted to the front wheels; you need only contemplate a cheap chain on the front wheels breaking and severing a brake pipe to make your mind up. At the time of writing most good quality chains appear to be of Austrian origin.

In most alpine regions you might see a road sign telling you that chains are compulsory when conditions get bad, and this applies to 4 × 4s too. If you don't fit at least two, you could be held responsible for any accident, and your insurance could be invalidated. You also need to remember that the ascending vehicle has priority, and that postal buses have priority over everything, at all times.

MORE ESSENTIAL EQUIPMENT

Another desirable piece of kit is a high-lift jack which is most useful for changing wheels, or for lifting a corner of the vehicle in order to place some rocks under a wheel if you find yourself high-centred and stuck; the high-lift jack will also lift one end of a stuck vehicle high out of ruts and cast it onto high ground. It also works as a short pull winch by attaching the top of the rack to a ground anchor and the toe of it to a recovery point with a chain. The chain can always be readjusted for another pull to get out of trouble.

A decent nylon tow rope, say 1in (24mm) with a 12-tonne breaking strain, is vital when towing or recovering off-road in low-ratio four-wheel-drive. Possibly the most useful off-road recovery rope is an eight-strand nylon rope, 27ft (8m) long with sleeved soft-eye spliced loops at each end. An ideal everyday towing rope is a 14ft 7in × 1in (4.5m × 24mm) three-strand rope, plus appropriate ¾ in (190mm) 'bow' or 'D' shackles. Whether it be Series I, II or III or a 90/110, the vehicle should have either a pair of bumper 'D' rings or Jate rings fitted to the front as securing points. Normally a good, strong and well fitted towing pintle or ball on the rear will suffice for most recovery situations, provided it is not one of the low-slung variety.

A pointed shovel is easier to dig with,

Vince Cobley gets cross-axled in his Pro-Trax 90 hard-top. Apart from a Warn winch, he also carries a pointed spade, a pick and a Jackall, and the vehicle exhaust is adapted for wading.

A unique winch bumper unit made by Glenfrome. The vehicle's front grille panel has been extended to house an air-conditioning radiator.

and one with an all-metal handle will last longer. The well prepared 'boy scout' should also carry a bow saw, a machete and a pair of long-handled pruners for cutting back undergrowth where necessary.

It is also advisable to carry a cable-operated hand winch, complete with 66ft (20m) of $\frac{5}{16}$in (8mm) wire rope,as it can be used on either the front, back or side of the vehicle, when the only way out is by winching. It is essential to secure all this equipment and spare fuel cans in the back of the Land Rover, because there is always a risk of a roll-over. An avalanche of tools, ropes, jacks and hand winches can be prevented by lashing everything down with rope, netting, mounting racks or lockers bolted to the floor.

Should the unthinkable happen, the drill is to switch off the ignition immediately to protect the engine and minimize the risk of fire. Then apply the handbrake to ensure that the vehicle doesn't continue rolling down the hill when it is back on its wheels. Check for acid leakage from the battery, and flush the area with water. Ensure that oil and fluid levels are correct before restarting the engine, and check lights, brakes and steering as well. It goes without saying that every off-roading vehicle ought to carry a first-aid kit and a fire extinguisher.

INSURANCE

Another requirement is insurance, and it is surprising that it can be difficult to get cover even for Land Rovers. Long-wheelbase multi-seater Safari models appear to be most problematic – though not all insurance companies are 'bad guys'. In the UK for example, NFU Mutual is a branch of the National Farmers' Union, founded in 1910, and many farmers, traditionally the most common Land Rover users, naturally tended to insure with them. The firm has since expanded to become the largest insurer of Land Rovers in the country.

OFF ROAD CENTRES

Off-road driving for novices need not be daunting, as certainly in the UK there are several excellent training courses in appropriate locations all over the country.

Crediton, Devon

One of the leading establishments is David Bowyer's Offroading Centre near Crediton, in Devon; at the time of writing there were three courses a week, each course catering for four or five vehicles. Typically, several instructors were on hand to give tuition and advice, the first day's instruction concentrating on off-road techniques, and the second day taking in the safe use of vehicle recovery equipment and winching. On each day 'pupils' attend a classroom session where they learn, for example, how to handle a failed climb, when to engage the diff lock, or use a winch safely. The various techniques for off-road driving are described, including use of gears, approach angles, and dealing with side slopes. Naturally, great emphasis is placed on driving safely and in a manner which does not harm the surrounding countryside or upset the environmental lobby, especially when greenlaning. The course advises on practicalities such as securing number plates and tow hitches, and checking oil, water levels and tyre pressures; and most importantly, if contemplating deep water driving, how to fit wading plugs to the clutch housing and cam-belt housing.

Much planning has gone into the layout of the 10-acre (4ha) site, set in beautiful countryside. The 1½-mile (2.4km) course has been constructed on a hillside, taking in plenty of hillclimbs, a wooded water section, some rocky terrain and a deep muddy section; and water levels are carefully maintained so that wading doesn't become too deep. Strategically planted trees add to the authenticity, and grassy areas have been maintained.

The instructors at the centre will also drive pupils individually around the course; then after a couple of circuits, they will take the passenger seats and pupils go solo under their watchful eye. One day's training is sufficient to give novices the confidence to tackle the whole course. The second day concentrates on vehicle recovery and winching, showing the different types and uses of recovery equipment, including high-lift jacks, kinetic ropes, shovels, chains and winches. Emphasis is placed on the safe use of all this kit, especially the importance of wearing a strong pair of gloves when handling winches and ropes, and the use of strops around trees when winching off them. You are shown how to shift a vehicle to one side using the high-lift jack; how to lower and pull a vehicle with the aid of the jack and chains between two vehicles; and how a hand-portable Tirfor winch can be used just as effectively as a battery-powered one. The centre also organizes longer courses and off-road tours.

Driving Lessons in Desborough, Northants

As the organizer of numerous off-roading events and competitions, it makes sound sense for Vince Cobley to pass on skills and techniques learned in hostile environments to novices – and to the not-so-inexperienced as well. I went back to school to find out how an expert teaches it. Vince Cobley has a wealth of experience off-roading in the hills around Llandiloes and Aberystwyth in Wales; his red Land Rover 90 is equipped with some impressive navigational aids. It is very much a working vehicle, and he has fitted a 300TDi for its performance and flexibility, together with new shock absorbers, although otherwise it's standard. 'Apart from driver ability it's tyres that really make a difference to off-road performance,' Vince explained. On some trips he swaps the Goodyear G90s he normally runs for General Grabbers which are better suited to certain terrain; and some people favour the impressive Goodrich Trac Edge or Mud Terrain tyres.

The key considerations with all greenlaning are checking that the routes are legal, and ensuring that no damage would be done by the vehicles. Those new to off-roading are advised to go in summer because as well as the weather being better, the lanes are easier to drive; on some terrain the water lies close to the surface, and in the wet winter months such places can be a very different proposition. Wales boasts an impressive variety of landscape, from forests to mountain tops, and what makes the principality such an attractive driving environment is that the wilderness areas include river crossings, rock steps, dense forest and steep gullies. You do not need expensive and highly equipped Land Rovers to use green lanes. But any off-road driving is more difficult with a leaf-sprung Land Rover like the Series III which I used as a journalist on *LRO*. With less overall ground clearance and much less axle articulation, in difficult gully sections the diffs of a Series Land Rover would be grounding and its wheels leaving the ground very easily, with the springs causing a powerful kickback in the steering wheel. Series Land Rovers also have much lower-geared steering which means more hard work on tight corners.

Petrol engines are not quite as good as diesels for slow first-gear work, because they lack the instant response of a diesel, and they won't idle along without any throttle, which a diesel will do in first or second in low box. A 90 would cruise over virtually anything in these gears in low ratios, such is its flexibility.

Lessons are held at Pro-Trax's West Lodge Rural Centre, based on a farm near Desborough in the lovely rolling countryside of the Northants-Leicestershire border. In effect there are three sites in one here: a gentle course through a new deciduous plantation for beginners; a far more undulating section of steep inclines, ruts and bogs; and then there is a dense woodland which featured as part of the 1995 Warn Challenge final. This section poses a great many of the hazards you might expect to find anywhere in the UK. There is also a formidable gully section, deep in a ravine, also used by the Warn competitors but not part of the Pro-Trax course. Depending on the state of the going at West Lodge, Vince also takes pupils to the quarry at Tixover Grange, because, as he says, 'to keep operational all year round, you have to have access to alternative sites as one may be bogged down and inoperable.'

Vince knows the land intimately. His 90 has the type of modifications you'd expect, bearing in mind the type of work it has to do: stiffer springs and dampers, a diff protector, a winch, a Range Rover gearbox, and significantly, no ball-hitch tow-bar – the enemy of the serious hill-climb. The vehicle was converted in 1994 from a truck-cab model and bears the scars of numerous altercations with obstacles. The spade and pick-axe which live on the front wing-tops are not there for display: they might be used to help get you out of a deep rut – and there are plenty of these in any off-roading situation.

Vince started by taking us through the most basic principles of off-roading: how to negotiate sloping surfaces where the vehicle is inclined to slide; ditches – go through one wheel at a time; ruts – not always a good idea to follow them, and best straddled; how to address hills, going up and down; and issues of safety – be prepared with equipment for all possible eventualities, such as high-lift jacks, strops and sand-boards. He stressed the importance of vehicle preparation, especially the need to check fluid levels.

Next step was a drive round the easy course, and we were shown how to cope with a failed climb – initially quite alarming as you restart the engine with the 'box already in reverse. With regard to difficult climbs and descents, we were advised only to tackle what we believed ourselves capable of: 'It's all down to the bum factor,' he laughed. 'You'll always back out first!'

We moved on to the more serious stuff, and it soon emerged that I needed smoother throttle control on reaching the brow of ascents, and that I was tending to turn in too late – 'get the lock on nice and early, as you can always wind it off.' My other vice, which comes from thirty-odd years of driving, was crossing arms when steering instead of feeding the wheel through my hands. I managed to keep my thumbs out of the way, though!

Benniworth Springs

It is interesting to see how some off-roading centres get started. One at Benniworth in the Lincolnshire wolds is a newer operation but is growing in status and it is a good example of how such a scheme gets off the ground. Farmer Keith Olivant started with an area of set-aside, including a wood, and moved in with a bulldozer to create a variety of topographical hazards. He walked the wood with his son and simply strimmed between trees to make a course, which is at times exceedingly tight.

Other demanding features are the dips and dunes, ribs, graves and bumps, and a hill named the Eiger. There is a special winching area, complete with an MoT failure parked in a mud hole to drag out. Most scenically attractive is the watercourse section with undulating streambed, and the water splash, which LR fans will be pleased to hear did the worst for a Mitsubishi on trial. Two Defenders are used for teaching, either a 90 or a 110 Safari.

Driving in the Welsh Mountains

The 4 × 4 Drive site at Glyndwr's Way, at Llandinam off the A470 near Newtown in Powys, is 'an adventure into the Welsh mountains': it covers more than 250 acres (100ha) of superb off-road driving terrain, comprising woodland and mountain tracks with an extensive area of open marsh and moorland; it is also the location of the largest wind farm in Europe. 'Our days incorporate driver training with off-road adventure, for which the venue is perfect,' said owner Richard Walsh.

Land Rover owners should find the terrain challenging enough for even the most experienced drivers. Recovery is on hand throughout so there is no worry about getting stuck. The courses cover driving controls, gear selection, gradients and side slopes, wading, fording, surveying the ground, tyre selection and care, recovery techniques and conservation.

On-Road Off-Roaders at Crowthorne, Berkshire

The main point of off-road driving courses is to show owners and enthusiasts how to handle their vehicles in the conditions for which they were built. However, prompted by recent controversy about the stability of swiftly driven 4×4s on the highway, DriveTech – based at the Transport Research Laboratory at Crowthorne, Berkshire – has included a lesson in on-road driving: 'What we aim to do is instruct owners of 4x4s how to use their vehicles on the road in safety. Many owners are unaware of the handling characteristics generated by the vehicle's high centre of gravity, and the degree of steering input required in a given situation. Many will overreact in a crisis, making a potentially dangerous situation even more volatile.'

Instructors are all ex-traffic policemen, qualified to ROSPA Advanced Instructor standard, which gives them unsurpassed first-hand knowledge of how such vehicles behave under duress both on- and off-road. As well as its excursion into the rough, the facility also includes a skid-pan and seminar tuition; but DriveTech can arrange lessons on-road anywhere in the country.

TOWING TECHNIQUES

Many Land Rover owners will tow agricultural machinery, light industrial plant, horseboxes, caravans and military equipment, and clearly there is nothing I can tell such owners about trailing techniques. However, certain tips for someone interested in towing may not go amiss:

Construction and Use regulations stipulate a maximum trailer length of 23ft (7m), the whole rig must not exceed 74ft (22.5m), and the trailer width mustn't be more than 7ft 6in (2.3m). Caravan and trailer brakes must act on all wheels while the vehicle is in motion, and on two wheels while it is stationary. The maximum distance allowed between Land Rover and trailer or caravan is 15ft (4.5m). Being a hefty vehicle, a Land Rover makes a fine tow-car; the chassis is absolutely ideal for attaching the tow bar to. Clearly, it is vital the Land Rover's clutch and brakes are in perfect shape.

The Land Rover should always be the boss, as it were, so that uncontrolled momentum does not allow the trailer to overwhelm the Land Rover. For instance, as a general rule when descending a hill, you need to engage a low gear at the top, and go down slowly to avoid over-revving the engine. Given their set of low ratios, Land Rovers are more compliant at this than any other vehicle, but if you are doing this sort of thing off-road, you obviously need to be more circumspect about it than on a normal tarmac hill.

Reversing into a site or through a gateway is always the most difficult thing to master. You need to remember that the trailer will go in the opposite way to the steering lock you apply on the Land Rover

RUSSIAN OFF-ROAD

There are countless things you can do with your Land Rovering expertise. For instance, if you want to go off-roading in Russia, there is a firm specializing in tours. Based in Moscow, Club 4 × 4 organizes six- to eight-day off-roading trips, taking in such delights as the historic city of St Petersburg, and travelling deep into the Karelian isthmus, bordering Finland. This vast wilderness has few metalled roads, and the climate is warm in summer, snowy in winter. The tours are flexible, and Club 4 × 4 can organize accommodation and airport transfer. The only snag is that they mostly run Lada Nivas. If you can handle that, it should be a worthwhile experience. Contact Club 4 × 4, Krilatskaya Street 10, Moscow, Russia. tel/fax: 095 140 44 83, or tel: 095 149 49 21.

Land Rover 90 hardtop with gymkhana favourite, the ubiquitous lightweight eight-wheeler Ifor Williams trailer.

wheel. So to make the trailer reverse to the left, first flick the steering wheel to the right to get it off in the appropriate direction, then apply left lock; but too much, and it will jack-knife and you will have to start all over again. There is no easy lesson to this; you have to do it again and again until you've got the knack!

CONTROVERSIAL ASPECTS OF LAND ROVERING

When you have mastered your vehicle and are keen to get out and about with it, there are certain environmental codes to observe. Two controversial aspects of Land Rovering which most members of the fraternity come across on an almost daily basis are the robust issue of bull bars, and the driving – or not – of green lanes.

Bull-Bars

Recent research in Germany has shown that even at speeds as low as 12mph

There has been mass debate about the worth and safety of bull-bars, and whether or not they are simply a fashion item. Serious off-roaders might disgree.

Off-roaders who drive green lanes are cast as social pariahs, but careful use of tracks which are not environmentally sensitive should not cause offence.

(20km/h), most small children hit by head-high steel bull-bars are likely to suffer fatal injuries. Without the bar, pedestrians, particularly children, are more likely to be flipped onto the bonnet, which gives a better chance of survival. Land Rover is not complacent on this and is always looking to improve the safety of its accessories and vehicles, and hopefully it will take a lead on these macho add-ons. An off-roader has an excuse for wearing one to fend off stray branches; otherwise, however, anything that protrudes from a vehicle is a limb trap, and the anti-lobby asks what use are bull-bars in this country anyway? If the bar saves the front of the vehicle from collision damage, there is an argument that you shouldn't have hit that object in the first place. My feeling is that they belong in the category of side steps and tilt meters.

Without regular use, most ancient byways and drove roads would soon become overgrown, so a certain amount of vehicular use is vital to keep them open.

Greenlaning

The other controversial aspect of Land Rover usage is greenlaning, and driving any route which is used by walkers and riders. Greenlaners seem to be viewed in the same light as bikers and speedboat owners, seen by many as social pariahs of their own particular patch. Certainly, there is a small number of irresponsible vandals who drive around abusing the countryside – having a right of way does not mean having a right to destroy. But equally, some councils are willing to impose restrictions on perfectly legal historic rights of way in the name of conservation, whilst allowing historic buildings, boundaries and such like to fall into disrepair. Another point worthy of mention is that while 4 × 4 traffic can and does cause damage to lanes, thousands of pounds have been expended in recent years repairing miles of footpaths devastated by thousands of walkers in the Dales and the Lake District. What is needed is more publicity for the country codes: associations such as GLASS deserve support, and for ten years the motoring organisations' Land Access and Recreation Association, LARA for short, has striven to get the 'tread lightly' message across to all users of 4 × 4 vehicles in the countryside, whether for sport or recreation.

Meanwhile in many places the damage has already been done by the mindless few, so that off-road driving may well have to be conducted in quarries and gravel pits, or disused mining areas. What we would then have is 4 × 4 play areas out of the way of environmentalists and noise lobbyists; in other words, greenlaning may have to be restricted.

When fighting for a right-of-way issue, there are always going to be difficulties. Even if 'proven usage' is established, nothing will stop a planning appeal if the appellants are determined enough – even the Department of the Environment will go against the wishes of parish councils, besides which a 'right of way' can always be

Unsuitable for some motor vehicles maybe? Sybil the Series I prepares to explore a typical green lane in Wales.

diverted or improved. But what about set-aside farmland? The majority of farmers have yet to wake up to the possibilities of opening their gates to off-roaders. While mountain biking and horse riding are considered healthy pursuits, 4 × 4s are easily portrayed as anti-social. However, the DoE does appear to be resisting the call for additional restrictions on greenlaning. One idea is to have local on-the-spot club contacts for each green lane, who will be in a position to say whether the lane is fit to use at any particular time. Hot air balloonists use a roughly similar system to avoid landing in sensitive areas.

Byway History

Most byways were created by wheeled vehicles and were durable enough to become established as rights of way. Some of these are now deteriorating, and it is all too easy to blame four-wheel-drive vehicles for the damage when in fact other factors may be damaging their structure. For example, the base of many byways is made up of a lattice of tree roots, supporting the banks and absorbing a significant amount of water from the soil. If the bordering trees disappear, the ground will collapse, and unless the trees are replanted the byways may well become impassable. If a byway is damaged by wheeled vehicles, it would be worth investigating what has made it less durable, instead of preventing vehicular use. As we have said, most byways were originally ancient cart tracks or drove roads, often created by wheeled vehicles, and without regular use they would soon become overgrown; so it follows that a certain amount of vehicular traffic is vital to keep them open.

The recent rash of anti-off-roading reports in the national press probably started in 1994 with the reclassification of a road used as a public path, or RUPP. Since then a steady stream of anti-greenlaning features has churned the waters, ranging from a byway in Berkshire being abused by poachers, to a High Court case concerning a Cambridgeshire RUPP, where rare great-crested newts inhabit the ditch-

BUYING GUIDE

Series I (1948–1958)

Prices:	From £500 to £2,000
Watch for:	Rusty chassis outriggers, bulkheads, missing components, backyard lash-ups, smoking engines.
Accept:	Noisy diesel engine, austerity, remanufactured parts. Any concours restoration will be worth considerably more.

Series II & IIA (1958–1971)

Prices:	From £400 to £4,000
Watch for:	Rusty chassis outriggers, holed footwells, high fuel bills of six-cylinder engine, poor restorations, smoky engines.
Accept:	Modest on-road performance, noise, austerity.

Series III (1971–1985)

Prices:	£500 to £3,500 for Stage 1 V8
Watch for:	Rusty chassis outriggers, rear crossmember, bulkhead; smoking diesels, noisy, leaking V8s, worn third and reverse gears.
Accept:	High oil consumption in six-cylinder engines, poor braking performance on 109s.

90, 110, 127 (1983–1990)

Prices:	£3,000 to £12,000
Watch for:	Corrosion at base of windscreen pillars, water leaks, worn suspension bushes, noisy propshafts, smoking diesels, fake County Station Wagons.
Accept:	Indifferent build quality, high fuel consumption of V8s.

Defender 90, 110, 130 (1990–)

Prices:	£8,000 to £16,000
Watch for:	Lack of service records, particularly turbodiesels, water leaking into cabin.
Accept:	Indifferent build quality of earlier vehicles, creaks and groans.

es on either side of the road. Happily for the off-roading fraternity, proposals for changes in the law were rejected by 90 per cent of highway authorities and the Department of the Environment. Damage to the surface by off-roaders is not regarded as a problem by 82 per cent of local highway authorities, the DoT, or the Rights of Way Review Committee (1992).

Interestingly, the 18 per cent of highway authorities who did report damage to byways blamed tractors and horses, and these results are supported by the Countryside Commission's report in April 1995 to the Environment Committee. It found that less than 1 per cent of the rights-of-way network is in poor condition through erosion, and that damage by recreational activity is heavily exceeded by industrialization, farming and urbanization. Consider that many footpaths and bridleways are ploughed up every year, and you could argue that a few tyre channels in a byway are relatively insignificant. At least the byway remains as a feature on the landscape, and a home for wildlife such as the newts. Thankfully, all the established associations, including the CLA, the National Parks Association and the NFU, encourage increased co-operation and discussion between landowners, users and authorities. Nevertheless, the world still continues to close in on the off-roaders.

There may be good reason to close a green lane, however: for example in June 1995, two byways near Luton in Hertfordshire were closed, along with their attendant feeder roads. Some were ready to object, but according to a Land Rover driver who attempted to drive the routes prior to the closure, local residents were delighted because they were fed up with people asking to be towed out and he confirmed that it was not possible to get through without a great deal of winch work. It appears that a combination of over-use and inconsiderate driving had churned up the tracks, leading to the closure. Devotees talked about taking several hours to winch vehicles short distances due to tracks being in poor condition - and surely, if this amount of time is spent on retrieving vehicles they should not have been there in the first place.

Generally though, it is entirely feasible to run a Land Rover without any of these sometimes controversial issues affecting your enjoyment of it.

7 Land Rovers Abroad

This miscellany begins with a typical Land Rover press trip, and gradually moves further afield to the far corners of the world, highlighting some of the contrasts of the Land Rover's domain.

IN THE HIGHLANDS OF SCOTLAND

It had been a long time since I had been on a press trip as thoroughly enjoyable as the Land Rover outing to the Highlands; and the vehicles were amazing too. For a product as specialized as a Land Rover there are few better places for showing off its capabilities than the wilds of Scotland. And it's not just the specialist 4 × 4 magazines that need to be informed of new developments; there are also the British and foreign Land Rover dealers. So the company spends a couple of weeks each year entertaining a few hundred guests with the Land Rover experience – and that includes a day's off-roading in brand-new vehicles.

These expeditions vary in complexity and level of difficulty according to the competence of the particular party of guests.

Led by Roger Crathorne of the Land Rover Experience, Solihull's press trips to the Scottish highlands found the author in breathtaking situations like this.

The author, left, shared the NAS 90 V8 with off-road writer Richard Thomas on a Land Rover Scottish press trip.

For instance, the lifestyle writers from the Sunday papers are merely driven along some scenic lanes; dealers are maybe taken a bit further into the sticks; and on this occasion Land Rover's PR team had decided that the specialist off-road writers possessed enough skills to handle Land Rovers in the wilderness proper.

We were to tackle some of the long-distance military roads which criss-crossed Scotland in the mid-eighteenth century, roads which have yet to see a motorized vehicle.

The press fleet consisted of three Defenders: a 110 Pick-up, laden with aluminium ladders, running boards, axes and shovels; a 90 Safari; and a US-spec 90 V8. There were also three new Range Rovers: a 4.0-litre diesel, a 2.5-litre Tdi and a DSE, and a Tdi Discovery. The NAS 90 V8 was a precocious little number in bright yellow, its occupants protected by the beefy roll cage; it was one of only three in the country at the time. So we set out, and after a short drive up to the vast Blair Atholl estate, began our ascent into the rough stuff. It all started gently enough, passing through a deciduous wood, the track offering little in the way of difficulty apart from a few exposed roots and rocks. We engaged low ratio – just press a button on the dashboard, with clutch depressed – and played with the Range Rover's air suspension, the touch of another dashboard switch raising or lowering the ride height.

As the convoy reached the tree-line, a narrow gateway in a drystone wall appeared in sight. It was sufficiently tight for us, in the luxury of the six-cylinder BMW-engined Range Rover, to pull in our door mirrors. There was then a mild descent to a stream in a culvert. Here was the first challenge, as the convoy gingerly edged off the bank, across the boulder-strewn stream bed, and up onto dry land. However, nobody had any particular problem here.

The procession then moved up a regular moorland track to wilder country, with no sign of human habitation in this vast space: whichever way you stood, the far horizon was of snow-capped mountains, with nearer, lower horizons emerging from the haze and folding one into another.

At this point we took over the US-spec V8. As we set off across trackless heather, I was bounced around in the austere back regions of the V8 – it felt like being in a dinghy in a rough sea. However, the roll cage provides plenty of bars to cling on to, and the best plan is to brace yourself rigidly from side to side.

Soon after a Range Rover became stuck in a rut: the problem was that the heather was as high as the cars' axles, making it virtually impossible to judge whether there were any gullies or boulders to avoid. From here on, the vehicles were led on foot to ensure no damage was sustained, showing where gaps were between rocks. It was mostly impossible to follow the preceding vehicle's tyre tracks in the springy heather and spongy peat. It didn't matter that we were proceeding at walking pace because there were almost vertical descents to negotiate, and it took some time to get each vehicle carefully down them.

The Land Rover team included a couple of mechanics who were on hand to cope with emergencies, such as towing out stuck vehicles. Their previous day's reconnaissance had included building a bridge over a small stream using aluminium running boards: it involved first-gearing your way down the side of a bluff, aiming the vehicle onto the boards, then as soon as the back wheels were clear, powering out and up onto a bank. I was driving the Discovery at this point, and having got used to the powerful performance of the V8, I found I hadn't got up enough revs on the Tdi to get through the boggy bit. It stalled – but swift and sure, I was hauled out by Colin in the 110 truck.

Perhaps the tyres were too much of a road-going compromise, I wondered, because everyone managed to get the Disco very stuck at some point or another. But probably this was just a coincidence, as the Range Rovers were similarly shod. They, too, were sometimes shifting more mud than they were getting a grip off, with clods of soggy peat flying over the roofs.

The latest Range Rovers come with traction control, of course, and we had its audible warning bleeping like mad in the boggy bits. In some ways, the Range Rovers and Discovery were at an advantage over the long-wheelbase 110 with its tow bar, because they had no overhangs in front or rear; whereas the pick-up sometimes managed to get its tow bar jammed in the earth. The Defender 90 also cleared such obstructions better than the pick-up. On one occasion the leading Range Rover became well and truly bogged down, and we had to use both the Defenders in tandem to tow it out. It was decided not to risk the rest of the convoy in the same swamp, and the rest of us were towed up a shale scree – I'm certain it was almost vertical, as all I could see was the V8's yellow bonnet pointing up at the sky! 'Put it in first, and let the rope do the work for you!' I was told.

We halted at what must have been the only building for miles, a tiny bothy in the lee of some hills amongst rocks and boulders, with a torrent of water rushing by to one side. Then we were off in the V8 again. I was very taken with the performance provided by the 3.9-litre engine; it felt so reassuring, and capable of getting you out of any sticky situation. We made a series of seemingly impossible descents through gaps in drystone walls and down a turf bank or two and we were on the banks of a river – a tributary of the Tay, but so remote I couldn't be sure. It was at least fifty yards (45m) wide at this point. The Defender went across first, and relayed back the best route across. We bounced and slithered over boulders, the water at floorboard level, and although the current was very fast flowing, the Land Rover showed no signs of being shifted from its course. We emerged without difficulty, although other vehicles – including the 110 pick-up – had to have more than one go at it.

As the river meandered along we had to cross it twice more, and on one of these crossings where the river narrowed and became appreciably deeper, the last Range Rover got stuck. Halfway across. Its hapless driver churned away in vain, searching desperately for traction, throwing great plumes of water skywards from the tyres like an empty barge on full throttle. It looked as if someone was going to have to take a cold bath. But now the pick-up was backed into the surging water, and the tailgate was dropped – just missing the Range Rover's metallic blue bonnet – enabling the rope to be attached to the eye on the stricken car. The Range Rover came out without any difficulty, and seemed none the worse for its immersion.

As we drove back on the broad swathes of the A9 to our hotel, it was time to reflect on just how versatile these vehicles are. I had seen cross-axling over dykes, Range Rovers performing the bizarrest of contortions, Land Rovers' undersides as they descended escarpments, driving themselves, almost, with no feet on their pedals; Range Rovers that looked for all the world like tottering drunks as they lurched their way over boulders down a heather-clad hillside. Yet here we were in what amounted to a luxury car cruising the tarmac at 70mph (110km/h) with no drama at all, and no hint of what trials the vehicles had just been put through.

The other lesson is that you can't rely on doing this sort of expedition without an experienced leader and a second vehicle to pull you out when you get stuck - or a winch.

Back at base, the Land Rover crew were faced with getting the vehicles washed

It looks incongruous, but Land Rovers can perform the most amazing contortions.

BP TRAVEL GUIDE

When motoring on the continent, even the simplest functions such as refuelling take on new significance: like, how do you ask the pump attendant for a tankful, and do they take your particular brand of plastic? Or interpreting road signs in Dutch or Greek, let alone coping with an emergency. The BP European Travel Guide can help, and these guides are available free from all BP service stations.

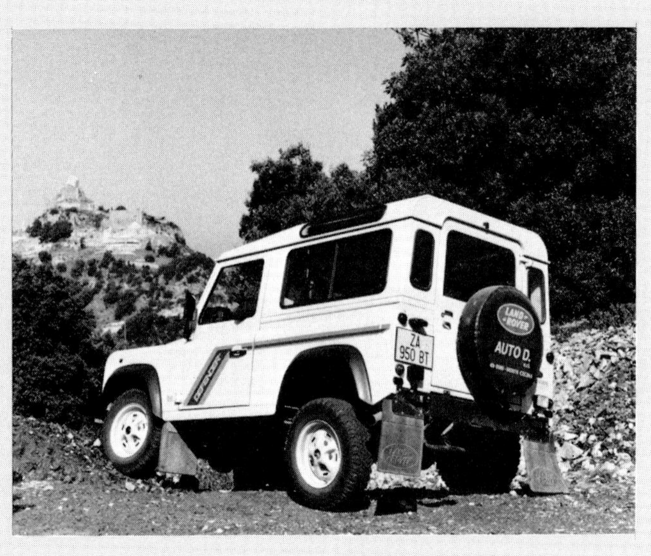

An Italian 90 used by conservators to reach the site of an ancient Etruscan hill-top village, in the throes of restoration.

down and all the heather and sods removed from their undersides before our evening visit to the Glenturret whisky distillery. Off-roading is not necessarily all hard going!

TRUSTY LANDIES

A mark of the vehicle's prestige is that the Land Rover of Heathrow Airport's duty manager Lisa Fedden is the only vehicle that can go absolutely anywhere on the airport. A fleet of Land Rovers is also being used by the National Trust in its membership recruitment drive in 1996. Land Rover actually sponsors the Trust's driver training scheme for its park wardens (to the tune of £26,000 in 1995).

AFRICAN ADVENTURES

Land Rover literature is mostly confined to histories or picture books, but one which deals with escapades in Africa is *Land Rover My Love* by John House. The author is a teacher in Zimbabwe, and has used Land Rovers as daily transport for most of his life. The book is set in the fifties and sixties, when he embarked on several adventures exploring east and central Africa by Land Rover with two or three friends; the Land Rover is effectively the fifth member of the party. John House charts their erratic progress through a variety of African terrain; they encounter all manner of hazards and exotic wildlife in places such as the Ngorongoro Crater – an extinct volcano – and the Serengeti Plain; they meet a wide variety of locals, too; and equally predictably, there are plenty of mechanical trials and tribulations and near misses. When the Land Rover's fuel pump gave up, for example, they used a length of hose and a broken beer bottle as a funnel to feed the carb direct.

As well as being an entertaining read for Land Rover lovers and especially anyone who has spent time in Africa, this book could prove inspirational for anyone considering a similar adventure.

The arid conditons of the Sahara make this a particularly punishing environment for Land Rovers. This is another Slavin expedition in progress.

MOROCCAN ROLLERS

One of the most rewarding adventures for Land Rover owners is the trip to Morocco. For cash-strapped students it can prove to be the trip of a lifetime driving to the Atlas mountains. It is vital to be prepared for such a trip, and the vehicles do duty as pack-horse.

The route leads via the Pyrenees. Boarding the ferry from Algeciras to Ceuta is the most direct sailing to Morocco and allows the traveller to get off the ship and pass through customs in one go. Crossing the border into Morocco can mean spending an hour or so filling in paperwork, then visiting various offices and caravans. Security guards often take exception to CB radios and mobile phones, and may confiscate them. Also the police and immigration checkpoints are an important and sometimes frequent procedure in north Africa and it is prudent to watch out for them, and to be respectful: the first step is to greet and be greeted, even offering a handshake, and to respond willingly to questions.

This modified Namibian Land Rover displays remarkable axle articulation. The beefy roll cage inspires confidence.

It can be convient to spend a night at the campsite just a few miles from the border, known as Restingasmir; ahead lie three days of travel on tarmac before heading into the high Atlas range.

Travellers unfamiliar with local climatic conditions often make the mistake of driving through the hottest part of the day, stopping every hour to blow-dry in the hot wind. During the first sixty miles (100km) around the edge of the Rif mountains it may seem that the local people, mostly children, are stationed every mile or so trying to sell drugs. Tarmac roads in Morocco are often narrow, sometimes with enough room for only a single vehicle, necessitating two wheels onto the rough when confronted with another vehicle.

After two days you can have skirted the base of the Atlas range towards Tinerhir and the Todra Gorge. This is a spectacular route, flanked by mountains on one side and the dunes of the Sahara on the other. The first ten miles (15km) of road is surfaced to allow the coaches to disgorge their tourists at the narrowest section of Todra gorge, where the pink rocky cliffs rise to over 1,000ft (300m) on either side. This is normally the furthest point that tourists reach, because beyond is a difficult 120-mile (190km) haul using unpaved tracks across the Atlas mountains to the next major point of civilization, and vital fuel supplies.

Probably the biggest danger in crossing the Atlas range is getting lost, so a map and a good compass which gives the altitude in the mountains are vital, and it also helps to give lifts to locals travelling on foot in exchange for directions.

In winter the route through the Todra Gorge is virtually impassable as it follows the course of a dried-up river bed, and while in full spate the whole gorge is flooded by the streams formed by melting snow from high up the mountains. When the rivers dry up, however, the track can be rebuilt – only to face destruction once again the following winter. About the only vehicles to use these roads are Bedford trucks, which are a lifeline carrying cattle and anything else to the Berber people on the Atlas beyond the gorge. Even Land Rovers find the road quite a test, as the size and dimensions of the ruts are established by the track and wheelbase of the trucks.

Tracks are harder to find west of the usual crossing from Imilchil to the Todra-Dades gorges; moreover the route is somewhat lacking in off-road adventure, although the scenery is spectacular. The tracks are rugged, and at altitudes of 8,380ft (2,600m), vegetation struggles to survive except where river oases irrigate farm terraces. Further south, a hostile stone desert extends into Algeria, comprising a hundred miles (160km) of dry river beds, plains and plateaux, blown by a constant dry wind.

Forsaking the desert, progress is easy on tarmac roads towards the coast reaching the Atlantic Ocean at Tan Tan Plage and thence along the coast to Tarfaya. Here are salt flats, dry lakes, huge depressions, and a harsh flat plateau ending in cliffs at the ocean. The 620mile (1000km) route from Guelmim to Dakhla is a tarmac road, thanks to the military and UN. Dakhla is in the desert in the far south of Morocco. Finally, travelling northwards and homeward bound, every town seems increasingly civilized.

Even though Land Rovers can perform some remarkable manoevres on home territory, nothing impresses quite like the versatility of running along the *péage* of France and then tackling the Atlas mountains on rough piste. Anyone who really wants a four-wheel-drive adventure should go to Morocco and drive over the Atlas mountains. It's not expensive once there, and really not very far, especially if you go via Santander or Bilbao in northern Spain. Just be sure your Land Rover is in good working order!

ON SAFARI

An interesting venture was launched in the summer of 1995: in association with Land Rover, travel agents Abercrombie & Kent Travel ran an exclusive range of guided self-drive African safaris. The three different nine-day expeditions took Range Rovers into Botswana, Discoverys into Zimbabwe and Defenders into Zambia. A maximum of three vehicles participated in each safari, each one accompanied by experienced guides. The Defenders were fully kitted out with expedition equipment, including heavy-duty winches, inter-vehicle short wave radio, global positioning system, spare tyres and coolboxes. Support vehicles carried satellite communications equipment, portable showers and toilets,

FRENCH RAID

Another way of getting into an African trip on a more organized basis is to go with a specialist firm. For example, Anglo-French off-road organizers CRTT included a selection of 4 × 4 'rally raids' in their 1995 programme. The Raid Atlas comprised eight days in the Moroccan mountains, and the Kenyan safari took in Lake Victoria, the Rift Valley and numerous game reserves.

Those seeking mountains and summer sun were catered for with week-long raids in the Pyrenees, Provence, Corsica and Portugal. On the longer event there was the chance to indulge in water sports such as white water rafting, canoeing and sub-aqua diving.

This fully equipped 110 is one of Land Rover's official African safari vehicles on the guided self-drive adventure holidays organized by travel agents Abercrombie and Kent.

MISSING IN AFRICA

It goes without saying that independent expeditions should not be undertaken lightly. People do get lost. In 1995 adventurer Audrey O'Neill was on safari in Africa with her 1982 blue 110 Station Wagon, and she and her two companions were intending to travel through Benin to Nigeria; but when she failed to rendezvous with a companion in Lagos, the alarms sounded. Her family alerted the Foreign Office and Interpol. At the time of writing, information, or news of sightings, was still being sought from anyone in contact with people travelling in these areas. Audrey was a seasoned traveller, and her vehicle was specially prepared by Mantec, the Nuneaton-based expedition specialists.

dining equipment and tents.

Starting from Victoria Falls, the Defender trip included trekking through the Kafue National Park and driving through the Zambezi. A support Defender transported mobile camps with attendants who set up camp and cooked each day.

GERMANY CALLING

Going to a Land Rover rally on the continent provides scope for a lot of fun. For instance, the Deutscher Land Rover Club staged its twentieth anniversary Jubilee rally at Cottbus, fifty miles (80km) south-east of Berlin. To travel there involves the Felixstowe to Zeebrugge, or Hull to Rotterdam crossings, and an 800-mile (1,288km) route across the Netherlands via Arnhem. The club was founded in 1975 and has about 550 members; it is the oldest and largest Land Rover club in Germany. Members organize regional meetings and camps and a yearly national. Their special international anniversary rally attracted some 350 Land Rovers and around 800 enthusiasts from all over Europe, including Switzerland, Denmark, Finland and the UK. The ex-military site at Cottbus included an easy off-road course in sand dunes and forest, catering for RTVs. A scaled-down Camel Trophy team event took place, and was well supported by club members and visitors, while the picturesque Janschwalde forest was the setting for non-competitive greenlaning for groups

The owner of this Series II navigated all the way from Austria to Britain and back to obtain the correct spares.

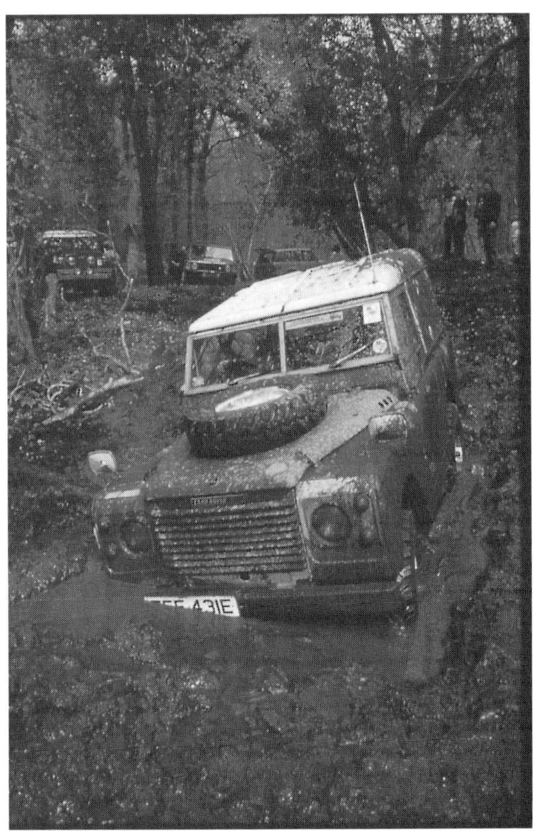

Some off-roading clubs stage scaled-down Camel Trophy-style events for non-competitive greenlaning.

consisting of ten vehicles at a time.

Since camping is very popular in Germany, Land Rover camper conversions were much in evidence. The concours for classic 'old-timers' and rarities attracted a variety of camper conversions, Series IIs, Series IIIs, current models, a 101, two monster 6X6s and four 80in Land Rovers. Other features of the meeting were, predictably, the beer tent, and a 'European Road Show' where enthusiasts could buy major spares for all models, including Series Is.

ROMANIAN RAIDERS

Another potential event for Land Rover owners is organized by the French *Moto Solidarité Roumanie.* It staged its fifth *Raid des Carpates* – Carpathian Raid – in August 1995, taking competitors into the heart of the unspoilt Romanian countryside, and one of Europe's wildest mountain ranges. The rally consisted of ten stages through deepest Transylvania, running to 1,243 miles (2,000km) and ranging in character from easy to very hard, although the most difficult sections could be avoided by novices. It included meals and accommodation, ranging from hotels, chalets and farms; and there was mechanical and medical assistance on stand-by – no bad thing since one of the stages ended close to the infamous Vlad castle, former home of Vlad the Impaler, and the legendary Count Dracula.

SWEDISH SAFARI

A fortnight's journey to the land of the Midnight Sun, from southern Sweden to the country's Arctic north, was billed as an 'educational adventure' into Europe's last wilderness. In midsummer 1995, off-roading enthusiasts covered 1,430 miles (2,300km) over seven days in the rough and six days on the road, from Simrishamn in the south to Kiruna in the remote and mountainous north. Off-road sections were over land given over to the military. The Swedish 4 × 4 magazine *4-Wheel Drive Magazine* sponsored the event, known as Terrain Touring Sweden.

PICK UP A CAMPER

If you are a camping fan and your Land

A convenient way of going camping with a Land Rover, this US two-berth tent comes complete with ladder and is designed to fold flat on the 90's roof-rack.

An ex-military ambulance like this Series III, originally made by Marshalls of Cambridge, makes a spacious camper conversion. Just remember to wipe your feet before getting in.

This German Variomobil camper conversion is mounted on a Tdi-powered Defender 130 chassis.

Rover is a long-wheelbase pick-up, the demountable camper conversion could be of interest; the European Adventure Pick-Up Camper is a fully-equipped module which simply mounts onto the truck portion of the Land Rover, and away you go. And although it is well secured to the vehicle, it can be completely removed in less than twenty minutes, leaving the 'Adventure' accommodation section as a free-standing unit, and the vehicle clear to drive off.

The Adventure is made of coated aluminium sides, with glass-fibre insulation and a galvanized roof; it is built in Ohio to US spec, but with UK-standard electrics. Standard fittings include a heater, twelve-gallon (54l) water tank, fridge, hob-cooker with extractor, 12/220 volt electrics, one double and one single berth, and of course windows and door.

At the time of writing the price of the basic Camper was £6,950, and options ranged from a chemical toilet to a shower and water heater. Contact Niche Marketing of Manby, Lincs, for more details.

A pair of Series Is, an 80in and a 107in spotted in Darjeeling. Series Land Rovers are kept going indefinitely in India.

SOUTH AFRICAN ASSEMBLY

Land Rover has recently tripled Defender and Discovery production capacity in South Africa. In 1995, on her visit to South Africa, the Queen officially opened Land Rover South Africa's new £10m assembly plant at Rosslyn, situated north east of Pretoria.

The new plant took over from the 800-a-year Defender assembly line run by AAD in Cape Town. The Rosslyn-based operation – not far from BMW's own complete-knock-down or 'CKD' plant, in operation since 1977 – will have an annual capacity of 2,500 CKD Defenders as well as 620 semi-knock-down Discoverys. The import tax structure relative to complete vehicles, CKD and SKD has been a major influencing factor for Land Rover. Import duty on fully built vehicles runs at 85 per cent.

As at Solihull, a final assembly line is fed from piles of components and sub-assemblies. The way it works is that batches of twelve completely knocked-down 110 Defenders are shipped from the UK in four 20ft (6m) containers to be united with appropriate body panels. These will have been through the final paint processes in Rosslyn's own low-bake oven system.

Assembly begins with axles meeting suspension components, and mated with the chassis. Lack of a moving conveyor system

Vehicles like this 90 truck-cab are built in South Africa from CKD kits dispatched from Solihull. The new Rosslyn plant will produce 2,500 Defenders a year.

is not a problem since the Defender's own wheels are fitted at an early stage to move the evolving vehicle through the assembly points. The process is just as labour-intensive as Lode Lane, and the line is staffed by ninety hourly-paid workers, each performing up to six operations. Three hands-on Land Rover UK personnel are in attendance as production line supervisors, supported by three ex-AAD operatives who bring the benefits of training and local experience to the job.

Production rate is currently running at half the plant's potential 2,500-a-year capacity, but Rosslyn is contributing to the build process by evolving a more accurate lateral alignment of side panels and shut-lines on the 110 Station Wagon. Instead of the bulkhead being mounted on the chassis with wings and front panel added later, the bulkhead, inner and outer wings are lowered on as a single assembly. Innovative door-aperture jigs are also in use, while air-conditioning is a popular option in South Africa.

Originally the product range at Rosslyn was restricted to 110 pick-ups and Station Wagons, and only in white, but by 1996, colour choice and Defender 90s were available. With petrol at only 32 UK pence a litre, the 3.9-litre V8 was a logical engine option, although the 300 Tdi was also attractive, with diesel at the equivalent of 20p a litre.

Land Rover South Africa has a modern headquarters at Midrand between Johannesburg and Pretoria, alongside that of BMW, and there are over fifty joint Land Rover/BMW dealerships. After years of trade sanctions and restrictions, it is a time of opportunity for Land Rover in South Africa.

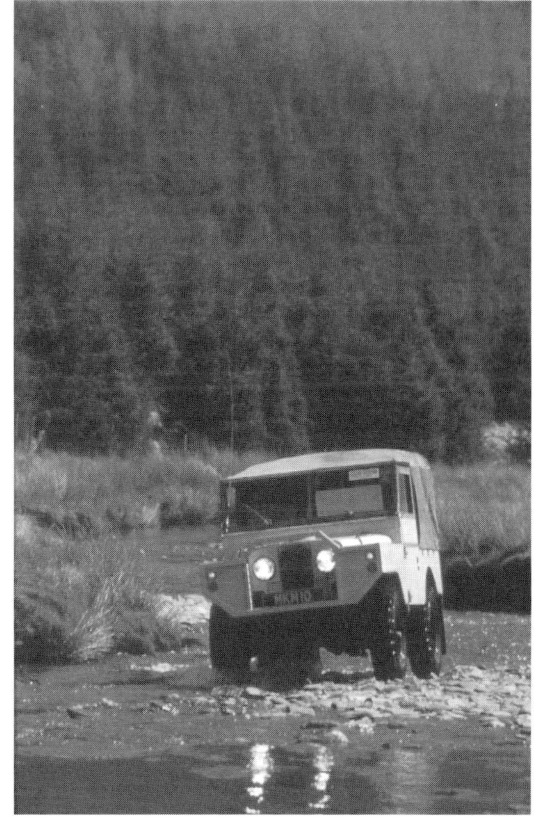

In some places you can make better progress by travelling along a water course than attempting to go across trackless country, as this modified Series I is proving.

8 The Restoration and Servicing of a Land Rover

Describing the restoration of a Series Land Rover deserves a book on its own, but since it is very much an everyday feature of the Land Rover cult, it has to be addressed. I have come across many restorations of varying depths, and was especially close to some friends in Essex who restored their beloved Series IIA from the ground up. I also include some of my own experiences of mechanical trials and tribulations as a pointer to the sorts of everyday occurrences which are part and parcel of Land Rover ownership. Before any restoration you make an appraisal of the value of the vehicle as it stands, and its projected worth once the work has been done. There are obviously degrees of renovation, from what is known as 'conservation' where you keep the vehicle going and make do and mend as necessary, to a new chassis-up refit with new or reconditioned drivetrain.

APPRAISAL AND TREATMENT

A cherished Land Rover which has doubled for years as the family pet is obviously going to get restored no matter what the cost, but broadly speaking, you never get back in financial terms what you put into a vehicle restoration: your only realistic option is to keep it forever once you've paid out.

Part-way through the restoration, you probably ask yourself if it is all worth it.

Chassis

A Land Rover restoration starts by taking off the body and removing all the metalwork. If the chassis is sound – which it probably isn't, because if it was any good, you wouldn't have got in so deep – sandblasting is the accepted way to go. Land Rover chassis and bulkheads are notorious for rusting, and plenty of smaller components corrode as well. A bit of preventive conservation with paint and wax injection could make them last indefinitely, but most are neglected.

There are doubts about the effectiveness of sandblasting. It is debatable whether the grains of shot or sand can penetrate microscopic rust craters effectively, and all the little components are too small to send for blasting, because they might get lost. So they get wire-brushed, and coated with anti-rust paint. However, there is a chemi-

Back to basics; a 1948 rolling chassis begging to be reunited with its bodywork.

It is quite feasible to repair a chassis by welding in fresh steel plates cut from templates.

cal called Corrodip, that dissolves rust on steel components; it comes in concentrate form: you mix 1.7 pints (1l) with water to make a total of 10.5 pints (6l). Corrodip attacks aluminium, but has no effect on plastic, paint or rubber and the makers claim that 'whole engines can be immersed without removal of water hoses, fan belts, generators or starters'. It will not work on grease-covered parts which should be washed first, and it can be re-used many times until it is too contaminated to work. Although at first it appears to do nothing and remains clear, gradually fragments of rust scale flake off. It helps if you first remove excess rust with a wire brush as this accelerates the process. After a couple of days, the treated parts should be clean, when they can be rinsed and dried off. Corrodip can be used as an alternative to sandblasting, as you can treat electrical assemblies, for instance, without dismantling delicate parts which are easily lost or damaged.

If you don't fancy this route, you might consider a replacement chassis, perhaps direct from Land Rover; you can have it galvanized if you want, and it will certainly outlive you and maybe your children. Otherwise it can be done the hard way with just a scraper, a wire brush and a rotary sander. If the chassis needs a little welding

Kriss and Sheila Evitts decided to restore their Series IIA at home. With the rear section and seats removed, the chassis looks a mess, with several holes visible.

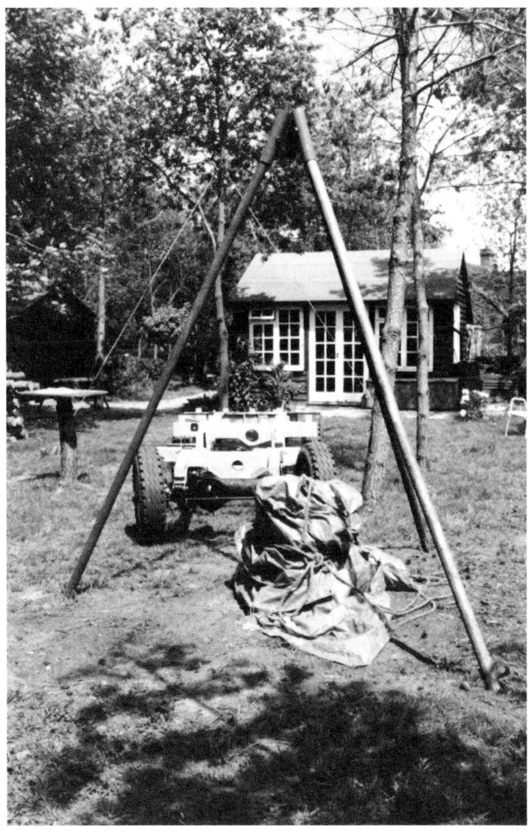

A new galvanized chassis was bought, and a tripod used to extract and replace the recon engine.

and patching up, it is likely to be in the area where the rear crossmember joins the chassis, a recognized weak spot in any Land Rover. The chassis can be abraded with a cup brush attached to an angle grinder, and any holes should be thoroughly cleaned back so that new plates can be welded over them onto sound metal.

Once the chassis is clean and repaired, it can be primed with a coat of red oxide or etch primer, followed by two coats of silver or black Hammerite (or indeed, whatever colour you like). If you want that silver-spangled effect of hot-dip galvanizing without the expense – at least on the outside surfaces – use any cold galvanizing paint. When it has dried for a few days, rub gently with wire wool to bring up a smooth finish.

Brakes and Brake Pipes

The brake piping should all be renewed and the brakes completely overhauled. The shoes and cylinder can be removed, cleaned and inspected, and new rubbers fitted. With luck the bleed nipples will not be seized. One way of checking whether drum brakes are sound is to hang each drum by

The spangled effect of galvanizing makes even the bare chassis look attractive. The drivetrain is now installed.

a wire and tap it lightly with the end of a spanner. It should sound like a bell with a clear sound; if it makes a dull thud, the drum is cracked and should be scrapped and replaced.

When you have the drum off it is worth checking for signs of scoring which indicates that the shoes have been allowed to wear down too far and the rivets have marked the drum. You can skim the drum if this is not too bad, but a replacement is advisable.

Always remove the rear drums after serious off-roading and clean the brake shoes and anchor plate, as they very quickly fill with mud.

Gearbox and Differentials

Depending on condition, the gearbox and differentials can be given an oil change and left alone. If the universal joints are also fine they can be refitted. Interestingly, differentials were stamped with a code: for example, T 4/57 would mean it was made at Tysley in April 1957.

Springs

Overhauling the leaf springs of a Series Land Rover is elementary, and should be regarded as routine maintenance. Perhaps the main reason for doing it is that clean springs can work wonders for your ride comfort, especially if the vehicle does a lot of off-roading.

It is actually more difficult to replace the springs than to remove them. The tools you need are ⅜in (9mm) Whitworth, ½in (13mm) AF, ¾in (19mm) AF, axle stands, hydraulic jack, high-lift jack, and a heavy-duty vice. It should take an hour to replace a spring, and an hour and a half to refurbish one. The workshop manual describes the procedure.

Dampers

Your vehicle's dampers may well prove to be all right. They used to be painted black, and were originally stamped Rover and Woodhead. Wire brushing might reveal a thin layer of Woodhead's standard blue, suggesting that Woodhead painted the dampers black when supplying Solihull.

Engine

The next major item is the engine. You may like to consider replacing an old engine with a reconditioned unit which will have had the bottom end overhauled, with new mains and big ends. The crank will have been reground, the block rebored and new pistons and rings fitted. The cylinder head will have been skimmed and new valves and guides fitted. The reconditioned engine may be refitted with the original clutch, but it depends on pre-op condition.

Refurbishing Bodywork

Before putting the body back onto the chassis, it pays to clean and prepare the underbody and waxoyl it. Some people replace the whole body assembly in the belief that is easier to refurbish bodywork when it is fixed to the chassis, but this is not necessarily true and individual panels can be treated more thoroughly if prepared and painted on the bench. They are all aluminium, of course, apart from the bulkhead, and also the radiator panel which is steel on 88in and 109in models and usually shows light rusting from stone chips.

My friends decided to renew the front wings and both lower door panels of their Series IIA, and painted them by hand with etch primer and a couple of top coats of Land Rover green.

They used a set of 109in wheels, which

The rear end features new aluminium plates, spring hangers and leaf-springs, plus a new exhaust system.

have a wider inset than SWB rims. These were cleaned up and hand painted inside and out before the tyres were fitted, and after two coats they looked as good as new, and really set the vehicle off nicely. The front bumper was new; good secondhand ones are rare and the straight new one smartened up the frontal aspect of the vehicle.

The seats were still serviceable, but a new wiring loom was installed for good measure. All the dashboard dials were working very well.

The cost of restoring my friends' Series IIA was around £2,000, and that does not take into account their time spent dismantling and refettling the vehicle. It must now be worth about £4,000, although that is rather academic since it is unlikely to be for sale.

SERIES III ENGINE SWAP

There are many solutions to the frequently felt need to swap engines ranging from GM

The new chassis shows off its new springs and transmission, while the restored bulkhead has been fitted.

Instrumentation, loom and pedals are in place. The footwells are to be replated.

diesel to Mazda/Perkins 3.0-litre to Ford V6. You can go for a later Land Rover Tdi unit, or a V8 perhaps, or convert what you already have. The on-going debate about increasing the performance of four-cylinder, petrol-engined Series model Land Rovers also extends to fitting a sports K&N type filter, an electric fan, an electronic ignition system, a free-flow exhaust system and a modified cylinder head. You get a more fuel-efficient and quicker Land Rover, but at some cost. A 2.5-litre Tdi probably does nearer 28mpg (10.1l/100km), which is poor reward for a life in the 50-55mph (80-90km/h) band, and this contrasts with Land Rover's claim for 43mpg (6.6l/100km) overall.

When I was features editor of *Land Rover Owner* magazine, I drove a Series III Station Wagon, and the engine issue was one of the first problems to be dealt with. In fact there were a number of mechanical problems to sort out. Body- and chassis-wise, the Series III was in excellent condition, but the engine was so badly worn it was known as Old Smoky. All diesels smoke a bit, even new ones, but this was so bad that a neighbour threatened to report us for polluting the environment.

Maintenance and repair work was done by 4WD specialists. They had a look at cold-starting difficulties, which proved to be due to old glow plugs, and other problems diagnosed included excessive movement in the water-pump bearings, and the coolant water which was as brown as a peat bog. It suffered from transmission- and engine-oil leaks, which were pinpointed to the transfer-box front-output shaft seal and the top of the gearbox casing, while the number and location of engine leaks indicated that a full set of gaskets

One Series IIA restored to pristine condition.

would be in order. As it turned out, a reconditioned engine was deemed more appropriate.

When you saw it parked up, at first glance it looked as though the Series III was lopsided. The offside rear spring swinging shackle bushes were worn, and it needed a new set of shock absorbers since all but one leaked. The transmission was prone to excessive backlash in the front axle, there was movement in the rear propshaft's front UJ, excessive movement in both front wheel bearings and both front swivels. This may have contributed to peculiar wear on the front tyres. The brakes pulled up unevenly and locked up, while the handbrake linkage was badly worn and loose on the chassis. In addition, the driver's door would not lock, which in view of the vandalism prevalent at the time, needed attending to.

The Series III's role was that of school bus for my two small children Alfie and Zoë, for which task it needed additional belts in the back. Old Smoky proved immensely popular with the children, who squealed with delight whenever there was a chance to go on outings in her. Our trips were mostly limited to the broad expanses of the north Norfolk coast, where there are one or two interesting off-roading possibilities.

After some discussion with the garage specialists, it was decided that it really did not matter where we started because basically, everything needed doing. The first step was to get the head off, fill the valve seats with fluid to check for leaks, and examine the pistons and bores. One of the cylinder head's hot plugs had burned out, which no doubt accounted for some of the engine's emissions.

The garage was mystified as to why the pistons were almost completely unscored and unburned, while the rings had no tension whatsoever, to the extent that they could be popped off with your fingertips. Ring gaps were in excess of 50-thou, when they should have been between 10- to 11-thou. The pistons themselves measured 7-thou variance in ovality, suggesting they were all right, give or take 1-thou wear.

They were also surprised that the oil rings at the bottom of the pistons had not been fitted, as they would to an extent have prevented some oil leakage. But putting the whole lot back together with the extra oil rings was a poor option, even in the short term, since they would take some 2,000 miles (3,200km) to bed in because of the bores' ovality. As it was, the top compression rings were badly grooved, and probably acting as suction pumps drawing oil up and past them. There was 9-thou clearance on these rings, and the fitter considered it was a waste of money just to fit new ones – he had never taken off any rings like that before.

A thorough check of tolerances revealed that the engine had been bored out to 60-thou oversize; Land Rover recommends not exceeding 40-thou. In addition, there was 4- to 5-thou mean bore wear, and 4- to 6-thou ovality of the bores. On the strength of this, the garage then considered fitting liners and new pistons as a way forwards. But there were other assessments to be made – for example, the valve timing would have to be checked, although if we ended up having a recon unit fitted, this would be simply an academic exercise to see just how bad it was.

Surprisingly, the 2.25-litre diesel can be a charger, but only if it is set up properly and is in good mechanical condition. The secret lies in the calibration and timing of the injector pump, and it is worth getting it set up professionally.

The injector pump on Old Smoky was turned as far as it would go for maximum adjustment, and sure enough, when they took the timing chain cover off, it was at its fullest extent. Also the adjusting idler sprocket teeth were worn. There should be flats on each tooth, although it does wear more than the other sprockets because it is moving around all the time. The timing chain bagging out had actually worn grooves in the outer casing, and the mechanic's impression was that the timing cover and sump had not been off for some 30,000 miles (48,300km).

Some good news, however, was that the valves appeared to seat quite well as there was no fluid leak from the head, and the heat plugs were also working well. But in short, everything was worn but the pistons, and it was becoming clear that a 'recon' unit would work out cheaper in the end. So while the concept of dropping in a V8 appealed to my performance instincts, in the interests of originality Old Smoky was given a reconditioned 2.25-litre replacement. The shiny new block included 40-thou oversize pistons, reground crank, new oil pump, chain, tensioner, gears and slap-pad: the old unit's slap-pad was missing, which in view of the inch of play in the old chain was unfortunate.

The fitter devised a convenient means of setting up the valve timing. It consisted of the front quarter of a cylinder head, and was gauged so that when number one exhaust valve was fully open, the exhaust peak EP mark on the flywheel whould be lined up.

Once Old Smoky was united with her new power plant, a running-in period of 500 miles (800km) was in order, and the basic instruction during that time was 'Don't thrash it'. That meant finding a spot where the engine felt easiest, maybe between 40 and 45mph (65 to 75km/h), and avoiding trunk roads where that speed would feel as if you were standing still. After running-in it had an oil and filter change and a general tightening up of nuts and bolts. After that, there was another 500 miles (800km) of easy use before it was considered run in.

MEASURES OF ECONOMY

A petrol Series III rarely betters 20mpg (14.2l/100km), but fitting a combination of overdrive, an electric cooling fan and, if not already fitted, some 7.50R16 tyres with a road-going bias and freewheel hubs will improve on this. It might also be worth considering having the cylinder head converted to run on unleaded fuel.

Most Land Rovers use the Fairey overdrive unit. It was designed by Fairey's technical director Herbert Fronicke, and can be used by all Series Land Rovers. It was introduced in August 1974, and apart from some minor changes during the first two years, it has remained essentially the same for over twenty years. It bolts on to the back of the transfer box, using the rear PTO position, and vehicles thus equipped then need an auxiliary PTO, bolted to the underneath of the transfer box. Superwinch Ltd bought Fairey Winches in October 1988, and the Land Rover overdrive units are available from Superwinch; they also supply a free parts diagram which serves to illustrate very well how the overdrive works.

The overdrive unit should be used like another gearbox, using the clutch to engage and disengage. Even though it has synchromesh, overdrive changes are leisurely, and with the relatively low power outputs of standard Series Land Rover engines, it can be used in any gear. More powerful diesels and V8s, or when towing, should only go into overdrive in third or fourth gear high range.

Performance figures are, pro-rata, significantly improved. Thus cruising speed for a Series I with standard 4.7:1 diffs and 600x16 tyres in high-box fourth is about 40mph (65km/h); in overdrive there is a 22 per cent improvement which means top speed would be around 50mph (80km/h). An overdrive does not necessarily bring better economy, as the increased gearing tends to translate into higher speed. The main benefits are a reduction in noise and vibration at cruising speeds, which makes long journeys more bearable.

Overdrive units for Land Rovers have been made by other manufacturers, but the Superwinch or Fairey unit is more authentic and spares are easily sourced. Second-hand units are available, but if any major parts need replacing, the price will approach that of a new one. The overdrive is preferable to the transfer-box conversion as it increases the versatility of the transmission instead of restricting it to a higher range, which might not always be appropriate. Altering the transfer or final drive ratio is usually preferential treatment for a V8 or slower-revving diesel. If retaining the standard engine, the overdrive should be seen as a way of lowering cruising speed rather than going faster.

FITTING A NEW CYLINDER HEAD

The Land Rover 2.5-litre petrol engine will

run quite happily on lead-free fuel, but in these days of green motoring it is entirely feasible to fit an 'unleaded' cylinder head to an earlier petrol Land Rover. I discussed the procedure with a mechanic friend who worked on his LWB Series III, although it eventually got a full reconditioned engine. One of the most likely problems with an old petrol engine is that the valve stem seals get worn and they become porous, necessitating a de-coke and head overhaul. Or you could simply exchange the head for a reconditioned unleaded item, available on an exchange basis from specialists. The DIY process is quite straightforward, provided you have a full set of tools and a correct manual.

The result is that engine response will be much improved, with the environmental benefit that you can now use unleaded fuel.

Another point that my friends attended to was replacing the alternator. It apparently failed because its diodes were damaged by someone inadvertently reversing the battery connections. All alternator-equipped Land Rovers have a negative earth. So best not do any electrical MIG or ARC welding on the vehicle without unplugging the alternator connection block, and removing the battery. Neither should you boost-charge the battery on an alternator-equipped vehicle without first disconnecting the battery earth lead.

Alternators superseded dynamos on virtually all vehicles from the early 1970s on, and Land Rovers were no exception. Although alternators are more delicate than dynamos, they are much better at generating electricity and most Land Rovers were equipped with them in around 1972. Until 1982, versions of the Lucas ACR unit were regular fitment, as used on the majority of British-made vehicles at the time. They are durable enough, and exchange units are widely available.

PROPSHAFT REPLACEMENT

Another vehicle I used while on the staff at *Land Rover Owner* was a 90. Its front propshaft UJ had been sounding rough for a little while, and after some modest off-roading in the hands of the editor at the ARC Nationals it was clearly on its last legs, and it wasn't altogether a surprise when it finally parted company with the transfer box. Thus the 90 joined its elder sister, Old Smoky, at the specialist garage, who took one look and diagnosed that the UJ had been on the way out for some time. It is not that common a failure, but it certainly happens occasionally. It would not happen with a part-time all-wheel drive Series Land Rover, because the broken shaft would just float, accompanied by a lot of clonking noises. But why does it happen? I was told that: 'Either you get a roller turn over, break up and lock, with the consequence that the propshaft has nowhere to go, and it locks up and the UJ rips apart or it can happen because something has seized in the front diff. Either way, something's got to give.'

It is easy to check that the front differential is all right by jacking up the front and rotating the wheels on lock. If there is no untoward graunching, that area is sound. The first move was to take apart the propshaft from the splined front differential output shaft, so the major length of it was out of the way. Once this was removed it was easier to get at the tortured nuts securing the universal joint to the central transfer box output shaft. Having removed the mud shield, the UJ was dismantled in a vice - and it was clearly in a worse mess than it had looked when still *in situ*.

The output shaft flange had fairly substantial grooves in it from where the seal runs, not connected with the UJ failure,

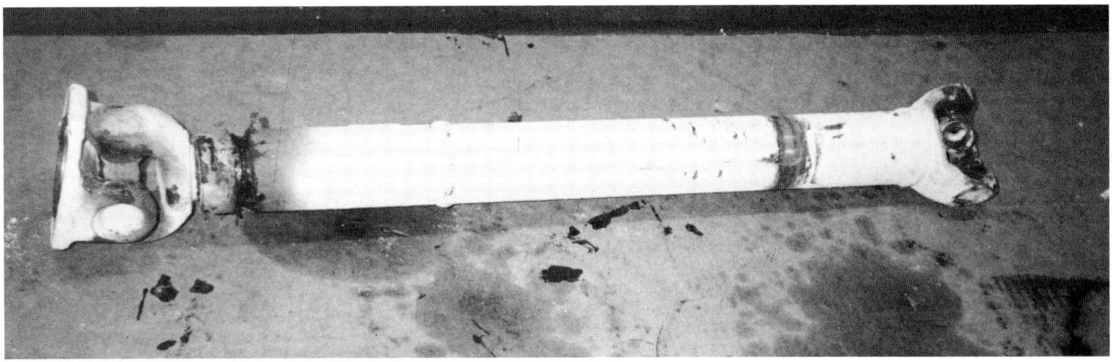

Forward prop shaft of the 90, with shattered UJ.

and needed replacing as it would have started to leak in the near future. It looked as though the propshaft steel itself was cracked, but after wire brushing we decided it probably wasn't. The propshaft thrashing around had damaged the nuts and bolt threads: the flange had to come off in order to get the studs out, and it was going to be difficult to remove the chewed-up nuts; a sharpened chisel was used to cut through them. It is frustrating, that these studs/bolts, which are unique to Land Rover, are only available in packs of five. They are an odd size, having a ½in (13mm) of thread but a longer shank to pass through the thickness of the flange.

Because of the broken UJ, the total time to do the job in this case was about one hour forty minutes, although a straightforward propshaft replacement should take more like forty minutes.

CHEAP DIFF-LOCK

When doing a rebuild, you may consider extending the range and effectiveness of the Land Rover's original spec. For example, since heavy-duty diffs and halfshafts have been successfully proven in events such as the Granada-Dakar and Warn Challenge, a heavy-duty ZF four-speed Autobox is now available which will fit all Land Rovers. For anyone who may be thinking of fitting a larger engine in their Land Rover, a ZF 4HP22 gearbox is recomended, to cope with the increased torque. This 'box incorporates the forward drive clutch from the larger 4HP24, giving an increased friction area and greater torque capacity. There are other reasons to consider exchange units, because even relatively young vehicles have mechanical maladies. I heard of a 1991 Defender which had terminal gearbox problems, and the Land Rover main agent told the owner that a new gearbox would cost £1,720.28. This is a major expense for such a young vehicle, particularly as it was out of warranty, and Land Rover had no obligation to rectify matters.

Another worthwhile product to come on the UK aftermarket recently is the Lock-Right diff-lock, representing a major breakthrough in terms of its simplicity and relatively low cost. The way it works is that the spider and side gears in the vehicle's existing differential are replaced by a pair of Lock-Right driver and coupler sets. No crown wheel and pinion set-up is required, and there is no bearing removal or fitment to do. There is no need to replace the carrier, and the system is fully automatic, in that it is fully locked until it recognizes the need for differential action, so it doesn't actually spin. It is claimed that it can be installed by anyone who is capable of changing a set of brake pads, and could be fitted in just two hours: apparently all you need are three spanners – a 9/16 (14mm), an 11/16 (17mm) and a 3/4 (19mm), plus some diff oil. Says one expert: 'If you want to get over a five foot vertical wall, here's your answer. It's half the price of any other diff-lock, and can be fitted by a novice. It's the product most people would like to have, but until now haven't been able to afford.'

The Lock-Right is made of nickel-steel alloy and was originally developed in the USA in 1979. It is claimed to be the most popular diff-lock in Australia, and there are applications for most vehicles, from Land Rovers to Chevrolet Corvettes. At the time of writing Lock-Right is only available from fifty authorized dealers in the UK,and the Land Rover kit costs around £300. There is a two years' unlimited mileage warranty, and it is said to be virtually indestructible.

SERIES III SERVICE

Most of us are capable of doing basic servicing jobs at home or in a friend's garage, maybe with the back-up of a local Land Rover specialist. Here are some basic ground rules, although to be thorough, a Land Rover or Haynes-type manual for your particular model will be a distinct asset. This servicing schedule is for the four-cylinder Series IIIs which I am most familiar with, but most of the procedures are the same for earlier and later Land Rovers, and the principles apply equally to the six-cylinder models.

SERVICING REQUIREMENTS

Tools and equipment

AF socket set, ring and open-ended spanners
Flat- and Phillips screwdrivers
Feeler gauges
Timing light/12-volt test lamp/voltmeter
Oil can, oil drainer

Capacities and Lubricant types

Engine oil
4 cylinder, 2.25-litre petrol: 11 pints (6.2l) plus 1.5 pints (0.84l) filter. Change engine oil and filter at least every 4,000 miles (6,440km). Use quality multigrade, eg 15 or 20W/50, to API SE (minimum), SF or SG.
6 cylinder, 2.6-litre petrol: 12 pints (6.8l) plus 1 pint (0.5l) filter. Change engine oil and filter at least every 4,000 miles (6,440km). Use quality multigrade, eg 15 or 20W/50, to API SE (minimum), SF or SG.
4 cylinder diesel: 11 pints (6.2l) plus 1.5 pints (0.84l) filter. Change engine oil and filter at least every 3,000 miles (4,830km). Ensure that the oil you use is specifically suitable for diesels.

Cooling System

4 cylinder, 2.25-litre petrol: 14.25 pints (8.08l) (1979 on, 14.5 pints/8.22l)
6 cylinder, 2.6-litre petrol: 20 pints (11.2l)
4 cylinder, diesel: 13.75 pints (7.8l)

Engine Settings

Compression pressures
4 cylinder, 2.25-litre petrol: 8.0:1, 160 psi; 7.0:1, 145psi
6 cylinder, 2.6-litre petrol: 7.8:1, 170-

This is a reconditoned 2.0-litre petrol engine in a Series I. This proved the most economical way to go with an engine rebuild the author was involved in.

175psi; 7.0:1, 140psi
4 cylinder, diesel: 400–500 psi (less than 350psi denotes serious wear)
(Note – maximum acceptable variation between cylinders 30–40 psi)

Valve Clearances

4 cylinder, 2.25-litre petrol: inlet and exhaust, 0.010in (hot or cold)
6 cylinder, 2.6-litre petrol: inlet, 0.006in; exhaust, 0.010in (hot)
4 cylinder, diesel: inlet and exhaust, 0.010in (hot)

Spark Plugs

4 cylinder, 2.25-litre petrol: Champion UN12Y or equivalent (7.0:1, N8), gapped to 0.029 to 0.032in
6 cylinder, 2.6-litre petrol: Champion N5, gapped to 0.029 to 0.032in

Firing Order

In all cases, no 1 cylinder is at the front of the engine.
4 cylinder, 2.25-litre petrol: 1-3-4-2
6 cylinder, 2.6-litre petrol: 1-5-3-6-2-4

Distributor/Contact Breaker

4 cylinder, 2.25-litre petrol
1971–83: Lucas 25D4 distributor. Points gap 0.014 to 0.016in; dwell angle 57° to 63°
1984: Lucas 45D4 distributor. Points gap 0.014 to 0.016in; dwell angle 52° to 62°. Or Ducellier distributor. Initial points gap setting 0.017in; dwell angle 54.5° to 59.5° (Lucas and Ducellier distributors are directly interchangeable)
6 cylinder, 2.6-litre petrol: Lucas 25D6 distributor. Points gap 0.014 to 0.016in; dwell angle 32° to 38°

Ignition Timing

Static – initial settings, normal four-star fuel
4 cylinder, 2.25-litre petrol: 8.0:1, TDC; 7.0:1, 6° BTDC (on late vehicles, TDC is centre mark of five on pulley, spaced at 3° intervals)
6 cylinder, 2.6-litre petrol: 7.8:1, 2° ATDC; 7.0:1, 2 ° BTDC

Tickover Speed

4 cylinder, 2.25-litre petrol: 500rpm
6 cylinder, 2.6-litre petrol: 500rpm
4 cylinder, diesel: 570-610rpm

SCHEDULE

Service interval: tarmac use, every 4,000 miles (6,440km) or approximately every three months. Vehicles used for off-roading require much more frequent attention, and may need servicing once or more a week.

Diesel models only:
Release accumulated water from fuel filter/sedimenter.
Clean sedimenter, and also sediment bowl near fuel pump.
Replace fuel filter element (preferably every 6,000 miles/9,660km).

Checklist for All Models:

- Drain and reverse-flush the cooling system every two years or 12,000 miles (19,310km), whichever comes first. Replace perished or damaged hoses. Replenish system with fresh anti-freeze mix containing corrosion inhibitors. This stays in the system all year round.
- Carry out a compression test every 4,000 miles (6,440km) and make a note of the readings. Regular checks reveal any gradual loss of compression.
- Clean the battery terminals and smear them with petroleum jelly. Make sure the battery is secure.
- Check all steel and flexible brake hoses, fuel pipes and the exhaust system for wear.
- Examine the suspension and steering components for wear, and check engine mounts, starter motor and manifold bolts.
- At each service, lightly grease the distributor cam lobes and administer a few drops of engine oil to the carburettor linkage joints. Similarly, do the top of the distributor shaft and the mechanical advance mechanism through the baseplate.

Engine Oil

Warm up the engine over a 10-mile (16km) run, so the oil drains freely. Use a ¾in (19mm) AF socket or ring spanner to loosen the sump plug, and allow it to drain for half an hour before refitting the plug.

Oil Filter

This will leak when undone, so place a suitable receptacle under it before releasing the central bolt (9⁄16in/14mm AF), which retains the filter bowl. Once removed, clean the casing in paraffin and wipe dry. Reassemble with a new filter element and sealing ring, and make sure the filter bowl is seating correctly on the seal.

Compression Test

If you do a compression test at each service and keep a record of the readings obtained, you can detect a gradual loss of compression on one or more cylinders and take appropriate action. For diesels you need a gauge reading up to 500psi.

Valve Clearances

For both four-cylinder petrol and diesel units, check and adjust valve no. 1 with valve no. 8 fully open, 7 with 2 open, and so on, in each case the sum of the valve numbers adding up to 9. This is called the 'Rule of Nine'. From the front of the engine, the valves run: exhaust-inlet-inlet-exhaust-exhaust-inlet-inlet-exhaust.

Rocker Cover Breather

The breather must be kept clean, and should be checked on a daily basis if the Land Rover is used in very dusty conditions. Release the bolt (7⁄16in/11mm AF) securing the breather, remove and allow it to soak in paraffin. Then shake or blow-dry and refit.

Spark Plugs

These are all easily accessible along the right side of the engine. As a matter of course you should keep the plug tops, distributor cap and high tension cables clean and dry, and on a vehicle which frequently goes off-roading, it is worth spraying the plugs and HT leads with a proprietary waterproof spray. When fitting new plugs, apply copper-based grease to the threads.

Distributor

Some later Series III Land Rovers used Ducellier distributors, while other Series IIIs have Lucas units. Whatever, all are easy to get at and straightforward to service. You need feeler gauges to get an initial points gap setting, then a dwell meter to confirm that the setting is correct. Then grease the cam sparingly.

Ignition Timing

The timing marks are notches in the crankshaft pulley rim, matching a pointer on the cylinder block. You highlight them with white paint, if it has not already been done, and check statically using a 12-volt test lamp or voltmeter, connected between the distributor low tension connection and earth.

Petrol Engine Air Filter

Types of air filter vary. On the oil bath type, you first release the single wing-nut and securing strap on the top of the unit, then carefully lift the whole assembly clear of the engine bay. Then release the three spring clips securing the two halves of the housing to get at the filter element and oil bath inside. Every 4,000 miles (6,440km), drain the oil from the casing and rinse it out in paraffin, together with the filter. Then dry and refill with fresh engine oil up to the level marked on the housing.

Petrol Filter

This needs cleaning frequently if the Land Rover operates in severe conditions. First, release the screw securing the sediment bowl, then remove and clean the bowl and its filter in paraffin. The cork gasket on which the glass bowl sits should be in perfect condition, otherwise it should be replaced. The securing screw should not be overtightened.

Carburettor Adjustments

Types of carburettor vary, and as a rule, they should only be adjusted with the air filter in place, the engine fully warmed up, and all mechanical and ignition settings having been checked. The throttle-stop screw raises tickover speed, then the mixture screw is adjusted to obtain the smoothest idle. Then finally, you reset the tickover speed.

Drive Belts

Examine the alternator belt for correct tension, and replace it if it shows signs of wear or cracking. If you press firmly with your thumb, it should give by approximately ¼ to ½in (6 to 13mm) halfway between the water pump and alternator pulleys.

Vacuum Pipes and Connections

The condition of the brake servo vacuum

pipes and their connections should be regularly checked. The hose clips should be in good order and tightly fastened. Any pipework showing signs of softening, brittleness or cracking, most likely at the hose clips, should be replaced.

Fluid Levels

The hydraulic fluid in the brake and clutch master cylinders should be maintained at the correct level, near the top of the reservoir. If the fluid level drops between routine checks, identify the cause immediately, and if there is a leak, get it fixed.

DIESEL CHECKLIST

Air Filter

Diesels need a great deal of fresh air to operate efficiently, so it is vital that the air filter is clean. If it is blocked the fuel will not burn efficiently, resulting in clouds of black smoke. The filter should be replaced frequently if the vehicle is used in dusty conditions.

Crankcase Ventilation

Make certain that the crankcase ventilation pipework and breathers are not obstructed, because if this happens, pressure builds up within the crankcase and oil is forced out at the weakest points, such as the oil seals.

Fuel Filter

The filter should be changed ideally every 6,000 miles (9,660km) to keep the injection system clean, and renewed much more regularly if the vehicle is frequently driven off-road. Filters are cheap when compared with injection pumps and injectors.

SELECTING THE RIGHT OIL

Before doing a service, it may be as well to assess what kind of oil to use. We tend to have our favourite brand, but it may not be the best for the vehicle. For instance, Series I and II Land Rovers use 20W/50 multigrade oil, rather than the lighter 10W/30 commodity often used today. Penrite and Castrol produce lubricants specifically designed for classic vehicles. These oils are multigrades of a similar concoction to the 20W/50 originally used by older engines in the 1950s and 1960s. They need the extra viscosity because of wider running clearances and lower operating temperatures than modern engines and because their oil pumps and oil seals were designed for thicker oils. For Series Land Rovers of both petrol and diesel variants, and early V8s as well, Penrite and Castrol recommend specific oils. Penrite's Classic Oil, a 20W/50 multigrade formula, meets the oil industry's highest performance standard, API SH/CD. Castrol offers GTX, a 15W/50 multigrade which suits older engines and high mileage vehicles. Both companies claim better oil consumption, less engine noise and reduced wear.

The original Castrol lubrication chart for the Land Rover Series II specifies intervals of 3,000 miles (4,830km), with 11 pints (6.2l) for an oil change and 3 pints (1.7l) for the filter. Both Castrol and Penrite have a range of products for gearboxes, differentials, CV joints and other Series Land Rover components. Brass or bronze parts used in pre-1960s differentials are prey to chemical attack from modern lubricants. Older gearboxes need a thicker oil to compensate for poor seals and for ease of gearchanging. Penrite's semi-fluid grease can be used to good effect in swivel pins, where it is less likely to leak than oil, and prevents mud penetration when off-roading.

Special Penrite running-in oil is a good idea for the first 300 miles (480km) after an engine rebuild. It will help the piston rings bed in, which a modern semi-synthetic will not do, being too efficient as a lubricant for running-in.

IDENTITY CHECK

There are so many Land Rovers out there that many are not quite what they seem. The vehicle's construction makes it relatively easy to interchange parts in order to upgrade its specification. If you were interested in buying a classic Series I for instance, how could you be sure that what you were looking at was the genuine article?

You begin with the V5 document which tells you the vital chassis number. This is stamped in two places on the vehicle, on its chassis and its identification plate. The 80in (2,032mm) models are stamped on the chassis by the near-side engine bearer. Later Series Is, including 86-,107-,88- and 109in (2,184-, 2,717-, 2,235- and 2,768mm) models, have the number stamped on the offside front or nearside rear spring hanger. Clearly you are checking that the numbers tally, and do not appear to have been ground off and re-stamped.

The identification plate is fixed on the top nearside of the bulkhead in the engine bay on early 80in (2,032mm), and the cabin side of the bulkhead on all other Series Is. If it appears to have been tampered with, there are questions to be answered. Replacement plates are available, but there has to be a reason why it has been substituted.

You will find the engine number stamped on the top front corner of the exhaust manifold mounting face, and it may be necessary to reveal it with a wire

Rover badge detail on restored Series I. Plates like these can be helpful in identifying accurate provenance.

brush. Gearbox numbers are more problematic. On 80in vehicles they are stamped on the offside rear of the top cover casting, and may be read using a mirror and a torch. Axle numbers are stamped next to the breather.

You will find clues to a vehicle's age, or the age of the components, in other places. For example, the month and year of manufacture are stamped on a disc soldered to the top of the radiator, and all Lucas components bear month and year stamps.

If the carburettors are stamped, it is the last two digits which identify the year. The bodywork has nothing to tell in the way of numbers. Sometimes specialist users such as the military or civil defence fix data plates, but these can be moved from one vehicle to another. In general though, there are enough clues to be pretty certain of what you are getting. You can refer back to Solihull to assess whether the numbers make sense.

FACTORY EXCHANGE UNITS

At the other end of the age spectrum, Land Rover's latest additions to its range of genuine exchange remanufactured parts enabled owners of vehicles built as recently as 1993 to choose either new or recycled replacement units. The Land Rover Genuine Exchange scheme was nearing full coverage for vehicles made between 1979 and early 1993.

The scheme's comprehensive range includes engines, gearboxes, differentials, alternators, turbochargers, starters, injectors, electronic engine management units and diesel fuel injector pumps.

Land Rover has established one of the most sophisticated and wide-ranging parts remanufacturing programmes in the motor industry since it began developing its 'alternative' range in the late 1980s.

'It began as a conventional exchange programme covering only major units but has grown to offer customers economic and fully warranted alternatives to expensive repairs or non-original substitutes,' the parts director explained. 'Our exchange parts are not simply repaired or reconditioned – they are remanufactured in the true sense of the word. Each unit is fully disassembled, inspected, measured and rebuilt to original equipment tolerances and specifications, using brand-new OE components to replace worn ones. The customer gets a factory-built unit which in

New Arrivals for Dunsfold

Five rare Land Rovers, including a Series II 109 chassis number 6, are the most recent vehicles on display at the Dunsfold Land Rover collection. The other unusual arrivals include one of the last Monteverdi Range Rovers ever made, an ex-Swiss railway 6x4 Range Rover Carmichael; Range Rover YVB 162H, pre-production number 15, which is presently undergoing restoration, and a 1993 cutaway Discovery. Donated Land Rovers play an important part in the large assortment. A Series II given by British Aerospace is currently appearing in the sequel to *A Fish called Wanda*, and a Judge Dredd vehicle has been supplied by Land Rover.

The collection has expanded over the years to include sixty Land Rovers. Alongside oddball and uncommon vehicles such as a Llama forward-control prototype there are more familiar examples. These include original and low mileage Land Rovers of most of the main models, as well as very early and late production examples.

A Series I in the workshops after restoration at Point-Two-Four 4WD specialists in Peterborough Petrol engine from a Lightweight nears completion.

every respect is as good as new – right down to the twelve-month, unlimited mileage warranty. Land Rovers are built to last ,and for us the exchange programme is a sustainable source of raw material to help our customers keep them going even longer and at a price which makes economic sense.' Details of the Land Rover exchange programme range are available from any of its 124 UK Land Rover Network Dealers.

9 Land Rover Specialists

There are many dedicated specialists involved in Land Rover service, restoration and conversion, and I have selected just a few to highlight the diversity of ownership, the aftermarket accessories and the extent of the Land Rover's scope.

DEFENDER OF THE FAITH

The Land Rover has fans in some of the highest places. The former Archbishop of Canterbury's Special Envoy and long-term Beirut hostage, Terry Waite, is a fine example. He was spotted by photographer Nick Dimbleby in his Defender 110 aboard the Portsmouth to Bilbao ferry, and chatted amiably with the British teams en route to the 1995 Warn Adventure in Morocco.

Terry's Defender replaced a TDi Discovery: 'I much prefer the simplicity of the old-fashioned Defender,' he said, 'so much so that the Discovery had to go'.

BIRD BRAINS

Some Land Rover interiors are more akin to pigsties, while some of us are happy to sleep out in the back. But treating the Land Rover as home from home is not confined to human beings: the staff of a caravan business were astonished to find a rare pied wagtail had built its nest in their Land Rover. Not only that, the bird didn't seem to be particularly alarmed when the vehicle was in use. The nest was built between the grille and the radiator, and the bird gained access via a couple of redundant spotlight holes in the former marine rescue short-wheelbase Series III.

The firm contacted the RSPB, who recommended they didn't touch the eggs - there were seven - during the three-week incubation period and until they flew the nest. The Land Rover was in daily use moving caravans around the three-acre (1.2ha.) site, so it never went very far or very fast. The mother bird flew out whenever the engine started up, and accompanied it around site, hovering over the bonnet.

BORN TO BE WILD

Given the Slavin family's disposition for heading off into uncharted territory, it would be surprising if their son Jonathan – or Johnny – was not of similar persuasion. His first memories are of a trip to Morocco on a North African expedition as a six-year-old, an adventure marked by the rumbling tanks and rebel gunfire heralding the coup which was taking place at the time. And now, twenty-five years on, he is following very much in the parental footsteps. He worked as a convoy driver delivering Aid Land Rovers to projects in Africa with his parents' company, and acted as a guide for a convoy of Norwegian Church Aid Land

Rovers down to Mali. For the last nine years, his home has been in California. He and his family – his American wife Bo and their two-year old daughter Caledonia Belicé – live off the beaten track near Pearblossom, some 75 miles (120km) north of Los Angeles.

Johnny's parents run a very successful business in Lincolnshire converting and equipping brand-new Land Rovers for Aid expeditions to war-torn or underdeveloped countries; although at the time of writing, business is booming in the States. The US government's Tied Aid policy commits it to buying vehicles on the domestic market, but American 4 × 4s are too sophisticated for Aid work. So using Johnny's premises as a bridgehead, the Slavins are fulfilling government contracts and selling their converted Defenders to US Aid. They have already seen action in Madagascar during Ken Slavin's Madagascan World Wildlife Fund expedition in 1994.

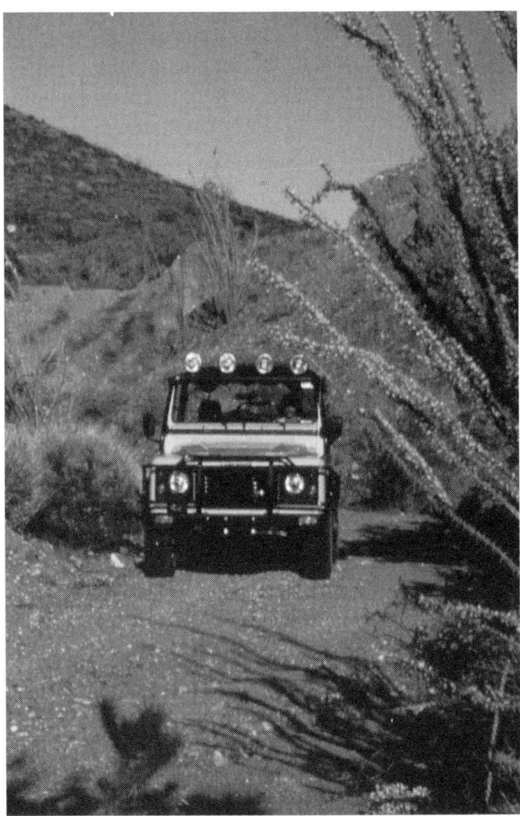

The Slavins have excellent opportunities for off-roading in the US, as Johnny visits Land Rover dealerships providing 4WD training. This is Bo Slavin in an NAS 90 in Mexico.

Johnny's job now is a significant one; he travels from one Land Rover dealership to another, giving instruction to the people selling the cars in how to drive them in their natural habitat – demonstrating to the demonstrators, in effect. This 'centre training' is at Land Rover outlets, which typically also sell other makes, being joint agencies. Land Rover's intention is to get them transferred to 'stand-alone' status, so the marque has more prominence. The numbers involved depend on the size of the dealership, but he is usually instructing around ten people at each stop; other qualified drivers are involved from time to time. 'We take LRNA's own demonstrator vehicles out to some suitable terrain – a motocross track is favourite – and generally show what they're capable of,' said Johnny. 'Often the guys selling them have no idea how versatile they are, so we really open their eyes as to what's possible.' It also opens up possibilities of what Land Rover might do in other markets.

Long days on the road, or more frequently, in planes, going from one side of North America to another, don't appear to have dampened Johnny's enthusiasm, although he does have long-term concerns for his daughter Caledonia's education. 'There are some worrying trends in education over there,' he said. 'The kids are very much influenced by violence in films and television and they take guns to school at a very early age. We have to think very hard about what to do in a year or so from now.'

Like all true car buffs, Johnny has one or two interesting machines back at the California cabin. For example, a 1965 Ford Galaxie 500, two Triumph motor cycles, a Bonneville and a T500; a Dodge D100 Half-tonne pick-up, 'the trash wagon' as he puts it, useful for lugging equipment around. His everyday car is a US-spec Discovery, which differs from British issue in emissions control equipment. And being a devoted Land Rover fan, he also has a Series IIA.

ENGINE CONVERSIONS

The rugged 2.25 BMC diesel was quite a common engine conversion in Land Rovers at one time, but naturally, was rather overshadowed by subsequent developments of Solihull's own units, and of course the influx of Japanese units. The only problems seem to have been the occasional cylinder head crack, but generally it seems to have been well liked as a hard-working if slow – 55mph (90km/h) maximum – power plant; an overdrive would increase top speed by about 12mph (19km/h) and allow slightly more relaxed top-gear cruising.

It is possible to fit an Iveco 2.5 litre diesel and a five-speed manual gearbox or even an automatic into a Series III, but whether the cost is justified is another matter altogether. Othrwise, three obvious alternatives are the Perkins 4128 non-turbo, a Nissan six-cylinder 2.8, or the Diahatsu 2.8. The Nissan 2.8-litre six is not a common engine in Britain; it is used mainly in the Far East to power the Nissan Cedric, a vehicle widely used as a taxi. The noise it emits is deep and powerful, while reliability and serviceability are said to be good. The timing belt is independent from the camshaft, so if it were to break, no serious valve damage would occur. It returns about 28mpg (10.1l/100km) and provides a top speed of about 80mph (125km/h), with excellent pulling power.

ROVER PARTING COMPANY

As you passed Wayside Garage on the outskirts of Norwich, you would probably identify it as just a regular petrol station and workshop. It looks like a cosy homespun business, and it's only when you see a Land Rover 90, a couple of Range Rovers and a TVR 3.5i wedged by the side of the forecourt that you start to take notice. The workshop gives the game away. Here are a pair of Range Rovers in the throes of complete refurbishment, and a number of Rover V8 engines on stands being dismantled. In a back room are pristine units in the process of being reassembled, with sparkling new blocks sitting on shelves.

RPi stands for Rover Parts international. The firm has been going for ten years now, and was started by Chris Crane and a young partner. They began by collecting and breaking V8-engined Rover saloons – SD1s mostly – and then rebuilding the engines and fitting them in customers' Range Rovers. To date, Chris reckons they have dismantled something over 1,500 SD1s and more recent 800s, and gradually, as they got to know more about the quirks, strengths and weaknesses of the engines, they were able to incorporate engineering changes to improve them. Over the years, RPi's business has expanded to include specialized options such as rocker covers, popular for show cars and with kit car owners, and ancillaries like four-branch exhaust manifolds and Rimmer's stainless-steel exhaust systems; and it quickly made performance tuning part of its service. It

RPi Engineering of Norwich specialize in rebuilding Rover V8s to provide performance with economy. This is a 4.2-litre version with Boxer RV8 manifold allied to four SU carbs.

also has a flourishing export business, recently supplying 150 trim items to the Spanish Land Rover concessionaire – hence the 'international' in the title.

When it comes to building high-performance V8s, RPi is really high class. It provides a range of engine options, to varying stages of tune. Most straightforward is the 3.5-litre reconditioned unit; this is based on a good used engine, with compression checked and crack-tested, cylinder heads honed with new piston rings, mains and big ends, bolts, standard camshaft and followers, timing chain, oil pump gears with high pressure springs and valves.

The next phase is a standard-spec reconditioned engine with more cleaning and extensive head work. You can buy a fully rebuilt engine which incorporates many new parts; or one with an additional 40bhp, gained by a Stage 1 head, including Piper 270/110 cam and a Piper Duplex full Vernier timing chain set, plus full gasket set.

RPi doesn't do machining jobs such as reboring or regrinding on the premises, but preparation and assembly is carried out by RPi's chief engine builder. He averages two or three engines a week, in varying capacities; during one of my visits he was working on units for customers from Norway, Hong Kong and Saudi Arabia. Engines are rarely kept in stock. Everything is usually built to customer specification, and the stores contain all the blocks, heads, cranks and ancillaries, ready for assembly depending on the customer's budget or requirements.

Having been asked on innumerable occasions for 'fast road cams', RPi has done considerable research into what provides the best compromise. Said Chris Crane: 'Obviously you won't want a full-race cam for your Defender, and it's most likely you'll want something which gives good mid-range increments without compromising torque.' The standard camshaft has to cope with every situation, so its profiles are something of a compromise. 'High-lift cams can find between 20 and 40bhp in an engine; but what counts is where it puts the extra power,' said Chris. 'If you want it spread across the rev range you have to settle for less of it; but you get a lot longer power spread, and that's what Land Rovers and Range Rovers want. So we go for 20hp cams that are in really early and stay until quite late. We've done a lot of research and think the Piper 270 is right for the 4.2 conversion.'

If you wanted an engine transplant or to upgrade your Land Rover's existing V8, RPi would be happy to do it for you; they work in conjunction with Norwich specialists JSF to modify the bulkhead if fitting a V8 to a four-cylinder Land Rover. Their first task in its rehabilitation would be to remove the engine and gearbox. The gearbox would then be treated to a Transfix overhaul kit comprising all synchros, bearings, oil pump, gaskets and seals. It would also be modified with higher ratio fifth gear.

To achieve the capacity hike from the regular 3.5-litres to 4.2, the bores are resleeved to 94mm, and filled with Rover 94mm pistons. The next stage would not be required if you were content with 3.9-litres. However, for a 4.2 stretch, a new, longer-stroke Iceberg crank is fitted. The standard mains bolts are not re-used or replaced as this is the most serious weakness in any pre-1994 engine; post-1994 factory mods included cross-bolting and more substantial main bearing caps.

Usually the original fuel injection system is retained, although the worn-out fuel pressure regulator may be replaced with the more efficient rising rate regulator. This power boost valve gives more pressure and is advantageous to any fuel injection system. As Chris Crane points out, 'It allows you to control your fuel pressure settings, which enhances performance and economy.' At this stage in the conversion, the fuel system added very little in the way of extra expenditure, and with the addition of free-flow air filters, a test vehicle was producing a theoretical 260bhp with 300ft/lb of torque. Fuel consumption was a frugal 25–27mpg (10.5–11.3l/100km) at a steady 65mph (105km/h).

With a fuel-injected engine you obviously do not have to change needles to change mixtures, which is where the power boost valve comes in, giving more pressure behind the injectors, so you do not need to modify the ECU for them to be open longer, you just have more pressure behind them.

RPi elected to try the Boxer RV8 manifold allied to four SU carbs instead of the fuel injection, because it represented an interesting research project. The Boxer gives equal length manifolding to each port, so all eight cylinders are supplied equally, and the result seems to be a gain in performance without significantly affecting the economy – although the vehicle still needs to be set up for optimum timing and mixture settings on a rolling road. And rolling roads catering for four-wheel-drive vehicles are few and far between.

'Our main goal is to make them accelerate, which they don't do in standard form, give them lots of bottom-end torque, and get them to do something to the gallon,' said Chris. Every single V8 which RPi has tackled has evidence of gasket failure on the valley side of the V – which isn't immediately obvious. 'The reason is the third row of bolts, which, when you torque them down, cause the head to tilt. And they've been doing it for thirty years! Now, on their post-1994 engines, Rover don't use the third row of bolts, and there's no problem.

THE BUSINESS

Some people are harder to please. Quite a few owners are happy with a regular engine rebuild, while others are content to install a regular 3.5-litre Rover V8 unit in their quest for more power. But Land Rover *afficionado* Tony Cable decided to put in one of the biggest units available: a rumbling GM V8 diesel. The look of Tony's 110 is dramatic enough by any standards, and once the GM V8 is running, you cannot fail to be aware that this is one monster of a vehicle: this 6.2-litres of throbbing American muscle is unstoppable, and the impression is that there is nothing, short of a mountain, that it cannot climb. If you have got the axle diff-locks in – not the gearbox one – it will go anywhere. Tony remembers being halted only once on his various expeditions, and that was by deep mud. And when it rolled in Morocco.

We met up near Dereham, Norfolk, at the Mid-Norfolk Off-Roading Centre. Here, in the water-filled sections where the channels leading in and out were full of sticky mud, we simply powered through, accompanied by great plumes of water and huge bow waves. There is really little point in comparing it with a 2.5Tdi, and it feels generally stronger than a 3.5-litre petrol V8; the 6.2-litre GM V8 has so much low-down torque there is no need to charge hills in the hope that momentum will get you to the summit. On one or two occasions where we lifted off early, the V8 carried on pulling on tickover, whereas a Tdi would simply have stalled. It is that confidence inspiring.

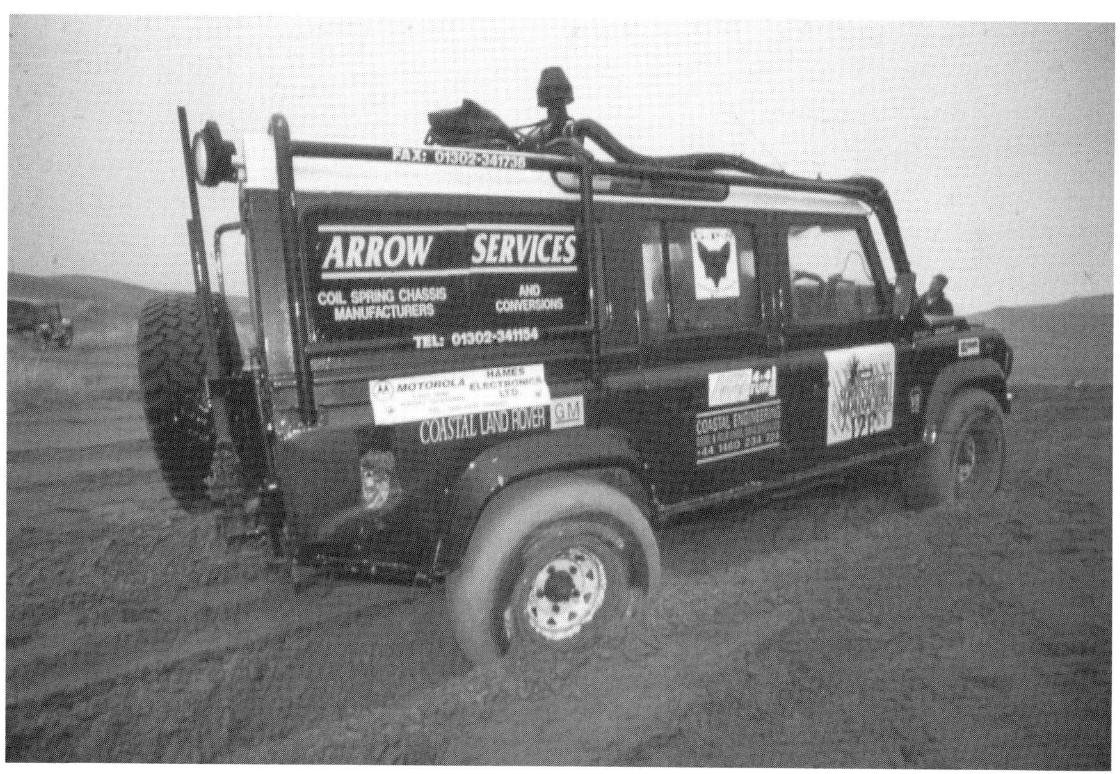

Tony Cable's monster 110 stands 2in (50mm) higher than normal, and is powered by the 6.2-litre General Motors V8 diesel. With its full roll cage and wading capability, there is almost nowhere it cannot go.

According to Tony, it will rev to 4,500rpm, but for the purposes of trundling around we were only using about 1,300rpm. Between sections, however, we got her to growl up to 3,500rpm.

It is responsive, too. Although the throttle is somewhat stiff, the pick-up is virtually instant, and in my opinion there was more power when creeping at tickover than a Tdi would have. In the long run, therefore, that makes it the quickest. We spent most of the time with low-box first gear selected on the auto box for the hilly section – and there was clearly so much power it could have gone up virtually everything on tickover. With all diffs locked on, steering is difficult, and you have to haul on the wheel a bit more, although Tony admitted that its steering lock is not exactly brilliant at the best of times: 'When the front diff-lock's in, you have hardly any control over the front axle.'

The extra 2in (50mm) of suspension height gives you the additional clearance that a regular 110 lacks, which prevents you getting caught out on ridges and summits; it also keeps the chassis and differentials clear in deep ruts. A series of farm tracks link the two aspects of the Mid-Norfolk site, and we travelled briskly in drive mode, which demonstrated just how much get-up-and-go this machine has at its disposal. It feels so sure-footed on its BF Goodrich 35/12.50 x 15 rubber, its Bilstein suspension set-up soaking up the bumps. But you really do have to hang onto it in the rough, when the big tyres pull it about a bit.

In the wooded section, the roll cage not only gives you a huge sense of security, it also does its job in the woods, fending off saplings and branches, and pushing the vehicle off bigger trees where to-and-fro manoeuvring is otherwise impossible. 'The cage is the first thing you look for if you're going off-roading,' said Tony. And, 'Let the cage earn its money!' as we eased through the gaps, brushing boughs to one side.

This 110 has been through several engines in a very short space of time. When Tony bought the vehicle it was a 2.5-diesel; this was quickly uprated to a turbodiesel, which he concedes 'isn't too bad an engine', and then having drowned it one day, they fitted another TDi unit. This took them through the 1994 Transylvania Trophy – but, said Tony, 'It just hadn't got enough go for something with this sort of weight in it.'

They installed a Nissan 3.3 next, 'Which,' says Tony, 'was a waste of time for us.' It was only in for a fortnight. 'I wanted something with more power, and it had to be diesel because of the wading, so we decided to go for the 6.2 litre GM V8.' The GM engine was fitted by Coastal Engineering in Chard, Somerset, who are the main importers of the GM unit; it was away for three weeks being done. 'I picked it up on the Friday night, and we left on the Monday morning for Morocco, so it was a tight schedule,' said Tony. The gearbox is basically an early Range Rover three-speed automatic; it has got two gearbox oil coolers, one of them being the item which looks like a brush on the front of the bonnet. The torque converter has been revalved, the gears are 'heavy-duty', and the transmission has been completely reliable so far. The axles and CV joints are heavy duty too, with Ian Ashcroft halfshafts and ARB lockers. Once everything was sorted, it was fine. 'It's now geared for speed on the road,' he said. I can believe it too, having followed him with some difficulty over a dozen miles (18km) of fast Norfolk A-roads. 'She's geared to do about 120mph, although she feels a bit like a boat on some corners because there's so much weight up top, and she's jacked up. She'll cruise all day at 90mph,' said Tony. I was in the following vehicle, and it appeared stable enough to me through the corners.

The chassis is straight Defender, but the vehicle's raised stance is really a one-off. It is achieved by fitting longer springs, 2in (50mm) taller, with the front turrets relocated 2in (50mm) lower down to compensate for the shorter length of the regular shock absorbers. On the back, they raised the shock absorber mounts on the axle by 2in (50mm), and fitted twin shocks on either side. (These were sourced from Transylvania veteran Dave Fletcher's ADI Engineering of Luton.) Unladen weight is something like 2¾ tons. At first sight, the proportions of the jacked-up vehicle make it look like a bigger Land Rover – a 130, perhaps – and if it stands next to a normal Defender, it is clearly 2in (50mm) higher.

'You really have to *drive* it off-road; with a 90, you can just put it into somewhere and you'll get out,' said Tony. 'But there are other compensations. Like all that stowage space, and Tony and Ivan can sleep in the back, so we don't have to mess about with tents. We can cook in the back as well,' he said. Tony is an electrical engineer by trade, and his East Coast Land Rovers business pays for his off-roading, although he is sponsored by two firms. He estimates that the 110 has probably cost him in total 'about £20,000, but you can't count the time it's taken to build it.'

Once installed behind the wheel, you notice the pedals are off-set slightly to the right, and this impression is caused partly by the seats, which are out of a Peugeot 205 GTi, and have wider sides than the regular-issue Defender. These seats have the effect of holding you in place better when the going gets rough, and are excellent on long distance runs.

The automatic gear shift is re-located in a higher position so the lever falls readily to hand, and the replacement transmission-tunnel cover was made up by Tony, where it houses fire extinguisher and sundry equipment. Beside the shift is the rev-counter and a console with four buttons: one for the compressor for the ARBs, one for winch control so it can be operated from within the vehicle, and one each for front and rear diff-locks. There is also a Terratrip ahead of the passenger seat for Ivan's use. They learned about navigation mostly while on the Transylvania Trophy last year.

Tony bought the 110 two-and-a-half years ago as a crashed vehicle. The only parts which are original are the chassis and the bulkhead – all the body panelling is nearly new. It took Tony and Ivan – an HGV fitter and Range Rover owner – just a couple of months to get it mobile, and over the following two years the dash and seats were altered, and suspension, sidebars, under-body protection and ARB lockers fitted. The vehicle is equipped with a compressor for the ARBs, which buzzes intermittently when it is pressurizing the system. Tony went for a Betterweld roll cage in the interests of economy, and his roll-over in the Moroccan desert proved that it works. 'In this game, you've got to pay for the right equipment.'

The downside of the 110 is the insurance premium. As with any engine swap – other than a recon unit – the insurance companies are loath to get involved. 'As soon as they discover you've put another engine in, they don't want to know.' Tony rang round several, and the only broker to fix him up with cover was Adrian Flux, a sporting specialist. 'At present the premium is £1,400 a year,' said Tony.

However, the old adage that there is no substitute for cubic inches is a very good one. Purists may be appalled, but I was left feeling that anyone who believes they need limitless power for their Land Rover, and has the budget, could do no better than follow Tony Cable's example.

SOURCING GM V8S

Tony Cable's Defender is not the only Land Rover in the UK with the GM V8 installed, but as far as I know it is the only one running automatic transmission. Ken Cottey of Coastal Engineering, at Chard, Somerset, explained that he mostly installs the GM V8 in Range Rovers, but there are a few Discoveries and 110s about with them. These engines are normally found in good old American pick-ups such as the GM Jimmys, and the US army and air-force Hummers and Chevrolet Blazers. They come complete with US-spec emission controls, so there is not a trace of black smoke. These devices swallow about 30bhp, but you are hardly going to notice that. A number of other places are fitting them now, which is not so surprising as it is basically a straightforward conversion, and more or less the same size as the Rover V8 petrol unit.

Coastal Engineering have been handling the GM V8 diesel for over a year now. They source their engines from Samurai Engineering, who are probably the UK leaders, as well as the States and Europe. They tend to deal more with used ex-military examples because new ones are becoming hard to come by. The engines are either reconditioned, or at least stripped down and inspected before being committed for sale, a task which takes one of Coastal's five-strong staff a week to do. Being ex-military spec, the electrics have to be converted from 24-volt to regular 12-volt system.

Fitting takes roughly sixty hours, and they like to have the vehicle between seven to ten working days; it may take longer if there is extra work to do on the gearbox, as in Tony Cable's case. If the GM unit is replacing a four-cylinder Tdi, the footwells need to be modified by sectioning them back slightly. This is because the gearbox sits further back than a Range Rover V8 110. In Tony Cable's vehicle, the automatic gearbox means that the GM engine sits further forward, so although it is tight down by the steering box and towards the back of the engine, the footwells did not need modifying. For this fitting operation, Coastal changed the gearbox crossmember and mounting points, the handbrake linkage, and fitted a Range Rover front prop to get clearance, and bolt-on chassis mounts.

'There are no short cuts with this installation,' said Ken Cottey. 'It is important to have the bigger radiator and bigger exhausts to suit this engine – you have to match the exhaust and air cleaner – so it's very much a specialist thing.' Coastal will do a part-exchange deal on the engine which is being taken out. The fitting kit comprises a gearbox adapter, flywheels, chassis mounts and special brackets.

MAKING MOVIES

One of the best-known faces on the Land Rover scene is Duncan Barbour. A veteran of the Camel Trophy and judge on the Warn Challenge, Duncan is now involved in the film business with his 4.2-litre, V8-powered 90, and was to the fore during the filming of the new James Bond movie *Goldeneye*. Over breakfast at the Haycock Hotel, Wansford, during the 1995 Warn Challenge, he told me about his work.

Duncan became involved with the movies when he was made redundant after five years as Camel Trophy event co-ordinator. At the time, all he was left with was a C-plate Land Rover 90, and his continued ownership of that was precarious, moreover as a 4.2-litre V8 model, it was a notorious gas guzzler. Duncan then offered his services and his Land Rover to the movie moguls as a mobile camera platform, reasoning that it would venture into places which were inaccessible to other vehicles. 'No one had done anything like this before,' said Duncan. 'A tracking vehicle is normally just a big truck with sloppy suspension, and nobody had tried to put together something specifically for both off-road and on-road tracking.'

The technique of tracking is when the camera moves along keeping pace with the moving subject – in the early days of the industry it literally ran on rail tracks a set distance from the action. At its most basic, a tracking shot involves filming a couple of people having a conversation as they walk down a street. But Duncan's Land Rover clearly covers more difficult situations. For example, in its very first commission for the Mel Gibson film *Braveheart,* the director wanted a vehicle that could out-accelerate a charging horse from a standing start. This was not a problem for Duncan's 4.2-litre 90, which features a 3.9 injection system. 'It'll do 0–60 in about 8.5 seconds,' said Duncan, 'but it's the mid-range acceleration that's really impressive. Floor the throttle in third gear, low 'box, and the power just keeps on coming.' Duncan has fitted a 1994 spec gearbox and competition clutch, which transmits the drive to Quaife torque-sensitive differentials front and rear. The brakes are also uprated with competition disc pads, which proved their worth when filming a chase between a Ferrari and an Aston Martin for *Goldeneye* at up to 85mph (135km/h) in the hills of Southern France. 'The faster we could go, the more realistic it looked on film,' said Duncan.

'A 110 would have been a better bet,' said Duncan. 'But when the Camel job finished, I already had the 90 – and I've modified the suspension quite a bit. I started off with Boge adjustable shocks and US-spec Range Rover springs, which were the softest and most progressive I could find. Then we added airbags to increase the spring rating when carrying heavy loads, and fitted modified Warwick Banks' handling kits front and rear, in order to produce the smoothest possible ride and control body roll at the same time.

'During shoots I found that it was crucial to be able to adjust the suspension from

Camel Trophy veteran Duncan Barbour leases his Land Rover to film companies as a camera platform for action sequences. He was heavily involved in 1995 hits Goldeneye *and* Braveheart.

inside the vehicle, without having to get out with a screwdriver. The 90 has now got Rancho air-adjustable shocks, which are excellent. On the road I use Pirellis at about 28psi, with the airbags set at about seven, and I swap to Goodrich Mud Terrains for off-roading.'

The movie *Goldeneye* was filmed in a variety of locations, including Russia, the south of France, Peterborough, and even Watford. A lot of big-budget Hollywood movies seem to be made at least in part in the UK these days, because there is an abundance of under-used talent here. Just a few minutes off the M25, suburban Watford has one advantage over the South of France, which is a disused aerodrome, ideal for the construction of film sets. For *Goldeneye,* one of these was the main street of St Petersburg, consisting of three-storey buildings peopled with Russian soldiers and citizens, and battered old Ladas. The façades were made of plaster, plywood and scaffolding, and it all looked highly realistic.

Duncan described how the Land Rover covered one of the *Goldeneye* stunts. There is a scene where two Jeeps hurtle out of a side street and plunge off a quayside into a river, and this was achieved in two stages, by rigging a ⅝in (6mm) steel cable between the Land Rover and each of the Jeeps, run at 90° over a pulley at the end of the alley. By accelerating hard, the Land Rover could tow the Jeep up to speed and shoot it into the river, while skilful camera angles hid the cable from view. However, rumour has it that one stuntman was killed in this episode.

One scene involves a stolen tank being pursued through the streets of 'St Petersburg' by Russian police, leaving crushed cars and pedestrians in its wake; for this, most of the filming was done from Duncan's Land Rover, which had to be kept ahead of the rampaging tank.

It is not just its performance which makes Duncan's 90 an attractive proposition on the film set: as well as for protection, the roll-cage tubing is ideal for mounting cameras in virtually any position, and it is this which makes the vehicle so versatile. The inner cage is made up from a Safety Devices 90 front one and an ex-Camel Trophy rear, and the outer cage was specially crafted and welded.

A simple tracking shot is done with just two crew members, one driving and the other operating the camera. But usually there is an extra person, the focus puller, who controls focus and zoom with a remote extension; he will either stand on the Land Rover's roof or sit in the front passenger seat. The camera operator sits in the back, using a video monitor to control the movement of the camera, which swivels on its mount or rises up and down on the crane. On set, Duncan is normally the driver, and he is expert at positioning the 90 so the camera operators can achieve some spectacular shots.

At the last count, Duncan had another exciting project in the pipeline: a film company which wanted to cover a Rallye Raid adventure across Africa was very interested in the vehicle and was talking with Duncan about shipping it to Africa for the event.

SHOCK TACTICS

One of the most effective ways of improving the handling of your vehicle – especially if it's getting on a bit – is to replace the shock absorbers. Many people never need to change them, because they don't hang on to the vehicle long enough, or they only fit new ones if they fail the MoT.

Off-roaders have a more specialized requirement in the way of shocks, and

RIPPING YARNS

When your vehicle's seat covers are exposed, as mine are, to the daily rigours of children and animals clambering about on them, the fabric or the stitching are bound to give up the struggle eventually. As a convenient and inexpensive way of refurbishing or protecting them, seat covers are your best answer. Chamberlain's make sets for Series IIIs, Defenders, Range Rovers and Discoverys. They simply slide on over the existing seats and you tie them securely underneath with the tape provided.

The material they use is called Moorland tweed, currently used in Defender upholstery anyway. They are machine-washable, and won't fade. Some other original Land Rover materials are also available, and they also do tailored polyurethane waterproof covers as well. Range Rover seat design has altered over the years, of course, so customers will need to specify seat type before ordering. Chamberlain's do a handy chart to help identify the right style. Contact Wendy Chamberlain, 2 Tremain Road, London SE20 7TZ, or phone 0181-778 7997.

BELTS AND BRACES

The firm of Safety Devices is well known in competition circles for its roll-over bars and roll cages for racing machines as diverse as Caterham Sevens and Renault 5s. They cater for virtually anything, in fact, and as readers will know, they produce the roll cages for NAS Defenders.

Now they offer a safety-belt range as well, which will be of interest to Land Rover enthusiasts who go in for competitive off-roading such as comp safaris and trials. There is no substitute for a good harness, and at the time of writing the three-point Sportsman belts start at £36.00, rising to £80.00 for the 2in (50mm) wide four-point fixing version. You can get them in either red or blue webbing, and they are FISA approved and ECE homologated.

Contact Safety Devices at Regal Drive, Soham, Cambridge CB7 5BE, tel: 01353 624624.

Warn have recently introduced the Black Diamond AT and XT dampers: AT for 'all terrain', and XT for 'extreme terrain'; these are said to be tough enough to cope with the toughest off-road situations, allied to on-road ride comfort as well. These shocks are designed to complement Black Diamond suspension systems and body lifts. For more information contact Ryders International, Knowsley Road, Bootle, Liverpool L20 4NW, tel: 0151-922 7585.

PAINT YOUR WAGON

We're all familiar with Hammerite products in the UK, but there is a French alternative on the market now. Deproma rust-proof paint has been used to paint barge superstructure in France for twenty-five years. Bearing in mind how the great *peniches* get bashed about in the continental locks, it obviously possesses special qualities. And now it's the latest weapon in the Land Rover restorer's battle against corrosion.

If necessary it can be applied to rusty, dirty or damp surfaces with minimal preparation - merely brush down to remove loose particles, no primer or undercoat is needed,but two coats are recommended. The pigment has a special ingredient which combines with the iron oxide to form a non-corrosive barrier against further rust developing. It is said to be usable under water as well. Its finish is very smooth, but not thick. There are eighteen colours to choose from, including suitable Land Rover colours. No solvents are necessary, and it can be diluted with regular thinners, and applied with a brush or spray. Drying time, abrasion resistance and gloss finish can all be improved if an accelerator is used.

Deproma's managing director Ted Elwes recently treated a 1985 Range Rover chassis using the product, and his account of the job is a copybook restoration. He used three coats, sprayed on, to a thickness of a hundred microns. It dried in three to four hours, but like all paint, it is best to give it twenty-four hours or so.

For more details, contact Deproma Ltd at Theocsbury House, 18-20 Barton Street, Tewkesbury, Glos. GL20 5PP, tel: 01684 291544. Deproma's Land Rover distributor is Tim Fry Land Rovers, King Alfred Way, Battledown, Cheltenham, Glos. GL52 6QT, tel: 01242 516028.

Most Defenders are ordered with Tdi engines these days, and only a handful of NAS 90s have escaped into the UK. On sale at Colchester dealers H.R. Owen, this one is being put through its paces by journalist Paul Horrell.

10 Clubs and Competitions

This modified 90 has sustained some scars on its Welsh excursion.

A major facet of Land Rover ownership is the club scene, with its many varied activities; there are clubs for nearly all models, and certainly for all UK regions, and there is at least one club in almost every country in the world. Here are just a very few of them.

THE HANTS AND BERKS ROVER OWNERS' CLUB

The Hants and Berks Rover Owners' Club was formed in 1983 and now has a membership of over 200. As with most other 'Rover Clubs', the majority of members are Land Rover owners, but owners of Rover cars are always welcome. The club's aim is to assist and encourage members in all aspects of Land Rover ownership. Members can indulge in all the usual off-road events, the treasure hunts, social outings, sightseeing trips, caravan and camping weekends and the annual holiday rally, which all adds up to something for everyone. The club holds club nights twice a month, one at Aldermaston and the other at Bishop's Waltham. The club is also involved with other events, such as the Bagshot Heath Off-Road Show; and, for example, HBRO members once held the record for the fastest drive to the summit of Ben Nevis.

The club's newsletter *Pants & Barks*, and its bi-monthly update sheet, keeps members informed of all events and activities; there is also news from other clubs, the ARC and event reports, plus a larger-than-average 'for sale' section.

For details, contact the club secretary: Gary Langton, 1 Hillside Court, 16 Solent Road, Drayton, Portsmouth, Hampshire PO6 1HH.

THE PENNINE LAND ROVER CLUB

The Pennine is one of the oldest Land Rover clubs in Britain, having been in existence, in one form or another since the early sixties. Nowadays it has a strong emphasis on competition – in fact it is regarded as one of the most competitive within the ARC, with club members at the forefront of competition vehicle development – but it still caters for members with interests in all aspects of Land Rovering. Pennine was also the first club to include 'night safaris', back in 1981, which today are regular features in most inter-club events; and it is one of the very few clubs still running point-to-point events, which enable both competitors and spectators to become involved.

The club holds a comp safari and a CCV trial on alternate months, with events taking place mostly in the Pennines on both sides of the Yorkshire–Lancashire border. The club's main event of the year is its annual August Bank Holiday Inter-club, regarded in past years as second only to the ARC National. The club's magazine, *Bottom Box*, keeps members informed of events, as well as providing news reports and classified ads. Club members are very active in other motor sport events, with Pennine recovery teams attending many international car rallies, hill climbs and the Hillrally.

Further details from club secretary Ivor Hill, 2 Westbourne Road, Pontefract WF8 4JY. Tel: 01977-707895.

Series I trialler hybrid being put through its paces at a club outing.

Great fun is had by all in trialling at Club level.

PORTUGAL'S *PASSEIO*

Clube Land Rover de Portugal's annual event is now in its sixth year, and the meeting held in mid-April – *Passeio 95* – was so successful that a second was convened in November. The main reason for its success was that membership soared to close on 1,000 members, and demand for places was very high. The venue is Monfortinho, a spa town some 280 miles (350km) north-east of Lisbon, not far from the Spanish border. Some Portuguese back roads are little better than mule tracks anyway, but the area is remote and quite mountainous, with forest tracks and fire breaks, some of which are very steep. By November, the nature of the terrain had changed with the onset of autumn rains, and the going was harder. Monfortinho had only limited accommodation, and the organizers had to restrict entries to eighty-five Land Rovers, or 260 enthusiasts.

Clube Land Rover de Portugal members receive a monthly news letter and quarterly magazine, and there is a special concours event called *Veteranos* for Series Land Rovers with £2,000-worth of prizes for the three best restorations. In addition to the *Passeio,* there are two other large national events, plus an off-roading school and a club boutique.

Further details of the Portuguese Land Rover Club can be obtained from the club secretary Carlos Duarte, *Clube Land Rover de Portugal*, Largo do Ministro, 3 – Porta 1, 1700 Lisboa, Portugal.

UNWELCOME GUEST

One 101 Forward Control Register member was amazed to discover that his vehicle was politically incorrect, and he described why in an issue of Register magazine *Six Stud.* Arriving early at the college where he worked, he parked his 101 at the front of the college car park, and left to attend an exam some miles away in a colleague's car. On seeing the offending 101 parked in a prominent position, the college principal went to great lengths to have it removed. Several attempts to get someone to 'hot wire' it failed, and the 101 stayed firmly in pole position.

The next day our friend received a memo saying that his 101 caused a 'health and safety risk being parked where it was', and that in future, if he must bring an 'army vehicle' to the college, he was to park it round the back out of sight. It may have

At home in its native habitat, a Series IIA splashes its way through the forests.

been no coincidence that the day the 101 was parked with such prominence in the car park was the same day that the Parliamentary Under Secretary of State for Education visited the college!

THE BAY STATE ROVER OWNERS' ASSOCIATION

Bay State is one of the largest Land Rover clubs in North America, if not the largest, with around 300 members. The bulk of the membership comes from the New England area, although it extends to the rest of North America and has a number of 'overseas' members, too. Membership of BSROA is open to Land Rover owners and anyone with an interest in Rover products, and the aim is to service the needs of owners and to promote the marque. To this end, club activities are wide and various. They include off-road events, inter-club meetings, regional and national events, as well as the annual BSROA gathering, special weekend outings, auctions and swap-meets, and much more. The association encourages full family participation of all ages, and the bi-monthly magazine *The Rover Reference* keeps all members up to date with BSROA events, plus Rover and Land Rover news from around the world, with members contributing travel and technical articles. *The Rover Reference* is published in a loose-leaf format to allow photocopying and ease of archiving, and binders are available to store back issues.

All members receive a full-colour BSROA sew-on patch and window decal, with a special members' discount on parts, and access to the club's 'Roverphenalia'. The association also supports environmental preservation, and this includes the 'tread lightly' philosophy. It is also affiliated to the UK's Association of Rover Clubs.

For details, write or call the Bay State Rover Owners Association, PO Box 342, North Scituate, Mass. 02060. Tel/fax (617) 545-4743. Anyone going over to the Bay State area of the USA will be made more than welcome. Alternatively you can contact their UK representative, Andrew Cutting, on 01394-448562.

KIWI CAPERS

The Land Rover Owners Club Auckland was formed in early 1994, and grew steadily to around fifty members by the end of its first year. The club also attracted people from further afield, to become the second largest club in the northern zone of New Zealand's 4×4 Association.

The burgeoning newsletter covers club events and articles of general interest to Land Rover owners, and keeps everyone informed of future events and trips. The club organizes a wide range of events throughout the year, with at least two club trips every month, varying from mud runs to camping trips through forests and tracks in some of New Zealand's more scenic and historic areas.

For further details on the club, or for anyone visiting New Zealand, contact: Jules Lee, c/o 41 Hastings Road, Mirangi Bay, Auckland, New Zealand. tel: (025) 968-376 or 473-0179.

Given a Good Grilling

The Land Rover Register 1947–51 club's *Full Grill* is always full of interesting observations, facts and finds connected with the original Series Is. According to the original spelling in the parts catalogue, *Full Grill* was spelt *Full Grille*. The reason given for the last 'e' being deleted was simply that editor John Smith thought it didn't look right. However, for the sake of correctness the 'e' has now been reinstated and the newsletter title is back to the original version: *Full Grille*.

SOUTHERN TIP

The Southland Land Rover Club, right down on the southern-most tip of New Zealand's South Island, is possibly the most southerly Land Rover club of all, and it is a close-run thing with the Falkland Island Land Rover Register. As far as dis-

Comp Safari is the next best thing to flying – as seen at the ARC Nationals.

tance goes, New Zealand is the furthest point from the UK anyway.

THE COMP SAFARI GUIDE

The 'Idiots' Guide to Comp Safari' is a dissertation written by Noel Cooper of the Leicestershire and Rutland LRC's bulletin *Tilting on the Hill*. He explains the procedure to do a comp safari:

> First, take care of the paper work: RACMSA comp licence, ARC logbook. The licence is no problem – just fill in the form and send it off, and it's returned seven days later. The ARC logbook is almost mission impossible: find two ARC scrutineers as close by as possible, then drive all over the country towing the Land Rover. Secondly, the event itself. The National – no less – get the vehicle scrutineered and helmets stickered. Attend the drivers' meeting, then go on a pleasant, romantic walk three-and-a-half miles (5.6km) in the pouring rain across land that time forgot, to familiarize yourself with the course.
>
> On the day of the event, load forty-two gallons (190l) of fuel and head for the quarry. Wait an hour or so for the green lights, then off – no police, no speed limits, no wife telling you to slow down, but always at the back of your mind a little voice telling you not to wreck the vehicle.
>
> After one or two events, the brain will have been sufficently damaged for that nagging feeling about not wrecking the vehicle to fade away. By next year's National you'll be in 'foot-down-all-the-way-and-drive-it-to-death' mode.

BRECKLAND SAFARI

As a counterpoint to the ARC Nationals, this is an event typical of the sort run by provincial clubs. It was Breckland Land Rover Club's mid-'95 competition in the heather hills of the 450-acre (182ha) CITB Bircham Newton training centre near King's Lynn, Norfolk. Unlike big-time meetings such as the ARC Nationals, it attracted just thirteen vehicles, all of which were machines converted specially for competitive off-road use.

Sponsored by Norwich specialists JSF Autos, the event consisted of timed runs staged over two miles (3.2km) of rough terrain adjacent to the board's plant training centre. The winner was Allan Roberts of Swafield, North Walsham.

LONDON 4 × 4 SHOW

You do not really expect to be able to go off-roading in the middle of London. But visitors at the first London 4 × 4 Show in Thamesmead in 1995 were treated to just such a display on private land overlooking the Thames. Featuring sandy cross-axles (the sand came from the bottom of the river apparently), a few steep hills and some pleasant wooded sections, the off-roading was extremely popular, attracting vehicles as diverse as a topless Series I and brand-new Range Rovers and Discoveries.

The London 4 × 4 Show was the inspiration of Victor and Helen Jones, and it also featured a trade area and main arena – site of the Land Rover ballet troupe and a 'pull-a-101' competition. Unfortunately, miserable weather put a slight dampener on things, so the turn-out was not as great as expected. Nevertheless, plans for future events are underway.

QUARRY PURSUITS

When it comes to winches, the North

GRAND NATIONAL

Off-roading competitions are many and varied, but they don't come much bigger than the All-Rover Club's annual British event, and the 1995 ARC National proved to be a huge success: thousands of enthusiasts converged on Lincolnshire for the ARC's annual jamboree. The host club, Lincolnshire Land Rover Club, has a reputation for putting on well run events, as well as setting out interesting and demanding trials sections. The prospect of a testing weekend meant that all the competitive events were soon booked up, with 240 entrants for the RTV class and 223 for the CCV category.

After a damp start, the weather was set fair for an excellent weekend of trialling, team recovery and all the razzamatazz generally associated with the ARC Nationals. The action took place in the quarries of Blankney and Metheringham, while the main arena site was a grass field surrounded by caravan sites and potato fields. Attractions here ranged from the beer tent to a fairground, plus trade stalls and marquees from regular Land Rover specialists, and a fine display of ex-military vehicles and Series I Land Rovers in the central area. By mid-morning on Saturday the trialling vehicles were assembled in the arena, and made their way to the first of the quarry sites. I joined the punters aboard a crowded Bedford army truck, one of three providing transport for spectators on the estate roads between trialling locations.

Trialling at Blankney quarry looked to be a straightforward affair, although the section which dived off into a wood caught out a few competitors. The most dramatic site was without doubt Metheringham, with its steep slopes, dramatic sand cliffs and terraces providing unbeatable viewing places for spectators.

Scrutineering for the RTV event was carried out under the watchful eye of Chief Scrutineer John Denniss. Vehicles lacking non-return valves in their fuel filler caps or breather pipes from the fuel tanks were dismissed to get them sorted out. Instead of having set times for scrutineering, as most competitive events, Lincs was open for twenty-four hours, and the special marquee was also equipped with power and light for major repair work in the evenings.

There were 240 vehicles in twelve groups for the RTV, and each group would drive six sections in one quarry before lunch and then swap locations afterwards. The winner was George McLay from the Scottish ROC, who only picked up two penalty points all day. On Saturday evening, many of those who stayed over adjourned to the Rover Restaurant adjoining the main marquee. The main bar proved an attraction for many, as did the fairground.

Typical V8-powered trialler at the 1995 ARC National. Such vehicles are often built on coil-sprung Range Rover chassis.

On Sunday morning everyone was away early for the drive across to the Metheringham and Blankney quarries for the National Trial (CCV). Clear winner of the Land Rover clubs' premier event was Tom Boydell of the Lancs & Cheshire ROC in a standard Series I, finishing the National trial six points clear, and showing all the specials the way to go.

Monday was comp safari day and the event was split between the two quarries, with the coilers in one and the leafers in the other; they swapped over after three runs in each. Action was of a similar quality to the previous two day's trials, although dusk was the main problem at the end of the day. On the whole, Metheringham quarry's comp safari section presented a tighter course than Blankney, which was more open and faster, possibly suiting the V8s better.

For many enthusiasts, Monday was a time to look round the trade and club stands and meet friends. There was plenty on offer, and several trade stands were selling spares necessary to replace parts broken in competition. The other competitions, including team recovery and winch recovery, also attract a decent number of entries and spectators, who get a grandstand view of the proceedings from the cliff-top. Six teams took part in the winch recovery, with Essex LRC team taking first place from the Midland ROC. Team recovery honours went to the Hants & Berks club.

There had been at least one spectacular accident in Saturday's team recovery in the daunting Metheringham quarry site: one competitor who was stalled half-way up a climb, succeeded in dragging his partner's tow vehicle over the top, and it crashed down on top of him, luckily with no injury to either driver; but there were two very sorry-looking Land Rovers at the foot of the cliff. Concours, gymkhana and trailer handling were once upon a time the National Rally's main attraction, but have been somewhat neglected by both competitors and organizers in recent years. Both gymkhana and trailer-handling events were run throughout the three days. The concours mustered just thirteen entries, while the gymkhana attracted a good field. These events might have been better supported had they been in the centre of the main trade stand field, where they would have attracted more spectators and entrants.

All you need is an SII with a roll cage and harnesses to really get stuck in.

American Warn company is a leading manufacturer of these vital devices, and every year it sponsors Land Rover-oriented winching events to promote its product. I watched competitors being put through the mill in the 1995 Warn Challenge.

One might expect the spring weather in mid-May to be reliable enough to make for easy going, but it was not, and this made for some slippery conditions in the Warn

Challenge finals. In two of the locations there was a great deal of slithering and sliding, and much use of the winch to assist bogged down vehicles. The finals were held in the weird moonscape of Tixover quarry, the soaring cliffs at Stainby quarry, and thick woodlands at West Lodge Rural Centre. Competitors were divided into six teams, comprising the winners of the twelve qualifying rounds, along with some invited crews – notably a couple of Dutch crews, including the winners of the recent Warn Adventure Trophy in Morocco – making twenty-two vehicles in all. Apart from three 'other' makes, all were Lode Lane products.

The organizer was at pains to point out that while there were time limits on getting through the stages and completing the tasks set, it was not a race as such, but a test of ingenuity, skill and stamina, and most of all, team co-operation. Competitors were assessed not only on their driving skills, but on initiative and planning, and how they dealt with the safety aspects of winching. The categories they were marked on – with points out of ten – were safety, driving skill, winching, teamwork and team spirit, and general approach.

A morning spent in the oozing sediments of Tixover Grange quarry saw most vehicles covered with a healthy deposit of mud, and in some cases, their occupants, too. While most drivers had little difficulty with the hard rock sections here, the pools formed in clay pits caught out a few. Some very contrived upward turns through rocky defiles caught out others. It was obvious that the short-wheelbase Land Rovers fared better than the long-wheelbase, and this was nowhere more evident than when one 110 became straddled over a ridge, with neither back nor front wheels completely in contact with the ground. A 90 was prepared to winch him off, and high-lift jacks were contemplated as a means of raising the rear of the Land Rover over the rim. Eventually the winch did the trick, but it was clear in a later trials driving section that with its shallow departure

Dutch 90 of Raul and Jean-Pierre Jacobs on the 1995 Warn Challenge at Tixover Grange quarry.

angle, the 110 was at a disadvantage.

After lunch, the entire company moved in convoy up the A1 to Stainby for the afternoon session. The cliffs hewn out of the landscape by long-defunct sand and gravel extraction provided a dramatic canyon-like setting for activities. There were six tasks to be completed, all with an accent on winching (bearing in mind who was sponsoring the event): bridge building, constructing an aerial runway, trials driving, winch recovery and winching down, and finally a theoretical debate.

Bridge building involved winching up a collection of telegraph poles and sleepers from a terrace in the 'canyon', and laying them out to replicate a rustic bridge. The objective was to drive one of the team's vehicles across it, so the poles needed to be secured with iron stakes, straps and boulders. And because it was notionally being constructed above a chasm, the bridge builders weren't allowed to touch the ground. Having completed their bridge and made a successful crossing, the team hurriedly dismantled it so the following contingent could start all over again.

The aerial ropeway demanded some nerve on the part of the team member who was to be dispatched down the rope. To begin with, however, the system had to be set up, with a Land Rover positioned at the top of the quarry, linked to another at the lower terrace level. The latter had to be thoroughly anchored to take the tension of the cable; also the pulley system needed to include a method of braking, otherwise the unfortunate transportee would have travelled rather swiftly. Once down, the team member was swapped for a log, which made the journey back up to the top. The operation was controlled by the winch man at the bottom.

A similar set of circumstances was used to lower a Land Rover doing duty as a crashed vehicle down the side of the quarry, and haul it back up again, except that it was controlled from the top. The winch vehicle was anchored to another at the top, which necessitated a right-angle attachment because of the narrow confines of the track there. Some teams also incorporated the vegetation, lashing their vehicles to trees to be sure of good anchorage. When all was set up, the third Land Rover, plus crew, could be winched down.

The long-wheelbase 110 was at a disadvantage, getting grounded over a ridge in Tixover quarry. Use of winches and high-lift jack got it over.

Another task involved winching a set of truck bogeys up the hillside, but first these had to be manhandled into a position where the winch cable could obtain access. A member of Team 2 drove his Range Rover down the access track to shove them along with vehicle power: that was lateral thinking, and there was nothing in the rules to say they could not.

Warn competitors build a 'bridge'...

...then put it to the test.

It was interesting to see how seriously some teams took the safety aspect of winching, bearing in mind the lethal potential of a snapped cable as the wire flies back to its source. Some teams wrapped a blanket over the cable to absorb its energy in the event of a severance, while others merely tossed a piece of matting over it. Happily no one suffered a cable breakage, but it's always as well to play safe.

When it came to the classroom stuff, most people's imagination ran riot. Teams were presented with drawings showing hypothetical situations in which they might find themselves – their Land Rover overturned in the jungle or on the edge of a precipice for instance – and they were then asked by one of the judges to work out what to do to recover the crashed vehicle.

Sunday's action took place in the narrow

woodland tracks bordering West Lodge Rural Centre, and they were sufficiently overgrown to replicate dense jungle; there were innumerable tree stumps to avoid, and the deep ruts and sharp bends required the Land Rovers to perform all kinds of contortions to overcome them. The teams covered the circuit in one direction in the morning session, then went back the other way in the afternoon.

Later, a presentation was held at the Lady Anne's Hotel Stamford and, for the second year running, Neil Hopkinson made off with the Warn Challenge spoils, navigated by his brother Manley. What is remarkable is that he did it using a virtually standard Series IIA in the face of considerably more sophisticated opposition. So what's the secret, then? 'Mainly down to thinking ahead and assessing the right lines to take through ruts and quagmires,' Neil told me. 'Unfortunately one or two people were a bit annoyed that I won it for a second time – but the judging was completely impartial.'

Having observed the event in its entirety, I can confirm that that was true. The judges picked for the occasion bore the highest credentials, being former Camel Trophy competitors plus a senior off-roading journalist; and the marshalling was first rate, too. In the event, Neil Hopkinson was very lucky to finish, as the carbon brush in the Series IIA's distributor cap burned out – but fortunately it happened just before the lunch break so he could effect a repair.

CLASSIC TRIUMPHANT

Adapting a Land Rover for competition use need not cost a fortune. Neil Hopkinson's low-budget modifications transformed his Series IIA into an off-road champion, his classic Land Rover running rings round younger, vastly more expensive off-roaders when he won the Warn Challenge final two years running in 1994 and 1995. Neil first became interested in Land Rovers when he was thirteen. Later he became a Land Rover test driver at Gaydon, he also organized a Land Rover safari in Kenya, and he used to manage his own off-road driving school. Since April 1995 he has been an instructor at Vince Cobley's Pro-Trax off-roading school in Northamptonshire. 'The old Series II draws a lot of comment these days,' he said. 'For some reason they doubt the IIA's off-roading ability – but I just love to prove them wrong!'

Neil bought the 2.25-litre petrol-engined SIIA five years ago: 'I wanted a cheap and capable off-roader, so a short-wheelbase IIA seemed an ideal choice,' he explained. 'People tend to forget just how good Series vehicles are off-road. They were built as stong, reliable working vehicles long before the sport became popular.' Neil was undeterred by the fact that when he bought it the IIA was virtually a non-runner: 'The engine was reasonably sound. The swivel heads were perfect and lots of new parts had been fitted,' he recalled. 'Although it looked quite tatty, I could tell it had been well cared for. I fitted new brakes and water pump, the faulty lights were repaired, and the pipe to the clutch pedal had to be replaced.'

Neil then set about turning the Land Rover into a potent off-road vehicle. But unlike some enthusiasts who spend a small fortune modifying their vehicles, he kept costs to a minimum by using cheap second-hand parts, often sourced from breakers' yards. 'A lot of my mechanical knowledge came from restoring a Series I when I was sixteen, so I've been able to do most of the work on the IIA myself,' he said.

The project began by raising the air

intake, which was made from a length of drainpipe. For added water resistance the joints were covered with silicone sealant: 'Many people rely on just screwing the joints together, but this doesn't make them 100 per cent waterproof and a small amount of water in the intake pipe can quite seriously damage the engine,' he explained. Neil fitted a Warn 9,000i winch which he won in the 1994 Warn Challenge. It is flush with the front bumper, making it less conspicuous, but more importantly, it does not diminish the vehicle's approach angle when off-roading. The winch has been welded back to the second crossmember on the chassis for extra strength.

Neil took part in the 1994 Transylvania Trophy in the Ukraine and, together with his brother Manley as navigator, competed in the 1995 Warn Adventure. Some adaptations were necessary to enable the Land Rover to cope with the tough African terrain. 'One of the major problems vehicles encountered during the Translyvania Trophy was damage to differentials,' he said. So the IIA was fitted with a specially designed underbody protection plate. Twin fuel tanks were added, a standard requirement for the Moroccan adventure. 'I opted for this because an additional tank spreads the load of the extra fuel better and more safely,' Neil explained. 'I also fitted a roll cage for the Moroccan trip; it was something I'd always wanted but never got round to installing before.'

Neil removed the sills and bottom rear wings which might have been damaged during serious off-roading, and fitted a set of modified Range Rover wheels, running on chunky non-standard tyres. 'I had to be extra careful when cutting the centres out of the wheels, as they tend to crack easily.' Other additions include a stainless-steel exhaust, a set of 100 watt halogen lights, and new outriggers for the bulkhead.

The IIA is hardly modified at all internally, although the holes in the front floor serve a very useful purpose: 'If ever I get stuck in deep water when I'm off-roading, the gaps will let in the water. Consequently, the vehicle will sink, the tyres can regain their grip, and away I go!' Always assuming the vehicle does not sink so deep that the Hopkinsons have to swim for it! The most expensive addition is a Terratrip, which Neil has fitted to read off the handbrake drum. 'This makes distances easily recordable, and was invaluable on the Moroccan event,' he explained.

A pair of wooden boxes over the rear wheel arches serve as tool storage. 'Not only does it keep things tidy, it also stops things flying around the vehicle and hitting me on the head when I'm off-roading,' he said.

During his five years of ownership, Neil reckons to have spent a modest £1,500 on the IIA which, considering it covers around 13,000 miles (20,900km) a year and is regularly put to the test on his frequent off-roading adventures, makes it an extremely economical vehicle by any standards. Its relatively light weight, soft top and reliable drivetrain make it an excellent off-road vehicle, and Neil intends to hang on to it for a long time. 'I just love driving it. Even if I won the lottery I'd still keep my IIA for off-roading.' And why not? It has done him proud so far.

STERN WARNING

The 1995 Warn Adventure Trophy was held in the Moroccan Sahara, and contrary to all expectations, it rained. The Warn event went to Morocco following the mixed success of the previous year's Transylvanian Trophy. The 1994 expedition had been dogged by endless delays caused by front

Neil Hopkinson showed everyone the way with his cross-axling Series IIA.

runners getting bogged down by too narrowly defined a route, leading to bottlenecks at the special task areas and traffic jams frustrating competitors further behind. Although sponsored by Warn, the actual running of the event was contracted out to a Spanish off-road company, and by holding it in Morocco, they hoped to circumvent these problems as well as providing more varied off-roading. Morocco has one of the most changeable landscapes in Africa, from northern forests and ski slopes to rock-strewn pistes of the Atlas mountains and the Sahara desert to the south. There are red sandstone cliffs, bleak mountain passes and flat, stony plateaux dotted with stunted trees.

There were plenty of Land Rovers on the Warn Adventure, although the event was open to all 4 × 4 vehicles, including Suzukis, Unimogs, Ford Broncos and Jeeps, and these made up half the entry list. Twenty-one teams took part in the 1995 adventure, from countries as far apart as the USA and Denmark. The diversity of vehicles demonstrated how different makes compare over the same terrain. It was also possible to judge the merits of short- over long-wheelbase, and old against new. For example, an elderly, bright green long-wheelbase Santana was frequently stuck in the sand because it was top-heavy and underpowered. Warn had included plenty of winch-based activity in the week-long programme, but the competition was also about navigation, logic and teamwork, as much as off-road driving skills. Competitors had to navigate with hand-held GPS units, referring to a number of waypoints supplied as map co-ordinates and photographs; by plotting a route from these co-ordinates, the teams had to get to as many waypoints as they could within the time allowed. These were invariably located in inaccessible sites, and most contenders failed to visit every one and reach the final control point; thus it was prudent to devise plans before setting off, in order not to have to retrace ground covered already.

There were special tasks to undertake en route between waypoints, intended to probe the quality of teamwork even further. For example, contestants had to winch out of a muddy lake bed and traverse a treacherous run of sand dunes as quickly as possible. The levels of professionalism varied widely between crews, the presence of a large amateur contingent being one of the attractions of the Warn Adventure, as compared with the increasingly disciplined Camel Trophy. Like the Warn Challenge, the Warn Adventure is open to anyone with an off-road vehicle, a state of affairs admirably illustrated by Neil Hopkinson in his Series IIA Land Rover: this was certainly the oldest, and probably the entry with the lowest budget, in the competition. Nevertheless, Neil's elderly Land Rover held its own in the sand dunes against the hordes of Defenders and 110s, partly because of its light weight.

At the other end of the scale were serious machines such as Tony Cable's 6.2-litre V8 110 (see Specialists chapter), which Tony rolled while crawling across a sideslope. Because of the snail's pace at which it happened, and thanks to the roll cage, little damage was sustained. The monster was winched back onto its wheels, although the photographer – none other than Nick Dimbleby – who was in the back when it flipped, found that his clothes and camera bag had got soaked in diesel.

Otherwise there were very few catastrophies, given the terrain. Diff protectors naturally proved useful, and most competitors were well prepared, particularly if they had been on 1994's Transylvania Trophy. Slightly less well prepared were the Spanish organizers, who were left in confusion by the unexpected onset of rain when the circus reached the Sahara. In a blustery wind and chill drizzle, the dunes looked more like the North Norfolk coast than Morocco, and by the end of the week some of the special tasks had been abandoned. However, the event was judged a success on the whole, and the Warn reps maintained international relations and kept the beer flowing.

The winning Dutch team comprised two Defenders and a Jeep, while the Italians came second with three Defenders. In third place came the Israeli team, running Unimogs and a Jeep; then the British teams, in fourth place with three 90s, closely followed by Tony Cable's 110 GM V8 and two 90 Tdis.

HILLRALLY SPONSORS

Like the Warn events, virtually all off-road competitions have major sponsors; at least, they are key names in the world of off-roading. Thus the event which many see as Britain's premier 4 × 4 showcase is backed by two major players in off-road driving, leading winch manufacturers Superwinch, and Safety Devices, the roll-over cage specialists.

The Safety Devices' boss Tony Fall is a veteran of the BMC Mini Cooper rally team in the days of Paddy Hopkirk, and went on to head the General Motors Competitions Department in Europe. Says Fall, 'We're manufacturing roll cages and roof-racks for 4 × 4s, as well as fitting kits for Superwinch. Hillrally competitors and spectators are one of our most important markets.'

The Superwinch/Safety Devices Hillrally is based in Builth Wells, mid-Wales, and covers over 90 miles (145km) of high-speed special stages, including the demanding Sweet Lamb section near Llangurig, with competitors taking to the forests to cover some exciting terrain. The 1994 event was won by the Simmonite sisters Stephanie

The Nene Overland 90 at speed in the Moroccan desert.

and Rachel in their Rover V8-powered Simmbuggini special. With Tony Fall's company now involved, more well known rallyists could be attracted to the event.

SOUTHERN HILLRALLY

Judging by its 1995 debut, the Sames Southern Hillrally looks set to become one of the key events on the off-roading calendar. Organized by the All-Wheel Drive Club, the first Southern Hillrally was held in August 1995, sponsored by a number of companies, with London construction firm Sames heading the list.

There were Land Rovers a-plenty, but it was really the province of the out-and-out triallers, with favourites the Simmonite sisters Stephanie and Rachel holding onto second place in their Simmbuggini, despite breaking a driveshaft and running with front-wheel drive only in the later stages. The Hillrally was also accorded both National and Clubmans' status, meaning that novices could try their skills over nearly 145 miles (230km) of special stages of the South Downs in Sussex. The National event was held over a slightly longer course, with some additional 120 miles (190km) of liaison tracks between stages.

No matter how important the event, it can not take place without marshals, those dedicated enthusiasts who do the donkey work at sporting events, from waving warning flags at dangerous corners, sorting vehicles out if they come off the track, and rescuing drivers when there is an accident, to sorting out spectator parking and liaising with competitors, organizers and commentators. Nothing in motor sport happens without efficient marshalling, and it happens to be something we do very well in Britain. In the case of the Southern Hillrally, the event has become so large that effective spectator control is necessary to avoid upsetting local residents and offending environmental pressure groups.

One of the problems the organizers had to sort out was obtaining permission for the

Andy Blois' Defender 90 raises the dust in Morocco.

Hillrally's special stages to cross over public footpaths and bridleways, of which there were a great many in the wide-open spaces of the South Downs. The All Wheel Drive Club's Andy Bush put together a team of rights-of-way experts to assist with marshalling at these sensitive points, in order to smooth out any public relations problems which might have occurred.

Tony Cable's stricken GM V8-engined 110 is about to be winched upright after rolling in Morocco.

CEVENNES RENDEZVOUS

One of the most interesting off-roading events in mainland Europe is the French *Trophée Cevenol*. It has been held seven years running and takes place in the idyllic setting of the Cevennes National Park in late May, based in the town of Les Vans, north-west of Nimes, and about 620 miles (1,000km) south of Calais. It is organized by the *Fédération Sportive Des Grands Randonneurs Motorisés*, or FSGRM for short. Leaving the *autoroute* at Loriol, you head west on the N104 via the towns of Privas and Aubernas, affording splendid views of what is a relatively remote area of France. It is a twelve-hour journey from Calais.

As with all such events, competitors sign on with the *Contrôles Techniques et administratifs*, followed by scrutineering, applying the obligatory sponsors' stickers and rally plate. The seventh *Trophée* began with a short trials section laid out on a compact area of wasteland adjoining the *stade municipal* on the edge of town. It consisted of a range of demanding climbs, descents, tight turns on side slopes, cross axles which had coil-sprung vehicles struggling, and a rock staircase which claimed several victims during the afternoon. The sections were sufficently testing for the marshals to be able to assess each driver and his or her vehicle's capability to mark the score sheets.

The main event is held over three days, with individual groups departing each day on one of three unique circuits marked red, blue and black; competitors then alternate on the following days so that they cover all three routes. At the start of each day contestants receive a comprehensive 'tulip' roadbook and are informed of any changes in the system. On the first day, competitors tackled the *Circuit Rouge* and began traversing a shallow stream-bed complicated by tricky climbs and descents in and out for 1½ miles (2km). The route into the mountains passed through huge tracts of forest.

From the summit, the descent was by way of narrow mule tracks, requiring total concentration in view of the precipitous drops waiting to send the unwary to oblivion. At the end of the track, an impromptu Camel Trophy-style bridge spanned a narrow ravine, its tree construction creaking under the strain of crossing Land Rovers. It was followed by an alarming descent back onto the tarmac road section. Next came another ascent on long, steep stony tracks which test vehicles to the limit with the tyres constantly grabbing on the loose rocks. For those with locking diffs, the climb presented few problems, but otherwise it demanded the correct line and a heavy right foot to succeed. The day ended at the picturesque village of Sablières where control cards were stamped.

Next day on the *'Circuit Bleu'* was wet, and during the briefing competitors were told that some of the descents had been cancelled as they had become greasy mudslides. Nevertheless, the route still proved extremely challenging as it followed tight tracks through the woods and in and out of a stream-bed. It culminated in a long, deeply rutted and muddy ascent, and it was here that the most serious vehicle damage occurred: a marshal's Toyota was positioned at the top to winch up vehicles which failed the climb. It had been left in neutral, unattended and unsecured, and while the cable was being pulled out, it started to slide on the slippery surface. It narrowly missed the Defender it was meant to be winching, bounced out of the tracks and careered into a tree. Having rolled over several times, it was a complete wreck. It took three hours to extricate it, while its owner lay on the ground in tears.

The most arduous stuff had been saved until last. On the *Circuit Noir* the day began with a 2 mile (3km) trek down a dried-up river-bed, followed by a short drive on tarmac, then onto a mule track deep in the woods. Here was a side slope with a number of tricky descents made even more daunting by the track's slippery surface. Finally a series of steeper, rocky descents and narrow ascents through the trees had the vehicles' external roll cage working overtime fending off branches. A measure of the severity of the conditions was that only six vehicles completed the final stages, and by the end of the event,

This 110 survived the 24-Heures TT de Paris *but sustained quite a battering.*

most vehicles showed signs of contact with the scenery. The prize-giving was held at the *mairie* in Les Vans, hosted by the federation's president, Jean-Louis Milelli. Competitors sampled the local wines and a buffet, which is all very agreeable: there's nothing like a good feast after a hard weekend's off-roading!

THE ORIGINS OF THE CAMEL TROPHY

The Camel Trophy has very quickly become an accepted part of the Land Rover scene, and is valued by the company as an excellent promotional medium. As far as this book is concerned, the key years were 1983, 1984, 1985, 1986, 1988 and 1989 because that was when 'genuine' Land Rovers, as opposed to Range Rovers and Discoverys, were used. Getting the Camel up and running entails twelve months of scouting for suitable locations, and another year of detailed planning and preparation. Nowadays everything is carefully organized, but in the early years of the Trophy, all kinds of things went wrong.

The idea of the Camel Trophy emerged in Germany in the late 1970s. Traditionally, it has always been hard to find places to go off-roading legally in Germany, and as a result, the off-road scene there has had a bias towards adventure in distant lands. The organizers obtained sponsorship for the first event from the makers of Camel cigarettes in Germany, RJ Reynolds Tobacco GmbH. The initial concept was that the Trophy should be a driving event combining a strong element of adventure, exotic location, and inhospitable and difficult terrain. There would be an element of competition among the drivers taking part, but instead of going against the clock and each other like a trial, the emphasis would be on off-road driving skill and a will to win.

Sponsors need to be able to justify their involvement in ways other than straight product sales. The image was right, and the elements of adventure and bravery in the face of adversity were just what RJ Reynolds wanted people to associate with their cigarettes. Now the event is firmly

French 90 truck-cab at speed; note the front diff protection.

established, a whole range of products associated with the intrepid Camel adventurers is available.

The first Camel event was held in 1980. It was called the Transamazonica, and was staged in 1,000 miles (1,609km) of the Amazon Basin. Only three teams took part, all from Germany, and all driving Jeeps. RJ Reynolds' publicity machine ensured that public interest in the event was captured, and there was sufficient interest to merit them sponsoring a second Camel Trophy in 1981.

At this point, Land Rover came on the scene. It is a mystery as to why Jeep did not get in on the act, but their lack of foresight was Land Rover's good fortune. Land Rover was entering a phase of major expansion calculated to give them a 75 per cent increase in production capacity by 1983. Part of the grand plan was to sell more vehicles in Europe, and Germany, home of the Camel concept, was a prime target. One way of promoting the product was by means of a high profile event such as the Camel Trophy, so a symbiotic relationship was formed with RJ Reynolds. Land Rover offered to provide the vehicles and technical support for the 1981 event.

The entry for the 1981 Trophy was again confined to Germany. The event was still in its infancy, and as far as the sponsor was concerned, there was sufficient reward in selling more cigarettes in Germany. Moreover there were plenty of administration problems without throwing it open to all-comers. Eventually, five teams of two competitors each were selected to go on the 1,000-mile trek across the equator on the Indonesian island of Sumatra. One pairing came from north Germany, one from Bavaria, two crews represented the military, while the fifth was a ladies team. Five Range Rovers were provided by Land Rover, specially equipped with roof-racks, winches and additional lighting, and they were finished in Austin Rover 'sandglow', which became the standard Camel Trophy colour scheme. The basic mechanical spec remained the same as normal however, because Land Rover wished to demonstrate that a standard two-door Range Rover was capable of handling such arduous conditions. Back-up would be provided by a Lode

Lane service team which included twelve support vehicles and a heavy truck. The support team's doctor was driving a Toyota, which was a public relations oversight: subsequently, Land Rover ensured that all the support vehicles were made in Solihull.

There were problems from the start, because despite the fact that full clearance for the event had been obtained from the Indonesian authorities, the local police in Jakarta apparently had no prior warning of it, and were fazed to find a seventeen-vehicle convoy making its way through the city. They pulled everybody over and forced the participants to wait out the next day and a half until the bureaucracy was sorted out, and it was a serious lesson for the organizers in not overestimating the power of Western frivolities. Once the event was under way, the vehicles negotiated seemingly impassable roads, and passed through debilitating climate changes as the route dropped dramatically from the mountain ranges of the north to the tropical swamps in the south of the island.

Amazingly no one fell by the wayside, and again the event attracted a great deal of media interest. The arrangement between RJ Reynolds and Land Rover was consolidated, and they began planning a third Camel Trophy. Land Rover's German subsidiary capitalized on the publicity by launching a limited-edition Trophy Range Rover, complete with bull-bar, extra lamps, compass, map-reading light, distance recorder and sundry expedition-style extras.

The 1982 Trophy lasted two weeks, and covered 1,000 miles (1,609km) of tough off-road driving. Additionally, the crews took part in a series of special tasks, including bridge-building, or any one of a number of other possibilities. The teams were awarded points for their competence in these tasks as well as off-roading skills, and the

Tight squeeze for a V8-powered 90 in a French forest track.

one with the most points at the end of the competition won the Camel Trophy. Thus teamwork became an increasingly important element in achieving success in the event. For the first time, the event was no longer restricted to West German entrants, and teams from Italy, Holland and the USA participated. Each of the four competing countries put forward two teams, making eight teams and sixteen participants in all. The venue chosen was Papua, New Guinea, part of the world's second largest island and an area populated by more than 700 tribes.

As the Trophy offered Land Rover a first-rate opportunity to promote their new vehicles, it was perhaps surprising that they provided the eight teams with two-door Range Rovers instead of the latest four-door models, which had been announced just too late for the 1981 Camel Trophy. However, two-doors it was which had to be guided around the narrow hairpin turns on desolate colonial tracks. The competitors were busy day and night building bridges, crossing rapids and completing challenging special tasks; and the winners at the end of this gruelling fortnight were the Italian team of Cesare Giraudo and Guiliano Giongo.

By the time of the 1983 Camel Trophy, the new coil-sprung 110 models had been announced. However, Land Rover decided against using them for the Trophy crews, because there was simply insufficient time between the launch and the start of the Trophy to prepare the vehicles and to train the crews on them. Instead, the company switched to Series III 88in (2,235mm) Station Wagons, which were of course still in full production because the new short-wheelbase coil-sprung models had not yet been announced.

That year's event established an important principle: vehicles used on the previous three years' Camel Trophy had all been petrol-drinkers, but the Series IIIs were oil-burners. It was not that the petrol engines had failed in some way, but the better economy of diesel engines meant carrying less spare fuel, as well as being less prone to water damage. The experiment proved a success, and no front-line Camel Trophy vehicles have been petrol-powered since then.

The following three years are of most relevance, as the vehicles used were 'proper' Land Rovers. For 1983, the Trophy was held in Africa for the first time. Its international nature was now established, and in that year the entries were broadened to include crews from seven countries. The 1,000-mile (1,609km) route ran from Kinshasa to Kisangani in Zaire, through terrain ranging from knee-deep mud to desert sand. The biggest hurdle proved to be the 113°-in-the-shade temperatures, with humidity up at 95 per cent. The Dutch

Defender 90 in the slush during the 1993 Mille Rivières.

Camel Trophy 110 takes a plunge. Land Rover 'utilities' were used by competitors on the event from 1983 to 1986, and again in 1988 and 1989. Although Discoverys have been the main Camel weapon since 1990, Defender 110s and 130s have provided back-up.

team of Bont and Heij overcame this slight impediment to emerge as the winners.

For 1984, Land Rover prepared a fleet of 110 Station Wagons, but again, the timing of the event failed to correspond with their new-model launch. The 2.3-litre diesel engine was replaced in the showrooms by a long-stroke 2.5-litre version in January 1984, but there was not time to prepare the newer vehicles for the Camel Trophy. With international interest now bordering on fever pitch, the organizers had to cope with over half a million applications from Camel wannabees. Participation rested on whether the Camel brand required promotion in the applicant's native country, so there were still no British among the twelve crews selected to take part, despite the fact that the Camel Trophy depended on Land Rovers built in Solihull. The crews were eventually chosen from the six Camel-smoking countries of Germany, the Netherlands, Belgium, Italy, Switzerland and Spain.

The 1984 Trophy returned to Brazil and the Amazon basin, beginning at Manaus where the 1980 Transamazonica event had ended. The event was meant to start just after the end of the rainy season, but the mighty Amazon was still swollen and 69ft (21m) higher than normal. In Holland the barges sail straight over the sluices under these sorts of conditions, but it never gets to be 69ft (21m) higher than normal. The substitute route was also virtually impassable, consisting almost totally of mud. At various times the contenders had to erect three 40ft (12m) bridges to span flooded rivers to get their vehicles across. Amazingly, the convoy got through and the winning team was the Italian duo Alfredo Redaelli and Maurizio Levi. The 1985 Camel Trophy was held on the Indonesian island of Borneo, which qualifies as one of the world's most remote places. With monsoon rains slowing the convoy's advance through the mountainous East Kalimantan jungle region, progress was sometimes down to just 1½ to 2 miles (2 to 3km) a day. The nadir of the expedition was when a helicopter had to be drafted in to hoist the participants and their vehicles out of the jungle. Understandably this was poor publicity for the new 90s, and Land Rover pointed the finger at organizational failure. Post-event analysis brought with it, among other things, the promise that a

British team would be participating on the 1986 Camel Trophy.

The winners of the 1985 event were the German team of Heinz Kallin and Bernd Strohdach. The dire conditions in Borneo prompted the organizers to present a second trophy, called the Team Spirit Award, for the team which had not necessarily won, but had tried the hardest. In Borneo it went to the Brazilians Tito Rosenberg and Carlos Probst.

Selections

The Camel entry list has grown steadily to eighteen countries, while destinations continue to be strictly off the beaten track: Borneo, Zaire, Siberia, the Australian outback, Madagascar, Malaysia and across the Andes. The most suitable applicants are invited to their national selections, where they are assessed in such disciplines as driving, orienteering, canoeing, abseiling, first aid, and also their ability to speak English, the official Camel language. In 1995 the Swiss, winners of the trophy in Guyana 1992, screened 400 contenders before sending fifteen to Portugal for further national selections in January. From these, three Swiss were shortlisted to go on to Turkey for the international selections in the spring. Finally, two qualified for the 1995 Mundo Maya in central America. A similar system is followed by most countries, and the competition is keen.

From the moment candidates arrive at selection, they are given little physical respite. The schedule is arduous and full of surprises; like, just when they thought the day was over, a 12 mile (20km) run could be announced. Candidates are split into four groups, and the disciplines are orienteering, pioneering, canoeing, bridge building, winching and driving. The latter abilities are assessed on timekeeping, vehicle navigation and slalom tests.

To a much lesser extent, events such as the Warn Trophy major on these activities, which can be seen much closer to home.

ORGANIZING THE CAMEL TROPHY

Land Rover's special events manager is Gwil Berry, and he is the man who makes sure Camel Trophy contestants actually have something to drive. Each year, the first news we get of the Camel Trophy is probably when the specialist press such as *Land Rover Owner* shows us pictures of half-submerged Land Rovers and contestants mud-wrestling with anacondas. But getting ready for a Camel Trophy isn't simply a matter of hauling a handful of Discoverys off the line and installing roll cages. Gwil Berry spends a whole year organizing what's needed to make it happen:

The Camel Trophy 1980 –1985

Year	*Venue*	*Vehicles*	*Teams*	*Nations*
1980	Amazon Basin	Jeep	3	1
1981	Sumatra	Range Rover 2-dr	5	1
1982	Papua New Guinea	Range Rover 2-dr	8	4
1983	Zaire	Series III 88	14	7
1984	Brazil	110	12	6
1985	Borneo	90	16	8

This ex-Camel Trophy Defender 110 support vehicle is now used as a course vehicle by Yorkshire 4 × 4 Exploration.

For example, if we take the 1995 build for next year's Camel vehicles, I first talk to Camel to find out how many teams there will be. Once we've got that, we know how many vehicles we've got to build. That includes support vehicles too. They will probably need camera crew, ambulance and maintenance vehicles.

Then I have to order those vehicles, and I talk to the people here who will load them into the system. After that, I liaise with the engineers whose job it will be to see the vehicles through production. In turn, they talk to the body-in-white people, the paint shop, and all the key areas in the process. We agree a specification, and all the elements then go into those vehicles on the production line. I'm the interface between all these key people.

The first people he is in touch with are World-Wide Brands Incorporated, which owns the rights to Camel, and Global Events Management, which actually runs the event, both owned wholly by Camel:

Then there's a requirement to train the Camel people, which includes the actual

Another Camel Trophy Defender Station Wagon support vehicle being put to good use in the 1995 Warn Challenge. These vehicles were kitted out just as if they were in the competition.

> contestants. I talk to Roger Crathorne at the Land Rover Driving Experience about what we need for the selection process, and this is true for international as well as UK selection. There could be specific needs in maybe Poland or Czechoslovakia, and I would organize special vehicles and perhaps sit with the participants to assist with the selection.'

Gwil's job is to have the vehicles built, equipped, prepared, loaded, shipped, landed, and ready to go on the expedition. He also recruits four Land Rover mechanics who go on the event with the participants. Their role is that of advisers, because the participants will have already been trained, to an extent, to look after their own vehicles. In reality, the mechanics are kept really busy.

> I also co-ordinate the cataloguing and packing of the spares which accompany the expedition. Last year I developed a 40ft (12m) container as a components store, so the expedition is self-sufficient for parts. It's just like walking into a distributor's spares department, and asking for a track rod or a brake pipe – items which commonly get damaged on the Camel. It's got its own generator and lighting, and its own crane. It's shipped out to the event with the vehicles.

This year there were no failures – such as alternators or water pumps packing up – only breakages, where for instance an axle was smashed on a rock. This meant only three components were drawn from the store, which was good from Gwil's point of view.

The Camel Trophy is supported by two vehicle workshops; these used to be based on Land Rover 130s, but because of the weight penalty of such heavy vehicles, Discoverys are now used, one positioned amidships in the convoy, and one at the back. They provide back-up to all the support vehicles as well.

Providing vehicles and back-up for the Camel Trophy isn't the only thing Gwil does. As special events manager, he's involved with other programmes on the marketing side, including the Land Rover hawk display team - a birds-of-prey display – which they take to events such as the Royal Show and Gatcombe Park. He looks after training for the Royal Geographical Society when their people are about to go off to remote parts of the world; and there's a big equestrian scene that Land Rover are involved with. In every walk of life and in every leisure activity, there's a Land Rover not far away.

Index